PRAISE FOR *COUNSELING INDIVIDUALS WITH LIFE-THREATENING ILLNESS*

"*Counseling Individuals With Life-Threatening Illness* helps clinicians to push the boundaries of the need for critical psychological support when facing anticipated losses. Full of useful advice about the tasks faced in response to the many phases of loss, Doka gives insight and experienced guidance in dealing with the painful reality most of us will face when confronted with the possibility that life will end."

—**Stephen R. Connor, PhD,** *Vice President for Research and International Development, National Hospice and Palliative Care Organization*

"Every professional counselor and other caregiver who seeks to help individuals with life-threatening illness and their family members should buy this book and consult it regularly! I gained a great deal from my first reading of this text and I intend to return to it again and again for guidance and enriched understanding of the issues involved."

—**Charles A. Corr, PhD, CT,** *Member of the Board of Directors, The Hospice Institute of the Florida Suncoast, Clearwater, FL*

"Where was this book when I was new as a counselor, and later when new as a life-threatened patient? Fortunately, it is here now, and with all the scope, depth, resourcefulness, and balance required for such situations."

—**Robert Kastenbaum, PhD,** *Professor Emeritus, Hugh Downs School of Human Communication, Arizona State University*

"On the cutting edge, extraordinary in detail, peerless in comprehensiveness, and making other treatments of the topic look anemic, *Counseling Individuals With Life-Threatening Illness* is the consummate professional resource.... Grounded in the very best of thanatological theory, philosophy, and research acumen, and integrated with the most efficacious clinical practices, this book gives new dimensions of wisdom to those who seek to serve this population."

—**Therese A. Rando, PhD, BCETS, BCBT,** *Author of* Grief, Dying, and Death: Clinical Interventions for Caregivers

KENNETH J. DOKA, PhD, is a Professor of Gerontology at the Graduate School of The College of New Rochelle and Senior Consultant to the Hospice Foundation of America. Dr. Doka's books include *Living with Grief: Children and Adolescents; Living with Grief: Before and After Death; Death, Dying and Bereavement: Major Themes in Health and Social Welfare* (a four-volume edited work); *Pain Management at the End-of-Life: Bridging the Gap between Knowledge and Practice; Living with Grief: Ethical Dilemmas at the End of Life; Living with Grief: Alzheimer's Disease; Living with Grief: Coping with Public Tragedy; Men Don't Cry, Women Do: Transcending Gender Stereotypes of Grief; Living with Grief: Loss in Later Life; Disenfranchised Grief: Recognizing Hidden Sorrow; Living with Life-Threatening Illness; Children Mourning, Mourning Children; Death and Spirituality; Living with Grief: After Sudden Loss; Living with Grief: When Illness Is Prolonged; Living with Grief: Who We Are, How We Grieve; Living with Grief: At Work, School and Worship; Living with Grief: Children, Adolescents and Loss; Caregiving and Loss: Family Needs, Professional Responses; AIDS, Fear and Society; Aging and Developmental Disabilities;* and *Disenfranchised Grief: New Directions, Challenges, and Strategies for Practice.* In addition to these books, he has published over 100 articles and book chapters. Dr. Doka is editor of both *Omega: The Journal of Death and Dying* and *Journeys: A Newsletter for the Bereaved.*

Dr. Doka was elected President of the Association for Death Education and Counseling in 1993. In 1995 he was elected to the Board of Directors of the International Work Group on Dying, Death and Bereavement and served as chair from 1997 to 1999. The Association for Death Education and Counseling presented him with an award for outstanding contributions in the field of death education in 1998. In 2000 Scott and White presented him with an award for Outstanding Contributions to Thanatology and Hospice. His alma mater, Concordia College, presented him with its first Distinguished Alumnus Award. In 2006, Dr. Doka was grandfathered in as a Mental Health Counselor under New York State's first licensure of counselors.

Dr. Doka has keynoted conferences throughout North America as well as in Europe, Asia, Australia, and New Zealand. He participates in the annual Hospice Foundation of America Teleconference and has appeared on CNN and *Nightline.* In addition, he has served as a consultant to medical, nursing, funeral service, and hospice organizations as well as to businesses and educational and social service agencies. Dr. Doka is an ordained Lutheran minister.

Counseling Individuals With Life-Threatening Illness

KENNETH J. DOKA, PhD

SPRINGER PUBLISHING COMPANY

New York

Springer Publishing Company, LLC
11 West 42nd Street
New York, NY 10036
www.springerpub.com

Acquisitions Editor: Sheri W. Sussman
Production Manager: Kelly J. Applegate
Cover design: YAY! Design
Composition: Publication Services

10/ 5 4 3 2

Library of Congress Cataloging-in-Publication Data

Doka, Kenneth J.
 Counseling individuals with life-threatening illness / Kenneth J. Doka.
  p. ; cm.
 Includes bibliographical references.
 ISBN 978-0-8261-1541-6
  1. Critically ill—Counseling of.   2. Critically ill—Psychology.
3. Death—Psychological aspects. I. Title.

 [DNLM:1. Attitude to Death.   2. Counseling.   3. Critical Illness—psychology.   4. Family Health.   5. Terminally Ill—psychology.
WM 55 D658c 2008]
  R726.8.D644 2008
  616.02'8–dc22

                                    2008022426

Printed in the United States of America by Hamilton Printing.

To my grandchildren,
Kenny and Lucy,
who each day bring new joy in living
and to their parents, my son and daughter-in-law,
Michael and Angelina,
for the gifts of grandparenthood and parental pride.

Contents

Chapter 6

Chapter 7   The Prediagnostic Phase: Understanding the Road Before   127

Chapter 8   ## Counseling Clients Through Crisis of Diagnosis   141

Chapter 9   ## Counseling Clients in the Chronic Phase of Illness   165

Foreword

Anyone who has provided companionship, counseling, or care to persons who are coping with serious illness knows how diverse the landscape of loss can be, with some itineraries through this terrain climbing to vistas of hope while others descend into valleys of despair. But most, perhaps, tread through a variegated terrain of threat, uncertainty, helplessness, action, isolation, acceptance, and connection, with too few markers to signal the way forward. Worse, those touched by the illness as well as those who help them may be presented with presumptive markers of a standardized, stepwise journey that departs substantially from the journey on which *this* patient, in *this* family, struggling with *these* issues, in *this* cultural frame, at *this* point in the progression of his or her illness, is embarked. Trying to find the way forward with a wrong map can be still more disorienting than having no map at all.

In this compact volume, anchored as it is in a deep history of personal and professional acquaintance with the topic, Ken Doka provides an authoritative and appropriately individualized guidebook for professionals who willingly accept the role of fellow travelers for patients and families contending with this unfamiliar terrain. With characteristic clarity Doka draws on the classic and contemporary literature as well as his own pedagogy and practice in death and dying to offer orienting concepts for the whole spectrum of care people may require when illness intrudes into their lives. For each phase of the illness trajectory, from prediagnosis through acute, chronic, and recovery/remission periods to the terminal phase, he offers intelligent attention to the problems and prospects people confront, and in countless examples of actual clinical situations he brings to life the concepts that inform compassionate care. What struck me was not only the simple practicality of the principles and interventions he described and illustrated, but also their comprehensiveness and sweep, encompassing concern with the physical, medical, psychosocial, and existential aspects of life-threatening illness. Implicit in this nuanced and multidimensional treatment of the topic is Doka's advocacy of interdisciplinary contributions to caring for people with life-altering conditions, as well as his encouragement, for all of us who do this work, to recognize its complexity and be willing to transcend sometimes-artificial disciplinary divisions to provide treatment to the whole person. In this respect I found this book to accord fully with recent developments in hospice and palliative care, which emphasize the importance of recognizing the integrity and diversity of patients in their own unique family and cultural contexts. However, in contrast to this occasionally abstract disciplinary rhetoric, Doka's gift as a storyteller consistently brings these principles to life, as in accounts of his counseling with a terminally ill 12-year-old who wants to grow up to be a lawyer; in his systemic intervention with dozens of members of the family and community to secure companionship and meals for a terminally ill older woman contending with the sudden death of her husband; or in Doka's own father's reinvention of his life after a brush with prostate cancer. In other words, as a skilled pedagogue, Doka tacks back and forth between abstract conceptualization and concrete experience, giving the reader useful models and methods for counseling in this challenging context but also illustrating their application to real people facing real problems. The result is a readable book that covers a surprising amount of ground without leaving the reader feeling winded from slogging through interminable theories or being bogged down with technicalities. As usual, Doka seems to have gotten the balance just right.

Although I am no stranger to this literature, I readily acknowledge that I learned a good deal myself from the perusal of these pages, and I am certain this will be the case for other readers, whatever their level of expertise. In consequence, I will find myself adding *Counseling Individuals With Life-Threatening Illness* to the recommended readings I use in classes with students as well as those I offer in workshops with professionals who work in end-of-life care. And I recommend it to you as well, confident that it provides practical counsel to all counselors who strive to offer guidance and understanding to persons negotiating the challenging terrain of serious illness and loss.

Robert A. Neimeyer, PhD
University of Memphis
June 2008

Acknowledgments

This work has been influenced and nurtured by many sources. Thus it is both fitting and pleasurable to acknowledge these diverse contributions. The contributions of Avery Weisman and E. Mansell Pattison are clearly evident in these pages. Others, too, through their writing or teaching, influenced my thinking about life-threatening illness. The ideas of Myra Bluebond-Langer, Herman Feifel, Robert Fulton, Barney Glaser, and the late Richard Kalish, Robert Kastenbaum, Nat Kollar, Elisabeth Kübler-Ross, Ilene Lubkin, Bruce Jennings, Victor Marshall, Rudolph Moos, Catherine Sanders, Edwin Shneidman, John Stephenson, Judith Stillion, Anselm Strauss, David Sudnow, Mary Vachon, and Hannelore Wass are all apparent in these pages. Charles Corr and Therese A. Rando have had a special role; not only did their ideas and thoughts influence me, but their constant encouragement sustained me. Donald Ford, a friend and physician, was always available to answer any technical or medical questions.

My many colleagues in the Association for Death and Counseling (ADEC) and the International Work Group on Death, Dying, and Bereavement (IWG) also provided constant support. Dana Cable, Terry Martin, Neil Heflin-Wells, Lu Redmond, Sherry Schachter, and Jane Nichols, as well as Robert Neimeyer, Britt Hysing-Dahl, Isa Jaramillo, Robert Bendiksen, Margaret Stroebe, Henk Schut, Leslie Balmer, Ron Barrett, and Stephen Fleming, to name a few, provided, over many years, encouragement, helpful criticisms, and camaraderie.

My own college has been supportive in many ways. The gift of sabbatical time provided an extended opportunity for writing. More importantly, I will always appreciate the freedom and opportunity to develop professionally that I have had at The College of New Rochelle. I hope I can provide the same to my students. I would like to acknowledge the support of President Steve Sweeny, Senior Vice Presidents Joan Bailey and Dorothy Escribano, Dean Guy Lometti, Associate Dean Marie Ribarich, and Wendi Vescio, Director of Human Services. I also should recognize the collegiality, stimulation, and support so freely offered by my colleagues and my students throughout the College.

This book would not have been possible without the secretarial and technical help so generously provided by Vera Mezzacuella. A research assistant, Mary Ryan Garcia, assisted with editing the earlier chapters. The Division's Administrative Assistants—first Mary Whalen and presently Diane Lewis—keep everything else operating with cheery efficiency.

Throughout the last number of years, I have had the privilege of being a consultant to the Hospice Foundation of America. This has helped me professionally in so many ways. Each year, preparation for a new teleconference and accompanying book continues to make me stretch my professional knowledge—moving me, for example, to study pain management or end-of-life ethics in a much deeper way. In addition, I have enjoyed the professional stimulation and personal friendships of the many wonderful people I have met there, including the late Jack Gordon, Myra MacPherson, David Abrams, Amy Tucci, Lisa Veglahn, Sophie Viteri Berman, William Lamers, Norman Sherman, and the staff, past and present.

Then there are all those in my own environment who, I like to think, keep me grounded. I am fortunate to live in a community that really is one. For that I thank my neighbors Paul Kimbal, Don and Carol Ford, Allen and Gail Greenstein, Jim and Mary Millar, Robert and Tracey Levy, Fred and Lisa Amore, and Chris and Dirotta Fields.

I, of course, need to acknowledge all those in my personal life who are always a source of joy. My son, Michael, and his wife, Angelina, and my grandson Kenny and granddaughter Lucy make it all seem so worthwhile. My godson, Keith Whitehead, graduates college this year—offering again a sense of vicarious pride in his accomplishments. Other members of my intimate network of family and friends, including Kathy Dillon; my sister, Dorothy; my brother, Franky; and all of their families, as well as Eric Schwarz; Dylan Rieger; Larry

Laterza; Ellie Andersen; Jim, Karen, and Greg Cassa; Linda and Russell Tellier; Jill Boyer; Lynn Miller; James Rainbolt; Scott and Lisa Carlson; Tom and Lorraine Carlson; Matt Atkins; Kurt Mulligan; Ken and Elaine Gilmore; and Don and Lucille Matthews, provide nurturing, encouragement, respite, friendship, and most importantly, laughter.

In addition, I have to acknowledge the help, encouragement, and infinite patience of my editor, Sheri Sussman, and her staff at Springer. And finally, I need to acknowledge all those people who in their own struggle with life-threatening illness and grief taught me much about dying and living.

Introduction

1

Counseling Individuals With a Life-Threatening Illness

- A 36-year-old mother learns that the tingling in her arm has been diagnosed as multiple sclerosis.
- A 64-year-old man, experiencing chest pains, is told he is having a heart attack.
- The parents of a two-year-old boy sit anxiously in a doctor's office, waiting to learn why their son has experienced continuous fevers and bruises so easily.
- A 28-year-old architect learns that he is HIV positive.
- During a routine examination a 69-year-old man is informed that he has a spot on his lung.
- A 41-year-old physician finds a lump in her breast.

In all these cases, individuals and their families are facing a moment of crisis, a terrible trial, a frightening encounter with mortality. Each must decide upon a course of action: when to seek medical help, how to choose the best treatment. The experiences of all these people may be very different. Some may find their worst fears are not realized. The lump may turn out to be merely a cyst; the spot on the lung may be benign. Some may undergo surgery or chemotherapy and eventually recover, but be forever changed by the experience of the illness. Others may struggle with chronic illness. And still others may face impending death.

The experience of life-threatening illness is one of the most difficult situations that individuals and their families ever have to face. From the first mounting suspicions about dangerous symptoms through the crisis of diagnosis and long periods of chronic illness, whether the result is recovery or death, any encounter with life-threatening illness leaves an indelible mark on ill individuals, their families, and even the people who care for them.

This book is meant to be a guide for anyone counseling or offering professional care to persons with life-threatening illness. Its very title, *Counseling Individuals With Life-Threatening Illness*, recognizes the medical revolution that has so radically changed the experience of illness. A few decades ago, to be diagnosed with any of a number of "fatal" diseases was to receive a virtual death sentence. A person with such a serious disease could expect to live but a short time; indeed, he or she might never leave the hospital. The experience of serious illness today is often dramatically different. Individuals can live a long time with life-threatening illness. Some—and these numbers continue to increase—will fully recover. Most will leave hospitals even as they carry on treatment. Many will resume their former lives, going back to work or school even as they continue to struggle with disease. Only at the very end of this process, often years after the initial diagnosis, will some finally reach the terminal phase of their illness. *Living* with life-threatening illness is the theme of this book, as it describes the particular challenges that individuals, families, and caregivers face at varying points during serious illness.

In the last 50 years, there has been another revolution in medical care evidenced by the growth of hospice and palliative care. Behind both is a simple yet critical premise: that care in life-threatening illness must be holistic. Life-threatening illness is not only a medical crisis; it is a social, psychological, and spiritual crisis as well. It not only affects the individual with the illness but also affects the family. Hence care must be not only holistic but also family centered. Both premises underlie this book.

Every book has its own biography. This book really arises from three sources. For the past 30 or so years I have taught courses on dying and death. In that teaching, particularly in a graduate seminar for nurses and other caregivers, I began to incorporate additional material that reflected the changed reality of illness, dying, and death that has occurred since the publication of Elisabeth Kübler-Ross's *On Death and Dying* (1969). My classes began to consider issues related to the diagnosis of illness, such as decisions about when to seek medical help or take diagnostic tests such as the HIV test. We also started to address issues associated with the problem living with chronic illness.

In short, we began to look at the dying process in the larger context of life-threatening illness. We studied the writings of E. Mansell Pattison (1969, 1978) and Avery Weisman (1980), two pioneering clinical researchers who emphasized the idea that life-threatening illness is a long process, best viewed as a series of phases, each with its own unique issues and problems. This book owes a heavy debt to their insights as well as to the work of many writers, researchers, and clinicians who are mentioned in the references.

The References lists all the sources I have found helpful while writing this book, but I wish to acknowledge my special debts to the classic work of Corr (1992), Kalish (1985), Moos (1977, 1984), Rando (1984), and Strauss (1975) among others, and the more recent insights of individuals such as Byock (1997).

Second, my father's bout with cancer also helped me to organize my own thoughts about the ways we look at life-threatening illness. It reminded me of the uncertainty we often face as we struggle with illness. Diagnosis can be an uncertain process, a roller coaster of good and bad news. Prognosis is rarely certain, and time frames can only be expressed as probabilities. The struggle is draining, not just for the ill individuals but also for their families and caregivers. My father recovered, and then lived a decade later to have a second, terminal bout with the disease.

This work draws from a third critical source: the experiences and responses that so many people have shared with me throughout these past thirty plus years. Although their names are not listed in any of the references, they too have taught me much about living with life-threatening illness.

Throughout my career I have resisted the term *patient*. I have always found the term *patient* to be inaccurate because it suggests that the ill individual is totally passive. For much of the struggle with life-threatening illness, individuals are rarely patients in the sense that they are spending much of their time in hospitals or physicians' offices. The root of the word *patient* actually means "someone being acted upon." That idea too was objectionable, for I have always stressed that individuals respond best to life-threatening illness when they are participants in their own treatment.

One colleague, Claire Kowalski, who once struggled herself with life-threatening illness, liked to call herself a *protagonist*. Drawn from Greek drama, the term *protagonist* refers to the central character around which all action revolves. It is the protagonist who sets the pace and direction for the ensuing drama. I have often felt that her perception of her role was admirable. Her demand to be the pivotal character in her own life struggle was the key factor in her own survival. I hope we come to the time soon when all persons with life-threatening illness will define themselves as protagonists.

Given my strong negative feelings about the word *patient,* I tried to avoid its use as much as possible in this book, often using the term *client* as more suitable to counselors. At times, though, *patient* seemed the best and clearest way to refer to individuals with an illness. Also, in certain contexts, such as a hospital, other terms such as "person with illness," "victim," or "client" seemed awkward, unclear, artificial, and sometimes even stigmatizing.

I deliberately choose to use the term *life-threatening illness* rather than terms *catastrophic illness, fatal illness,* or *terminal illness* that seemed to overemphasize the crisis nature of the illness. Though there are times of crisis, and a diagnosis can be truly catastrophic, the term *catastrophic illness* tends to underemphasize the reality that many people strive to maintain a normal life even when faced with impending death. For similar reasons, I avoided terms such as *fatal* or *terminal,* since these terms focus on the dying process. In this book, people are referred to as *dying* only when they are in the final, terminal phase of life-threatening illness. In the terminal phase the illness has progressed to such a point that recovery or remission is highly improbable, health has declined, and death is likely to occur within a specific time frame. I also avoided the term currently in favor, *life-limiting illness,* since many people do recover from such illnesses and go on to lead normal lives. Not every life-threatening illness is life-limiting.

As stated earlier, this work follows a long history of others who have contributed much to the care of persons with life-threatening illness. Chapter 2 reviews those that have had an impact on history, placing this work in its context.

Chapters 3 and 4 address the particular ethical and systematic stresses that those persons who counsel or care for individuals with life-threatening illness may experience, causing moral distress. These chapters also recognize the special sense of loss that is part of that role as well as the critical skills and attributes needed of caregivers who are privileged to work with persons with life-threatening illness and their families. While emphasizing the importance of self-care at both individual and organizational levels, the chapters affirm a central paradoxical message of work in hospice and palliative care: that few other jobs are as exhausting or as rewarding.

One of the central lessons that I have learned is that every experience of life-threatening illness is distinct, and individual responses are therefore very different. Chapter 5 explores and emphasizes that individuality. People respond to life-threatening illness in a variety of ways. A wise instructor once told me that she could predict the way I would die. When I asked "How?" she answered, "The same way you respond to any life crisis." Chapter 5 then considers the range of responses to life-threatening illness that individuals, their families, and their caregivers may experience.

Responses to illness are affected by many factors. No two experiences of illness are alike. Each disease creates its own special issues and particular problems. Nor is coping with a disease an isolated process; rather, it is a part of the continuing process of life, influenced by all the developmental, psychological, and social factors that influence response to any life crisis. These factors are described in Chapter 6.

Corr (1992) indicates that these challenges include physical ones (for example, the physical challenges caused by disease and treatment); psychological ones (for example, maintaining a sense of psychological comfort in the face of the disease); social ones (for example, negotiating relationships and the roles changed by the fact of illness); and spiritual ones (for example, finding meaning and value in the midst of illness). All dimensions of our lives are affected by an encounter with illness and death.

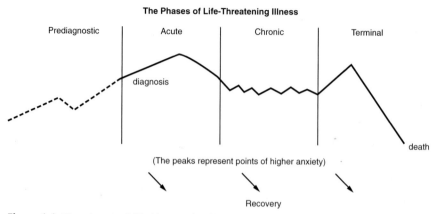

Figure 1.1 The phases of life-threatening illness.

Chapters 7 through 11 describe particular issues that arise at different points during the experience of life-threatening illness. Underlying this book is a perspective or model that views life-threatening illness as a series of phases, each with its particular challenges or tasks (see Figure 1.1).

I use the term *task,* since that word does not imply any order or sequence. Each task simply refers to challenges posed by the illness, so that people might face a given task at different points in life-threatening illness. As Corr (1992) notes the use of the term *task* also reinforces a personal sense of freedom in meeting each challenge. Just as any individual can decide on any day that he or she will choose to do or not to do particular chores, so individuals struggling with life-threatening illness can also choose to confront or not to confront particular challenges or tasks presented by the illness. Moreover, the term *task* emphasizes individuality. Just as different individuals may do even the same chore in their own unique manner, persons with life-threatening illness will find their own individual and idiosyncratic ways to complete their tasks. And as with any set of tasks, persons will vary in how quickly and competently they can tackle these tasks. These tasks in life-threatening illness can be outlined in the following ways.

A *prediagnostic phase,* discussed in Chapter 7, often precedes diagnosis. Here, someone recognizes symptoms of an illness or risk factors that make him or her prone to the illness. That person now needs to select strategies to cope with this threat. The tasks here include:

1. Recognizing possible danger or risk
2. Coping with anxiety and uncertainty
3. Developing and following through on a health-seeking strategy

Chapter 8 considers the *acute phase*, which centers on the crisis of diagnosis. At this point an individual is faced with a diagnosis of life-threatening illness and must make a series of decisions—medical, psychological, interpersonal, and so on—about how, at least initially, to cope with the crisis. Here the tasks include

1. Understanding the disease
2. Examining and maximizing health and lifestyle
3. Maximizing one's coping strengths and limiting one's weaknesses
4. Examining internal and external resources and liabilities
5. Developing strategies to deal with issues created by disease (disclosure, coping with professionals, treatment options, life contingencies)
6. Exploring the effect of illness on one's sense of self and relationships with others
7. Ventilating feelings and fears
8. Integrating the present reality of the diagnosis with one's past life and future plans

Chapter 9 describes the *chronic phase*. During this period the individual is struggling with the disease and its treatment. Many people in this phase may be attempting, with varying degrees of success, to live a reasonably normal life within the confines of the disease. Often this period is punctuated by a series of illness-related crises. Tasks in this phase (see Lubkin, 1986; Strauss, 1985) include

1. Managing symptoms and side effects
2. Carrying out health regimens

3. Preventing and managing health crises
4. Managing stress and examining coping
5. Maximizing social support and minimizing social isolation
6. Normalizing life in the face of disease
7. Dealing with financial concerns
8. Preserving self-concept
9. Redefining relationships with others throughout the course of the disease
10. Ventilating feeling and fears
11. Finding meaning in suffering, chronicity, uncertainty, and decline

In many cases people will not experience all of these phases. Moreover, sometimes in the acute or chronic phase, or even rarely in the terminal phase, a person may experience recovery. This *recovery/remission phase* is described in Chapter 10. Even here, however, people may have to cope with certain tasks such as

1. Dealing with psychological, social, spiritual, and financial aftereffects of illness
2. Coping with fears and anxieties about recurrence
3. Examining life and lifestyle issues and reconstructing one's life
4. Redefining relationships with caregivers.

Chapter 11 reviews the *terminal phase*. This describes the situation in which the disease has progressed to a point where death is inevitable. Death is no longer merely possible; now it is likely. Death has become the individual's and family's central crisis. Tasks (see Rando 1984; Kalish 1985) here include

1. Dealing with symptoms, discomfort, pain, and incapacitation
2. Managing health procedures and institutional procedures
3. Managing stress and examining coping
4. Dealing effectively with caregivers
5. Preparing for death and saying good-bye
6. Preserving self-concept
7. Preserving appropriate relationships with family and friends

8. Ventilating feelings and fears

9. Finding meaning in life and death

To summarize, this model holds that in any experience with life-threatening illness one is faced with four major tasks:

1. Responding to the physical fact of disease

2. Taking steps to cope with the reality of disease

3. Preserving self-concept and relationships with others in the face of disease

4. Dealing with the affective and existential/spiritual issues creatd or reactivated by the disease.

At each phase of the illness, these basic tasks may raise different issues, concerns, and challenges (see Table 1.1). There is one additional advantage to the term *task*. It reminds counselors that they are facilitators—their role is not to do task work for clients but to assist clients as they assess and complete their necessary tasks.

It is important to remember that while this model can be useful, at best it offers a general description of a complicated and highly individual process. Not every individual will experience the same situations and reactions I describe here. Nor will every life-threatening illness proceed methodically or precisely through these phases. In many cases an individual will seek medical treatment, fearing the worst, and happily learn that the symptom is minor and the condition itself easily treated. Even a diagnosis of life-threatening illness can result in successful surgeries or other interventions that minimize or eliminate any further risk. In many illnesses, such as multiple sclerosis, a chronic phase can last indefinitely, while with other illnesses decline into a terminal phase will immediately follow diagnosis.

There is another limitation to this model. We need to remember that life-threatening illness is only a part of life. Throughout the time of illness, at whatever phase, individuals continue to meet many needs and to cope with all the issues and problems that they had prior to the diagnosis. The experience may affect the person's perception of these needs and ways of coping with those issues, but the needs and issues themselves continue throughout the illness. While this model

Table 1.1

TASKS IN LIFE-THREATENING ILLNESS

GENERIC TASKS	ACUTE PHASE	CHRONIC PHASE	TERMINAL PHASE
I. Responding to the physical fact of disease	1. Understanding the disease	1. Managing symptoms and side effects	1. Dealing with symptoms, discomfort, pain, and incapacitation
II. Taking steps to cope with the reality of disease	2. Examining and maximizing health and lifestyle 3. Maximizing one's coping strengths and limiting weaknesses 4. Examining internal and external resources and liabilities 5. Developing strategies to deal with issues created by disease (disclosure, coping with professionals, treatment options, life contingencies)	2. Carrying out health regimens 3. Preventing and managing health crisis 4. Managing stress and examining coping 5. Maximizing social support and minimizing social isolation 6. Normalizing life in the face of disease 7. Dealing with financial concerns	2. Managing health procedures and institutional procedures 3. Managing stress and examining coping 4. Dealing effectively with caregivers 5. Preparing for death and saying good-bye (if necessary)
III. Preserving self-concept and relationships with others in the face of disease	6. Exploring the effect of illness on one's sense of self and relationships with others	8. Preserving self-concept 9. Redefining relationships with others throughout the course of the disease	6. Preserving self-concept 7. Preserving appropriate relationships with family and friends
IV. Dealing with affective and existential/spiritual issues created or reactivated by the disease	7. Ventilating feelings and fears 8. Integrating the present reality of the diagnosis with one's past life and future plans.	10. Ventilating feelings and fears 11. Finding meaning in suffering, chronicity, uncertainty, and decline	8. Ventilating feelings and fears 9. Finding meaning in life, dying, and death

emphasizes the experience of the illness itself, it is necessary to recognize that, for the person living with life-threatening illness, all the previous challenges of life—dealing with family and friends, coping with work and finances, even keeping up with the demands of a home or apartment—remain an ongoing part of that larger struggle.

Life-threatening illness is inevitably a family illness, because the life of everyone within the family is changed when one member of a family experiences disease. Chapter 12 considers the way in which families might be affected by the illness. It also offers suggestions for counseling families to cope with the illness of a family member. Chapter 12 also applies this general discussion to the special needs of specific populations such as children, the developmentally disabled, and older persons, as well as those of different cultures.

A number of years ago one of my students, soon after taking my dying and death course, found that her brother, with whom she was very close, had cancer. She nursed him, helped her parents, and struggled with her own emotions. One day she came to class to talk about her experiences in coping with his illness and subsequent death. Someone asked her whether the course had helped. She answered, "It didn't change my feelings or situations and crises we faced. It did make them more understandable." That really expressed the goal of this book: to make the struggle with life-threatening illness a little more understandable and perhaps less lonely and frightening.

REFERENCES

Byock, I. (1997). *Dying well: The prospect for growth at the end-of-life*. New York: Putnam.

Corr, C. A. (1992). A task-based approach to coping with dying. *Omega: Journal of Death and Dying, 25*, 81–94.

Kalish, R. (1985). *Death, grief, and caring relationships*. Monterey, CA: Brooks/Cole.

Kübler-Ross, E. (1969). *On death and dying*. New York: Macmillan.

Lubkin, I. (1981). *Chronic illness: Impact and interventions*. Boston: Jones and Bartlett.

Moos, R. (Ed.) (1977). *Coping with physical illness*. New York: Plenum Press.

Moos, R. (Ed.) (1984). *Coping with physical illness 2: New perspectives*. New York: Plenum Press.

Pattison, E. M. (1969). Help in the dying process. *Voices, 5,* 6–14.

Pattison, E. M. (1978). The living-dying interval. In C. Garfield (Ed.), *Psychological care of the dying patient* (pp. 163–168). New York: McGraw-Hill.

Rando, T. A. (1984). *Grief, dying, and death: Clinical interventions for caregivers.* Champaign, IL: Research Press.

Strauss, A. (1975). *Chronic illness and the quality of life.* St. Louis: C.V. Mosby Company.

Weisman, A. (1980). Thanatology. In O. Kaplan (Ed.), *Comprehensive textbook of psychiatry.* Baltimore: Williams & Wilkins.

2 Historical Perspectives on Dying and Illness

INTRODUCTION

Although many people associate the historical roots of the study of dying with Kübler-Ross's epochal book *On Death and Dying* (1969), the origins of the field are in fact both earlier and more varied. In this section, I will explore some of the early and contemporary contributions to the study of the dying process. This chapter begins with a brief history of some of the early formative work, reviews the development of the concept of anticipatory grief, describes more contemporary efforts to develop task models of dying, and discusses theorists who have viewed dying as a developmental and transformative experience. This is, in no way, a comprehensive review of all the work that exists in the field. Rather, it represents the author's perspective of influential work that has contributed to the care of the dying as well as to the task model developed in this book. Persons who wish a more all-inclusive view may wish to consult varied social histories of the field (Pine, 1977, 1986; Corr, Doka, and Kastenbaum, 1999).

Perhaps one of the earliest efforts to understand some of the psychosocial processes of dying was the study by Lindemann (1944) of grief reactions based on samples of survivors of persons who died in Massachusetts General or the Cocoanut Grove Fire (a Boston tragedy in which a fire in an overcrowded and locked nightclub killed 492 patrons). Although the study naturally emphasized grief reactions, it introduced the concept of *anticipatory grief*—a topic that will be explored later in this section.

Herman Feifel's *The Meaning of Death* (1959) was one of the first publications and early efforts in thanatology. Feifel's book emerged from one of the first organizational efforts in the study of death. Herman Feifel had made a suggestion, somewhat radical at the time, that the American Psychological Association sponsor a seminar on dying and death at its 1956 Annual Meeting. Although many thought death more a topic for religion than psychology, the seminar attracted wide attention. *The Meaning of Death* was a natural outgrowth of the seminar. Feifel invited a range of authors including psychologists, psychiatrists, and theologians as well as individuals in medicine and the humanities. In many ways this project set the tone for the field of thanatology. It would remain multidisciplinary rather than merely the province of one academic discipline.

THE STUDY OF DYING: EARLY EFFORTS

Although Feifel and Lindemann both touched on the dying process, their major focus was on the study of grief. Glaser and Strauss also published, in that early era, two books that would contribute some enduring concepts to the study of the dying process. In *Awareness of Dying* (1965), Glaser and Strauss studied what dying people knew or suspected about their impending deaths. It is important to remember that in that period, general practice was not to discuss death with individuals who were dying. Nonetheless, Glaser and Strauss documented that dying individuals experienced four different awareness contexts. In *closed awareness*, the dying person had no inkling of his or her impending death. As Glaser and Strauss noted, this context was unstable and unlikely to last long, as dying individuals began to respond to both external and internal cues. Internally, patients were likely to realize that they were getting weaker rather than stronger.

Externally, patients could see the worried and saddened looks of their families, the discomfort of family members and medical personnel over future-oriented questions that the patients might ask, and the hushed tones and private conversations that seemed to surround their care. Patients would soon suspect that they might be dying. In *suspected awareness*, dying individuals expected their impending death—often trying to test their suspicions with medical staff or family. A third context, *mutual pretense*, was the most common. Here patients and family were aware of the impending death, but each person attempted to protect the other by pretending that the patient would recover In the last context, *open awareness*, both patients and family were aware of and could discuss the possibility of death. The work of Glaser and Strauss (1965) played a significant role in questioning the veil of silence that had surrounded the dying process.

Their second work, *Time for Dying* (Glaser & Strauss, 1968), focused on the temporal organization of death within the hospital. They noted that most deaths followed certain expected trajectories—such trajectories where the descent into dying was slow or "lingering" as well as others that were "quick." Glaser and Strauss emphasized how medical staffs organized their efforts around an expected trajectory, using their expectations not only to organize own efforts but also to manage family reactions to the loss. "Badly timed" deaths, when the death did not follow an expected trajectory, often created great difficulty for staff.

Strauss's interest here presaged later work on the process of chronic illness (Strauss, 1975). This work, often barely recognized, was important for several reasons. First, Strauss sought to broaden the emerging study of the dying process to ask a larger question: "How do individuals cope with life-limiting illness even when death is not an immediate expectation?" Second, Strauss's work was one of the first studies within the behavioral sciences to really examine the strategies that individual patients and families use to cope with the multiple problems of living with illness, such as managing medical regimens, controlling symptoms, and coping with the inevitable social isolation that often occurs in illness.

Sudnow's *Passing On: The Social Organization of Dying* (1967) was an ethnographic account of dying in two hospitals. Sudnow's work also was far reaching. Many of his observations reinforced those of Glaser and Strauss (1965, 1968). Sudnow also documented the medical staff's attempt to manage the family's reactions. Hence, unpredicted deaths were problematic, and in some cases, staff went so far as to manufacture a "crisis of dying" even after the patient was already dead. Sudnow emphasized the social context that surrounded dying, sensitive to the varying ways the medical staff treated patients based on their age or social status. One of his most enduring contributions was the introduction of the concept of *social death*. Social death referred to his observed phenomenon that family and staff often treated many comatose patients, although technically alive, as if they were dead.

In 1962, Weisman and Hackett published a study on dying patients and the predilection to death. Weisman and Hackett found that patients' strategies of coping actually seemed to influence their survival. Patients, for example, who prematurely accepted death, in effect "giving up," were likely to have lower survival rates than patients who retained hope, denied death, or actively fought to remain alive. This study led Weisman to more general investigation of the role of denial in illness (Weisman, 1972) as well as to the range of ways in which persons coped with cancers and other illnesses (Weisman, 1979, 1984). In his work on coping, Weisman noted a wide range of coping responses, such as seeking information, sharing concerns, suppression, displacement, using humor to deflect, redefining, passive acceptance, disengagement, taking appropriate actions, compliance, escape, or blaming oneself or others. Weisman noted that these strategies not only affect survival but also help the individual patient as well as family and friends determine whether or not the death was "appropriate." To Weisman, an appropriate death was a highly individual concept; that is, that persons decide whether or not a particular mode of death is a fitting or meaningful end to life as that individual wished to live it. This is a critical concept, very different from the notion of Kübler-Ross (1969), which sees the acceptance of death as a hallmark of appropriateness.

HOSPICE: A WAY TO CARE FOR THE DYING

In this early period, Cicely Saunders founded St. Christopher's Hospice, often credited as the first hospice, in the London area. Saunders emphasized that dying was not simply a biomedical or

physical event but also had psychosocial, familial, and spiritual implications (Saunders, 1959). Care of the dying then needed to be holistic
and centered on the ill person and his or her family as the unit of
care. St. Christopher's tried to create a "home-like" atmosphere that
sought a holistic, family-centered way to allow dying persons to live
life as fully as possible, free from debilitating pain and incapacitating
symptoms. Both the hospice philosophy and the growth of hospice
did much to improve the treatment of dying persons and to encourage the study of the dying process.

The hospice movement's remarkable history is well noted in
other sources (see, for example, Stoddard, 1978). It is, perhaps,
one of the most successful grassroots movements in the last quar-
ter of the twentieth century. The holistic philosophy of hospice has
permeated much of medicine now—at least in terms of recognition
that a patient's quality of life means meeting not only physical needs
but psychological, social, and spiritual needs as well. Moreover, the
success of hospice has led others to seriously question how well the
medical system generally meets the needs of those who are dying as a
result of multiple serious chronic illnesses (Myers & Lynn, 2001).

St. Christopher's became a beacon of both research and practice,
generating seeds that would grow throughout the world. Many of
the pioneers who would influence the development of hospice and
palliative care visited or trained there.

In the United States this resulted in the development of Hospice,
Inc., outside of New Haven, Connecticut, in 1974. Branford (Connecticut) also had a small home care unit. But it was Dr. William
Lamers, a founder of a hospice in Marin County, California, who
viewed home care as both the heart and the future of hospice. To
Lamers, the idea of a home-like environment could best be offered
within the patient's actual home. Lamers offered a model that freed
interested individuals from fund-raising for new facilities. This home
care model of hospice quickly spread throughout the United States,
sponsored by a range of groups from churches and interfaith groups
to junior leagues. Hospice then took a very different cast in the United
States compared with England, in that in the United States hospices
offered home care primarily and heavily stressed psychosocial care
and the use of volunteers (Connor, 1998).

Not everyone learned the same lesson at St. Christopher's. St. Christopher's impressed Dr. Balfour Mount, a Canadian physician. However, Mount was convinced that the lessons of St. Christopher's need not necessarily lead to a new form of care but could be applied even in the high-technology environment of the modern hospital. When he returned to the Royal Victoria Hospital in Montreal, he pioneered the development of a hospital-based palliative care model. In recent years, this movement has become a major force in American medicine, evident in attempts to educate physicians, nurses, and other hospital-based personnel, such as chaplains and social workers, in end-of-life issues through programs such as EPEC (End-of-Life and Palliative Care), ELNEC (End-of-Life Nursing Education Consortium), and ACE (Advocating for Clinical Excellence) as well as efforts to create standards for assessing the quality of palliative care (Lynn, Chaudhry, Simon, Wilkinson, & Schuster, 2007; National Consensus Project, 2004).

To Saunders and Kastenbaum (1997), the growth of hospice was a reaction to several trends. First, technology-driven medicine focused on cure, seemingly abandoning those who were no longer responsive to treatment. Second, hospice resonated with two other themes of the era—"consumerism" and "return to nature." Both trends converged on the idea that individuals could create alternative, more natural organizations, in which persons could take control of their lives—and their deaths.

KÜBLER-ROSS AND *ON DEATH AND DYING*

Few of these efforts, at least in the very beginning, captured as much public attention as did the publication of Kübler-Ross's *On Death and Dying*. The book appeared at the right moment. Kübler-Ross was a charismatic woman who spoke of a "natural death" at a time when there was an increased aversion to technological and impersonal care (Klass & Hutton, 1985). Her message found a ready audience.

Kübler-Ross posited that dying persons went through a series of five (now famous) stages—*denial, anger, bargaining, depression, and acceptance.* It also should be noted that Kübler-Ross stressed that, within and all through these stages, *hope* was a constant reaction—although the content of hope may change from "perhaps I beat this" to "I hope I see my brother before I die."

The stages, although still popular in lay literature, are far more problematic. Evaluations of her theory of stages (see, for example, Doka, 1993) note many problems. Some are methodological in nature. Kübler-Ross never really documented her material or her methodology. It is unclear how her data were collected or how many patients experienced which reactions. Nor has research supported the concept of stages (e.g., Schulz & Aderman, 1974).

There are other problems as well. Later work would demonstrate that denial and acceptance were far more complex than presented by Kübler-Ross (Weisman, 1972). In addition, although Kübler-Ross insisted that the stage theory was not to be understood literally or linearly, the book clearly offers an impression of linear stages. As such, individual differences and the diverse ways in which persons cope are often ignored. In addition, it is unclear whether the stages represent a description of how persons cope with dying or a prescriptive approach that stresses that dying individuals ought to be assisted to move through the five stages and eventually embrace acceptance.

Yet despite these serious criticisms, Kübler-Ross, in her many case vignettes, offered a model of communication that made a powerful plea for the humanistic care of the dying patient. In an excellent evaluation of Kübler-Ross's contributions, Corr (1993) suggests that this call for humanistic care and her affirming message to talk to dying persons, along with the heuristic value of the work, are the enduring legacies of the book.

TOWARD A MORE INCLUSIVE CONCEPTUALIZATION OF THE DYING PROCESS

The work cited so far in this chapter played a critical role in the evolution of thanatology—moving the field from a primarily theological and philosophical endeavor to one more broadly rooted in many disciplines. However, as the study of the dying process continued, other work began to emerge that would more directly influence the paradigm developed within this book.

Avery Weisman and the Complexity of Denial

As stated earlier, one of the critical criticisms of Kübler-Ross's stage theory was that denial and acceptance were far more complex than acknowledged in her work. In Kübler-Ross's work, denial was essentially a negative state—a buffer brought on through shock of a terminal diagnosis. The dying patient had first to surmount this denial—to recognize, even in an existential anger, that death was imminent—and thereby to begin the journey toward a more peaceful acceptance or, at the very least, a passive resignation to death.

Perhaps the earlier work of Weisman and Hackett (1962) on predilection toward death had already suggested that denial was not as problematic as Kübler-Ross perceived. In any case, Weisman's 1972 work, *On Dying and Denying. A Psychiatric Study of Terminality*, suggested that denial and acceptance were highly complex processes. Weisman first described *orders of denial* emphasizing that patients might deny several realities in the course of the illness. In *first-order denial*, the patient denies the symptom. For example, the patient may deny that a lump is a new and possibly malignant lesion, insisting that it was always there or the result of an injury that will soon heal. A patient in *second-order denial* no longer denies the symptom, but denies some aspect of the diagnosis. A few examples may illustrate. A patient may describe the lump as a "neoplasm," eschewing the far more charged word "cancer." In one of my counseling cases, a patient would carefully describe his condition as "acquired immune deficiency syndrome," correcting those who called it AIDS. To this patient, they seemed different disorders rather than one an acronym of the other. *Third-order denial* means that the patient accepts the diagnosis while avoiding the prognosis that usually accompanies it. A 40-year-old patient with late-stage pancreatic cancer shared with me that he had a dream in which he was promised that he would live "three score and ten" or 70 years, the average age at which males in his family tended to die.

While delineating the complexity of denial, Weisman also notes that denial is not always negative. It allows patients to participate in therapy and sustain hope. Denial is a defense mechanism. In the absence of denial at some level, there is little reason to engage in painful therapies.

Weisman introduces a very significant concept of *middle knowledge*—meaning that patients drift in and out of denial, sometimes affirming, other times denying the closeness of death. Denial, then, is not a state that patients leave on a journey to acceptance. Rather it is a constant companion as patients deal with the reality of illness. Persons even in the later of stages of illness may deny the possibility of death in one conversation even as they acknowledge it in the next.

When I first began in this field, in 1971, most children with leukemia lived only a few years with the diagnosis. I was called in one night to deal with Brett, a bright 11-year-old boy who was highly anxious as he realized in the quiet of the night that he was unlikely to live to see his 14th birthday.

It was a powerful conversation.

Throughout the early hours of morning, the child struggled with all the things that he realized he would probably never do, from driving a car, to finishing school, to romance with a girl he would never likely meet. The next morning when I dropped by, he was watching *Perry Mason,* a popular television show of the time about an attorney. As I sat down, he turned to me, just hours after our painful dialogue, and announced, "When I get older, I think I would like to be a lawyer." We made small talk about the challenges of law. I realized how important *both* conversations were. Brett needed to know that I could talk to him about death. But he also needed to know that he could control that discussion, and that I would not intrude when he was not ready to address it.

The concept of *middle knowledge* expands considerably the understanding of denial. It reminds us that individuals with life-threatening illness must, at times, use denial simply to cope with the realities of life—one could not constantly focus on one's own death. Yet, as Weisman also points out, true and sustained denial in persons with life-threatening illness is rare. Such individuals, even children, are constantly assessing internal cues. They know they are getting weaker, they can feel the disease progress. They are reminded of their condition by external cues—the visits, glances, and guarded comments of others. In an Internet era, information is no longer controlled by medical monopoly. It is easily available with a few clicks of a mouse.

Although that is true, individuals with life-threatening illness will want to set the pace, to determine when and with whom they wish to discuss the possibility or even the inevitability of death. To Weisman, the important question was not "Does the patient accept or deny death?" but rather "When, with whom, and under what circumstances does the patient discuss the possibility of death?"

The Evolution of Anticipatory Grief

In the closing section of his study on acute grief, Lindemann (1944) noted that individuals anticipating a loss could experience grief reactions. Later, Fulton and associates (Fulton & Fulton, 1971; Fulton & Gottesman, 1980) attempted to develop this concept. They viewed anticipatory grief as a more common reaction, because illnesses were generally now more prolonged, and they viewed these grief reactions somewhat ambivalently. They hypothesized that as individuals slowly die, others might experience grief reactions such as sadness or depression, rehearse the death, and even prepare to live with the consequences of the death. The potential difficulty was that as family members continued to grieve in anticipation of the eventual and inevitable death, they might disengage from the person who was dying— further isolating that individual. In addition, if the dying period was highly prolonged, family members' grief may very well be "spent"; that is, most of their grief was completed by the time of death, leaving little visible reaction at the moment of death. Because the immediate family felt little reaction, they might well decide to forgo a traditional funeral, thus depriving the extended family and intimate network of a meaningful ritual that would facilitate their grieving process.

Later, Fulton became concerned that the term was easily misused. Fulton wrote at a time when many clinicians attempted to "encourage" family members to experience anticipatory grief under the assumption that the acknowledgment and processing of the grief prior to the loss would mitigate grief experienced after the death. He later described this as a "hydrostatic" perspective of grief—indicating a zero-sum notion of grief; that is, that there is just so much grief or tears that can be expended. Therefore, whatever is experienced earlier on in the illness will not need to be encountered later (Fulton, 1987). Moreover, foreknowledge or forewarning of death does not seem to necessarily imply that anticipatory grief occurs. It is little wonder that research showed little evidence that the anticipation of loss positively influenced later grief outcomes (see Rando, 2000, for an extensive review). Fulton has since reevaluated the concept, stating, "I have serious reservations regarding the heuristic value—either theoretical or practical—of the concepts 'anticipatory grief' and 'anticipatory mourning'" (Fulton, 2003, p. 348).

Rando (2000) has offered an extensive revision of the concept. Rando acknowledges that the term *anticipatory grief* is a misnomer. Yet, she still finds it useful. Rando redefines the phenomenon as *anticipatory mourning*. This is a critical distinction. Anticipatory *grief* refers to a reaction, but anticipatory *mourning* is a far more inclusive concept that refers not only to reactions experienced but also the intrapsychic and interpsychic processes that one uses to adapt to and cope with life-limiting illness. Rando also redefines the concept as referring not only to the grief generated by the possibility of future loss but primarily as a reaction to the losses currently experienced in the course of the illness. The patient is not the only person to incur these losses. Family members and even professional caregivers may experience these losses as the patient continues to decline.

For example, in the early 1990s a good friend of mine, Kurt, a man in his 40s and married with two young adult children, developed ALS (amyotrophic lateral sclerosis), popularly called Lou Gehrig's disease. ALS is a motor neuron disease characterized by progressive deterioration. Eventually, victims may lose much neural functioning and may become unable to use their limbs, to speak or even to swallow, or, eventually, to breathe without respiratory support. As Kurt continued to decline, he once commented that his greatest loss was his ability to hug his children. He was a bright and witty conversationalist prior to the illness. At the funeral, his wife commented that her greatest loss, even beyond that of the death itself, was when he finally lost the power of speech.

Rando never saw disengagement from the person with life-threatening illness as an inevitable result of anticipatory grief. Rather, she viewed the family as struggling with three different and contradictory reactions—striving to be with the person in the present, longing for and grieving the person as he or she was, and simultaneously planning for a life with the possibility that the ill individual may not be part of that future. Because this reaction is far more complex than simply an anticipation of the death, it has little relation to the grief reactions that may be experienced should the individual with the illness eventually die. Rando's reformulation then frees the concept from much of the earlier misconceptions that proved problematic.

The Possibilities in Dying

In addition to coping with dying, there has been some work on possibilities for continued growth and development throughout the dying process. Kübler-Ross, in her edited book, *Death: The Final Stage of Growth* (1975), suggested that accepting the finiteness of life allows us to more fully live life—discarding the external roles and petty concerns that are essentially meaningless. Dying persons are our teachers, she asserts, because when they accept the limited time left in their lives, they can focus on what is truly important and meaningful.

Byock, in his excellent book, *Dying Well: The Prospect for Growth at the End-of-Life* (1997), suggests that, once a dying patient is freed from pain, that person retains the human potential to grow and the possibility to use his or her remaining time to express love, finish significant and meaningful tasks, and reconcile with others.

This may be true at any phase in the illness experience. My father was a child of the Depression. He took his work very seriously, sometimes in a consuming way. He was anxious about his work as well. Despite that he was a valued employee, he constantly worried about his performance as well as the stability of his firm. He rarely took vacations, and when he did, he seemed to get little enjoyment from them. We feared, as often was the case, that a call from the office would abort our trip. He was like many fathers of that era; families were the responsibility of the mother.

When I was a teenager, my father showed symptoms of prostate problems. This was a cause of great anxiety, because his father had died painfully from prostate cancer. My father made many promises to my mother, and I suppose to God, if he could be spared a similar fate. The biopsy showed benign enlargement—nothing more.

My mother kept him to his promises, however. Family became more important. Less fearful at work, he stood his ground and offered his opinions more often. He even countered a threat from his supervisor with an offer to resign—knowing that he could always find work. The result was not what he initially expected. His supervisor turned white, offered him a raise, and met whatever modest demands my father had asked. He worked for the man in a number of different roles, including as a postretirement consultant well into his 70s. He often joked throughout life that an enlarged prostate was one of the best things that ever happened to him.

Such growth can happen at any phase of an illness, even or perhaps especially as death nears. This time can offer unique opportunities to express love or to ask forgiveness, and even to bring a sense of completion to one's life. The key caution is to remember that these are possibilities—possibilities that need to be embraced by the dying person. They become a danger when others, whether family members or health professionals, see it as their goal to induce the dying person to achieve such possibilities. Shneidman (1982) offers a fitting caution that no one has to die in a state of "psychoanalytical grace."

Intervals and Phases

One of the limitations of Kübler-Ross's work is that, at the time it was written, many individuals diagnosed with a disease had a limited life span that was often lived exclusively within a medical setting. As time and treatment progressed, the reality of illness changed. A diagnosis in many diseases was not necessarily a death sentence. Individuals experienced treatment—often as an outpatient—and even returned to their earlier roles. Counseling persons with diseases such as cancer did not initially or automatically meaning counseling individuals who were dying.

The work of both Pattison (1978) and Weisman (1980) began to reflect the changing nature of the illness experience. Pattison (1978) spoke of a *living-dying interval*, or the time between a diagnosis and a death. As Pattison noted 30 years ago, this is a new stage in the human life cycle, enabled by medical advances that allowed individuals to extend life considerably. In the years since Pattison first wrote about the living-dying interval, not only has this time been extended but, for many diseases, even the certainty of death has been challenged.

Pattison further divided this living-dying interval into three phases. The first phase, an *acute crisis phase*, is characterized by the crisis of a diagnosis that disrupts the assumptions and patterns of life. The *chronic phase* is the period of time during which one lives with the disease, seeking treatment, and, to Pattison, coping with a multiplicity of fears as the disease continues to debilitate. In the *terminal phase*, the patient begins to disengage as he or she approaches death.

Similarly Weisman (1980), studying cancer patients, spoke of several stages in the course of the illness. The first of Weisman's psychosocial stages of cancer was *existential plight*. Here there are two substages—impact distress at the time of diagnosis and existential plight proper as the patient continues to adjust to the diagnosis, initial treatment, the reality of cancer, and the threat of death. Weisman recognizes that some of these fears and issues can even arise prior to diagnosis as the patient begins to notice signs and possibly suspect cancer. This phase usually lasts about three or four months.

The second stage, *mitigation and accommodation,* can last indefinitely depending on the course of the disease. Here essentially the patient learns to live with the diagnosis, adjusting to the limitations imposed by the treatment or the disease.

In stage three, *decline and deterioration* occurs when the disease begins to progress. Here the patient's quality of life begins to suffer, and the patient moves to a fourth stage, *terminality and preterminality,* as the declines become steeper and death becomes inevitable.

Myers and Lynn (2001) remind us of another reality of death in contemporary Western societies. Many people today, especially older persons, often face multiple, chronic, life-threatening illnesses as they approach the end of life. This not only complicates care; it makes a definitive prognosis difficult. The result is that many individuals today die suddenly—in the middle of multiple chronic conditions.

Task and Phase Models of Coping with Life-Threatening Illness and Dying

Worden's publication of *Grief Counseling and Grief Therapy* (1982) represented a paradigm shift in the way we understood mourning—one that would contribute to the study of dying as well. Whereas prior models offered a more linear stage or phase theory to explain the mourning process, Worden conceptualized mourning as a series of four tasks. As Corr (1992) noted, the use of tasks offered certain advantages. Implicit in the concept of tasks was an inherent assumption of individuality and autonomy not often seen in stage models. Bereaved individuals might find it easier to cope with some tasks than with others. They would complete tasks in their own unique ways. They would also complete these tasks on their own timetables or even choose not to address certain tasks. Also, in contrast to stage theories, there was no assumption of linearity. Moreover, a task model had clear clinical implications. A grief counselor could assist clients in understanding what tasks they were struggling with and facilitate these grieving clients as they sought to work on these difficult tasks.

Both Corr (1992) and I (1993, 1995) applied the concept of tasks to the dying process. To Corr, coping with dying involved four major tasks that correspond to the dimensions of human life—physical, psychological, social, and spiritual. The physical task was to satisfy bodily needs and to minimize physical distress in ways that are consistent with other values. Corr defined the psychological task as to maximize psychological security, autonomy, and richness. The social task was to sustain and enhance those interpersonal attachments that are significant to the person concerned, and to sustain selected interactions with social groups within society or with society itself. Corr's spiritual task was to address issues of meaningfulness, connectedness, and transcendence and, in doing so, to foster hope.

Building on the work of both Pattison (1978) and Weisman (1980), I suggested that a life-threatening illness could be understood as a series of phases, noting that not all phases would appear in any given illness (1993, 1995). The *prediagnostic phase* concerns itself with the process of health seeking. It refers to the time prior to the diagnosis.

One of the most common, but not the only context, would be the time between when an individual notices a symptom and seeks medical assistance. The *acute phase* refers to the crisis period surrounding the diagnosis of life-threatening illness. The *chronic phase* refers to that period where the individual struggles with the disease and treatment. Many individuals may recover from the illness. However, it is important to remember that, in the *recovery phase*, individuals do not simply go back to the life experienced before illness. They still have to adapt to the aftereffects, residues, and fears and anxieties aroused by the illness. The *terminal phase* revolves around adapting to the inevitability of impending death as treatment becomes palliative (see Figure 1.1 in preceding chapter).

At each phase, individuals have to adapt to a series of tasks. These tasks derive from four general or global tasks—to respond to the physical facts of disease, to take steps to cope with the reality of the disease, to preserve self-concept and relationships with others in the face of the disease, and to deal with affective and existential/spiritual issues created or reactivated by the disease (see Table 1.1 in preceding chapter).

Although these models seem to have interesting implications for understanding the ways in which individuals cope with dying and life-threatening illness, they have not been widely applied. Yet they still represent a possible direction toward which we strive to develop new approaches and models of the dying process. It is this model that underlies this book.

REFERENCES

Byock, I. (1997). *Dying well: The prospect for growth at the end-of-life.* New York: Putnam.

Connor, S. (1998). *Hospice: Practice, pitfalls and promise.* Washington, DC: Taylor and Frances.

Corr, C. A. (1992) A task-based approach to coping with dying. *Omega: Journal of Death and Dying, 25,* 81–94.

Corr, C. A. (1993). Coping with dying: Lessons we should and should not learn from the work of Elisabeth Kubler-Ross. *Death Studies, 17,* 69–83.

Corr, C. A., Doka, K. J, & Kastenbaum, R. (1999). Dying and its interpreters: A review of selected literature and some comments on the state of the field. *Omega: The Journal of Death and Dying, 39,* 239–259.

Doka, K. J. (1993). *Living with life-threatening illness: A guide for patients, their families, and caregivers.* Lexington, MA: Lexington Books.

Doka, K. J. (1995) Coping with life threatening illness: A task based approach. *Omega: Journal of Death and Dying, 32,* 111–122.

Feifel, H. (1959). *The meaning of death.* New York: McGraw-Hill.

Fulton, R. (1987). Unanticipated grief. In C. A. Corr & R. A. Pacholski (Eds.), *Death: Completion and discovery* (pp. 49–60). Lakewood, OH: The Association for Death Education and Counseling.

Fulton, R. (2003). Anticipatory mourning: A critique of the concept. *Mortality, 8,* 342–351.

Fulton, R., & Fulton, J. (1971). A psychosocial aspect of terminal care: Anticipatory grief. *Omega: Journal of Death and Dying, 2,* 91–100.

Fulton, R., & Gottesman, D. J. (1980). Anticipatory grief: A psychosocial concept reconsidered. *British Journal of Psychiatry, 137,* 45–54.

Glaser, B., & Strauss, A. (1965). *Awareness of dying.* Chicago: Aldine.

Glaser, B., & Strauss, A. (1968). *Time for dying.* Chicago: Aldine.

Klass, D., & Hutton, R. A. (1985.) Elisabeth Kübler-Ross as a religious leader. *Omega: The Journal of Death and Dying, 16,* 89–109.

Kübler-Ross, E. (1969). *On death and dying.* New York: Macmillan.

Kübler-Ross, E. (1975). *Death: The final stage of growth.* Englewood Cliffs, NJ: Prentice-Hall.

Lindemann, E. (1944) The symptomatology and management of acute grief. *American Journal of Psychiatry, 6,* 193–199.

Lynn, J., Chaudhry, E., Simon, L. N., Wilkinson, A., & Schuster, J. (2007). *Improving palliative care.* Oxford: Oxford University Press.

Myers, S. S., & Lynn, J. (2001). Patients with eventually fatal chronic illness: Their importance within a national research agenda on improving patient safety and reducing medical error. *Journal of Palliative Medicine, 4,* 325–332.

National Consensus Project for Quality Palliative Care (NCP). (2004). *Clinical practice guidelines for quality palliative care.* Retrieved from http://www.nationalconsensus-project.org

Pattison, E. M. (1978). The living-dying interval. In C. Garfield (Ed.), *Psychological care of the dying patient* (pp. 163–168). New York: McGraw-Hill.

Pine, V. (1977). A socio-historical portrait of death education. *Death Education, 1,* 57–84.

Pine, V. (1986). The age of maturity for death education: A socio-historical portrait of the era 1976–1985. *Death Studies, 10,* 209–231.

Rando, T. A. (2000). *Clinical dimensions of anticipatory mourning. Theory and practice in working with the dying, their loved ones, and their caregivers.* Champaign, IL: Research Press.

Saunders, C. (1959, October 9–November 13). The problem of euthanasia. . . . When a patient is dying (a series of articles). *Nursing Times* 960–961, 994–995, 1031, 1091–1092, 1129–1130.

Saunders, C., & Kastenbaum, R. (1997). *Hospice care on the international scene.* Beverly Hills, CA: Sage.

Schulz, R., & Aderman, D. (1974). Clinical research and the stages of dying. *Omega: Journal of Death and Dying, 5,* 137–143.

Shneidman, E. (1982, September). *Reflections on contemporary death.* Keynote presentation to the Forum for Death Education and Counseling, San Diego, California.

Stoddard, S. (1978). *The hospice movement: A better way of caring for the dying.* New York: Vintage Books.

Strauss, A. (1975). *Chronic illness and the quality of life.* St. Louis, MO: C. V. Mosby Company.

Sudnow, D. (1967). *Passing on: The social organization of dying.* Englewood Cliffs, NJ: Prentice-Hall.

Weisman, A., & Hackett, T. (1962). *The dying patient: Special treatment situations.* Des Plaines, IL: Forest Hospital Publications.

Weisman, A. (1972). *On dying and denying. A psychiatric study of terminality.* New York: Behavioral Publications.

Weisman, A. (1979). *Coping with cancer.* New York: McGraw-Hill.

Weisman, A. (1980). Thanatology. In O. Kaplan (Ed.), *Comprehensive textbook of psychiatry.* Baltimore: Williams & Wilkins.

Weisman, A. (1984). The *coping capacity: On the nature of being mortal.* New York: Human Science Press, Inc.

Worden, J. W. (1982) *Grief counseling and grief therapy: A handbook for the mental health practitioner.* New York: Springer.

3 Effective Professional Caregivers: Seven Sensitivities

A woman institutionalized in a nursing home was praising her nurse, describing her as gentle and warm, caring and considerate. "Of course," the woman added, "I wish I never had the opportunity or need to meet her." This comment expresses the ambivalent way in which caregivers can be perceived as they care for individuals and families struggling with life-threatening illness. They are important, critical allies in the struggle, and are sometimes perceived as having almost magical powers. Caregivers, families, and individuals can forge powerful bonds. Caregivers can become deeply concerned about and involved with their clients. Indeed, occasionally caregivers are the ones who are unable to let go, even when individuals themselves and their families are ready to accept death.

Yet the caregiver role can generate more than a little ambivalence. Sick individuals and their families may have mixed feelings toward their caregivers. Caregivers, after all, are unwelcome reminders of disease. Individuals who are ill, as well as their families, may resent their dependence on caregivers. Certainly, patients may wish that the circumstances of life had never brought them together.

To function effectively, caregivers will have to demonstrate sensitivity; sensitivity to the individual is paramount. They will also need to be sensitive to the culture of the individual, whether ethnicity, lifestyle, or social class defines that culture. They will need to be sensitive to the constraints and nature of their own roles. In all, there are seven sensitivities that the most effective caretakers manifest:

1. sensitivity to the whole person
2. sensitivity to the problem of pain and discomfort
3. sensitivity to honest, open, and mutual communication
4. sensitivity to the individual's autonomy
5. sensitivity to the individual's needs
6. sensitivity to cultural differences
7. sensitivity to treatment goals

This chapter addresses these seven sensitivities of effective caregiving. It puts these sensitivities at the center of any caregiving role—whether for the physician, the health aide, the counselor, the nurse, the chaplain, or the social worker. I have seen caregivers in a variety of roles taking a special place in an individual's struggle with life-threatening illness. In each case, it was that caretaker's combination of skill and sensitivity that enabled him or her to contribute in a positive manner in that struggle. The next chapter then identifies some of the key attributes of the skilled counselor.

SENSITIVITY TO THE WHOLE PERSON

I remember one doctor on grand rounds stopping by the bed of a man who had cancer. As the interns surrounded the bed, the doctor began to lecture. Still lecturing, the doctor and his entourage departed, never having said a single word to the ill man himself. The doctor was highly skilled technically; indeed, on that level he had much to recommend him. But he was seriously flawed as a healer because he saw people as patients with various conditions, such as bad livers or swollen spleens. He was blind to the fact that patients are people: husbands or wives, fathers or mothers, baseball fans or balletomanes, cat lovers or dog fanciers.

The persons one cares for are not just patients but people—living human beings who are struggling with all the concerns of life. Life-threatening illness, at any phase, is more than just a physical or health problem. Life-threatening illness is a multifaceted crisis, one that affects an individual physically, psychologically, socially, financially, and spiritually.

Effective caregiving means maintaining consistent sensitivity to all the dimensions of this crisis. That holistic approach is the heart and strength of the hospice philosophy. But most caregivers do not have the luxury of taking a holistic approach when a patient has reached the terminal stage of illness. Nor do caregivers always have the luxury of "specializing." Individuals themselves will often choose the person with whom they wish to discuss specific concerns. It is not unusual for a patient to address psychological or spiritual concerns to a nurse, rather than to a psychologist or a chaplain. One woman, for example, reminded her nurse that the chaplain was not available at that moment, 2:00 a.m., but that she needed to talk now. Her nurse was able to listen, provide support, and later provide referral to other caregivers as well.

A holistic approach affirms the reality that life-threatening illness takes place in the context of life. Throughout the time of illness individuals continue to struggle with the same issues and needs that preceded the illness. Naturally, these issues can and will be complicated by the experience of illness. Caregivers who recognize these struggles will not only facilitate an individual's response to illness, but also reaffirm his or her human identity.

SENSITIVITY TO THE PROBLEM OF PAIN AND DISCOMFORT

Pain will be a major focus of attention for individuals experiencing severe symptoms or physical discomfort, leaving them little energy for anything else. Intense pain can exacerbate psychological distress, disrupt social relationships, and intensify spiritual alienation, but none of these issues can be addressed until individuals achieve at least minimal comfort. One of the most important tasks of caregivers is to help individuals who are experiencing pain to achieve a reasonable degree of physical comfort.

The good news is that there is both an increased recognition, even by regulatory bodies, of the importance of pain control as well as an increasing array of pharmaceutical, radiological, and surgical strategies as well as complimentary therapies to achieve effective management. In addition, many hospices and hospitals now recognize the need to treat pain holistically. A distinction can be made between *pain*—a physical sensation—and *suffering* as mental and spiritual anguish (Puchalski, 2006). The point is that in a life-threatening illness both pain and suffering may be contributing to the patient's discomfort. Hence effective pain management must be accompanied by spiritual and psychological counseling.

The bad news is that despite these advances many patients still suffer and experience pain. Although there has been considerable progress in understanding, assessing, and treating pain, there are still considerable barriers to effective pain management. Some barriers relate to policy. In the current regulatory climate, many physicians are reluctant to prescribe opioids because this may attract the unwelcome attention of state and federal authorities (Doka, 2006; Edmondson, 2006). Some barriers are related to the education of physicians and the organization of medical care. Many physicians and nurses were trained at a time when effective pain management was underemphasized. Physicians may be suspicious of patients who constantly complain of pain (Doka, 2006). Hospital care is often fragmented. One of the lessons of hospice is that pain management is best achieved with multidisciplinary teams. Yet, it is not only the problem of medicine; many patients and their families may be fearful of pain medications—worried that they may lose consciousness and control or become addicted. There may even be a *Dubose syndrome*, which is a belief much like that of the character Mrs. Dubose in *To Kill a Mockingbird*, that suffering is a mark of moral fiber and that it is heroic to die unbeholden to any drug (Doka, 2006).

Caregivers may use several strategies to manage pain. In some cases they may serve as patient advocates, reminding doctors and nurses about the pain problems of the individual. In other situations, they may have the ability to directly intervene. They may be able to provide more effective pain treatment.

Pain management is a shared responsibility. Each professional caregiver should take pain seriously and respectfully—remembering that "pain is what the patient says it is." Each caregiver shares a responsibility to assess pain and advocate for the patient's needs. Although physicians retain primary responsibility for medically treating pain, other caregivers may have a role in managing pain within the parameters of their role.

Caregivers also may be able to teach patients and families both how to assess and report pain and alternative, nonpharmaceutical techniques of pain control such as imaging and visualizations, relaxation techniques, and other behaviorist and cognitive approaches. Such help will not only allow individuals to experience increased comfort and permit them to consider other issues, but it may also assuage anxieties, reaffirm an individual's sense of control, and build trust and rapport.

SENSITIVITY TO HONEST, OPEN, AND MUTUAL COMMUNICATION

Honest and mutual communication is an essential prerequisite to care. Open communication means responding honestly to an individual's concerns. This is the essence of patient rights and is central to effective caregiving: caregiving cannot be effective in a context characterized by deceit and evasion.

Whereas it is important to provide individuals with information about their illness, it is equally important to do a good job communicating this information. Hogshead (1976), for example, suggests eight principles to employ when delivering "bad news":

1. Keep it simple.
2. Ask yourself, "What does this diagnosis mean to this patient?"
3. Meet on "cool ground" first. Get to know a patient prior to presenting the news.

4. Wait for questions.
5. Do not argue with denial.
6. Ask questions yourself.
7. Do not destroy all hope.
8. Do not say anything that is not true.

These suggestions were addressed primarily to physicians, but they are useful for all caregivers. They remind caregivers of the need to establish a context of open communication.

Avoid cryptic messages that leave people in suspense. It is cruel to say to a person struggling with illness something like "Well, the tests were not as positive as we hoped; we'll talk about it next Tuesday." It is better to say nothing than to provide people with partial information that can only increase their anxieties. Full disclosure, with time allotted for discussion, is the only way to present unsettling news.

There is a nonverbal dimension to open communication as well. The caregiver needs to convey both by the use of space and demeanor as well as words that he or she welcomes communication. Providing privacy, maintaining eye contact, and, when appropriate and acceptable, including reassuring physical contact, facilitate communication. Sitting near an individual rather than behind a desk communicates equality and respect.

An open communication process is both honest and person centered. Here the caregiver honestly responds to the individual's concerns. For these concerns are cues to what the person is able and willing to hear at any given time. Thus, if the individual does not ask about, or does not wish to discuss, prognosis at the time of the diagnosis, it need not be addressed. And if the individual does ask or wish to discuss such issues, they ought to be considered in as tentative and hopeful a manner as honesty allows.

An open communication process tries to accomplish three goals:

- It lets the individual set the pace and tone.
- It is reflective. It allows individuals to reflect on their concerns, in effect, to find the answers to their own questions. For example, once a man asked me whether I thought he would live to see his new grandchild, expected in about four

months. When I asked what he thought, it became an opportunity to share his fear, anxieties, frustrations, and unfinished business. Previous queries to his physician yielded only vaguely hopeful reassurances that showed a reluctance to consider his question.

■ An open communication process provides reassurance that any topic is open to consideration.

Open communication also means trying to understand the individual's perspectives. It is essential that one try to understand an individual's own biography and perspective. That biography may include items that are part of an individual's history: personal and familial characteristics, religious and spiritual beliefs, cultural perspectives, and informal and formal social support. But it is also critical to understand the individual's perspective on health, illness, treatment, and perhaps, at a later phase, even death.

It is important to understand how an individual became the person he or she is now. To do that, one has to understand the ways in which that individual has struggled with the illness. Often the individual's thoughts and fears about a diagnosis can be very revealing.

Health professionals can be dismissive of, or even threatened by, an individual's attempt at self-diagnosis. Yet self-diagnosis can be very informative: it reveals much about the individual's medical sophistication, fears, support systems, and early attempts at detection and treatment. Rather than avoiding the individual's perspective on diagnosis, health professionals should encourage such discussion. Beyond providing insight into the person's basic beliefs, this discussion can convey an attitude of respect and help facilitate a context in which the individual is a full participant in treatment.

This step leads naturally into a larger area of concern, understanding the person's perspective on health, illness, treatment, and death. But understanding of that perspective is not easy. Whereas caregivers may or may not differ from individuals in terms of psychological attributes, social attributes, and philosophical ideas, they are certain to differ from them in role and perspective. It has often been noted that doctors are accorded almost mystical prestige in our society. The caregiver brings prestige, knowledge, and authority to the encounter, and the ill individual or family member is clearly dependent. Perspective too is dissimilar. The caregiver is dealing with scientific generalities, but the individual is concerned with a specific life, his or her own. Language too, is different. Scientific language is always tentative and probabilistic: "The chance of X occurring is very remote." But individuals who are struggling with illness speak a more concrete language and seek to hear certainty: "X will never occur," or "X is inevitable." Sometimes educational, class, and cultural differences that cloud the communication process can also complicate these differences.

Words may have very dissimilar meanings for caregivers and ill individuals. Each person has a personal construction or meaning of the disease that includes images of the disease as well as ideas about its etiology, treatment, and outcome. Susan Sontag (1988) noted that metaphoric meanings connected to a disease might include connotations of weakness, punishment, and/or inevitable decay and death. A person receiving a diagnosis of AIDS, for example, may perceive the disease as being rapid and horrifying, disfiguring and disorientating. Another individual receiving the same diagnosis may have an image of a long, uncertain struggle, but one that allows interludes of remission and perhaps the opportunity of benefiting from a still-to-be discovered cure.

Perceptions of etiology can also differ. Some may perceive the disease as an unlucky event, others as divine wrath. Given current knowledge that emphasizes lifestyle factors in disease, it is not unusual for individuals to identify lifestyle factors that they believe contributed to the disease. But the degree to which someone attributes illnesses to his or her own behavior, and the feelings he or she has about personal responsibility for illness, can differ widely.

People habitually reinterpret the past to make sense of the present. Individual perceptions concerning the etiology of a disease may include numerous segments of biography that the individual believes brought him or her to this moment. And there may be considerable affect, including anger and guilt, in that reconstruction.

Images and theories of treatment may vary as well. Certain individuals with cancer may have a deep fear of surgery because they wrongly believe that once the cancer is exposed to the surgeon's knife it will inevitably grow and spread. Others may have heard horror stories about chemotherapy or fear that radiation will lead to impotence or cause new cancerous growths. Individuals may have self-fulfilling expectations concerning side effects.

People with illness may also have divergent images of outcome. Some may see death as inevitable, others see it as a risk, and still others see it as a remote possibility. They may have images of other outcomes too. The person who suffers a heart attack may envision a postattack life of near-invalidism. A woman facing a mastectomy may believe her sexual life is over. Individuals may fear that disease will lead to financial impoverishment and familial disintegration.

Even meanings of death can differ. To some, death can be the great enemy, to be fought at all costs. Others may be resigned to death. Some may fear death greatly; others may show less anxiety. Some may see death as an entry to a new form of existence, others as the end of existence.

Images arise from a number of sources. Individuals may have had different experiences with death. Knowledge of the disease may differ. All the variables that affect attitudes—class, culture, age, place in the life cycle, education, religious beliefs, gender, and personality—will influence images of illness, treatment, and death.

There may be societal influences as well. Sontag (1978, 1988) suggests that many diseases have a public meaning. She notes that diseases are often used as metaphors—for example, "The cancer of poverty that eats away at the heart of the city." These metaphors influence private meanings of the disease, often complicating responses to a diagnosis. These meanings may change over time and may not be consistent from society to society. Cancer and leprosy, for example, no longer hold the terror they once held. Historically, even at times when leprosy was prevalent, it was not always perceived in the same manner by different cultures. In some cultures leprosy was greatly feared and lepers ostracized, but in others there was little fear or disgust. AIDS, in the early years of the epidemic, and to an extent, even now, provides a similar example. AIDS was one of most dreaded diseases in our society, perhaps because it combines characteristics of other diseases feared throughout history—mysterious origin, disfiguring symptoms, and inevitable fatality—and perhaps because it is passed through blood and semen, bodily fluids that have had universal mystical significance as the fluids of life.

Whatever the roots of patient images, caregivers should try to explore the individual's perspective on the disease during the time of diagnosis. Exploration will enable the caregiver to better understand what issues significant for the individual are likely to crop up during the course of the disease and treatment. Every disease creates its own distinct issues, both medically and psychosocially, for care. Colon cancer, and subsequent colostomy, may create deep feelings of shame and possible social isolation. One task of the caregiver in counseling an individual through a life-threatening illness is to understand how the unique issues raised by any given disease and its subsequent treatment will be understood, interpreted, and acted upon by that person.

A second reason for understanding the individual's perspective is to guard against what might be called self-fulfilling prophecies. Sudnow (1967), in his book *Passing On,* offers a vivid example of the potency of self-fulfilling prophecies. A man diagnosed with a particularly virulent form of cancer exhibited the normal symptoms and decline characteristic of the disease. Only after his death did the autopsy indicate that the tumor was benign and should not have been life-threatening. In recent years the recognition that a person's perspectives on disease may influence outcome has increased. Certainly, the individual's perspective will influence responses to the disease and treatment. As Rosenbaum (1978, p. 171) states, "The successful long-term treatment of any patient will depend to a great degree on a patient's attitude. If he can strive for and maintain a positive attitude, which means he is willing to fight for his life and believes he can live longer by doing so, he often will respond better to treatment."

Caregivers need to understand and to work through individual's anxieties about treatment. Siegel (1986) claims that "the most important thing [for an ill individual] is to pick a therapy you believe in," and believes that most negative side effects are the result of self-fulfilling prophecies fostered by physicians and patients. Other research (Chandler, 1965) has indicated that individuals who have a strong presentiment of death—that is, a feeling that death can occur at any time, an attitude often found in heart attack and stroke victims—exhibit higher levels of anxiety, interpersonal difficulties, and acting-out behaviors. Although the topic of impact of an individual's perspective on treatment and prognosis needs more extended investigation, it already seems clear that an individual's perspective does play some role on outcome. At the very least, it can be said that individuals who harbor some hope that the disease can be slowed, if not stopped, have a stronger motivation for treatment.

A final issue in reviewing an individual's biography is to understand earlier crises and the ways in which that person coped with these prior crises. Such discussion may provide a good sense of the individual's circumstances as well as his or her perspective. Some may have lived a life characterized by crises whereas others may have lives that are less tempestuous. Some may define a wide range of events as crises whereas others are far more selective. A discussion of the responses to these crises also reveals basic coping strategies. These strategies will often be used throughout the current crises. Becoming aware of them at this early point allows caregivers, individuals, and families opportunities to discuss the ways that their characteristic coping styles both facilitate and complicate adjustment. And it alerts caregivers to the need to explore what may be occurring when these formerly characteristic coping styles are not used in the current crisis.

SENSITIVITY TO THE INDIVIDUAL'S AUTONOMY

Sensitivity to the individual means respecting that individual's autonomy. The very experience of life-threatening illness thrusts persons into dependent roles. At times in the illness individuals may be physically dependent. Even if they are not always physically dependent, they are dependent for treatment and information from caregivers. Often they may feel that their lives are out of control.

The sensitive caregiver tries to reaffirm that sense of control by offering choices when possible, rather than simply making dictates, or by allowing families and individuals as much control over treatment and daily routine as possible. Sometimes this can be very simple: for example, allowing an individual to choose one time slot for treatment from among three or four possible time slots gives him or her a sense of participation in his or her treatment.

Respecting autonomy also means respecting a person's choices. Every individual will make his or her own choices on how to cope with the illness, how to choose appropriate treatments, and—if necessary—how to face death. These choices may not always be the choices caregivers would make. Someone else's styles of coping may be very different, as may be his or her ways of responding to illness or death. One nurse, for example, was very troubled because a very special elderly patient had no interest in reconciling, prior to his death, with an estranged son. In another situation caregivers were dismayed that an individual chose to discontinue treatment. Caregivers cannot force people to do this or that; all caregivers can do is to help individuals to understand and evaluate their actions. They cannot make choices for others. Shneidman's (1982) dictum that "no one has to die in a state of psychoanalytic grace" is wise advice.

SENSITIVITY TO THE INDIVIDUAL'S NEEDS

Having sensitivity to the individual means, of course, having sensitivity for all of that person's needs. Throughout this book there are many needs—physical, financial, psychological, social, spiritual—that life-threatening illness intensifies. These needs complement and, at times, complicate the health needs of individuals as they continue to try to live their lives. Sensitive caregivers seek to support individuals as they meet those needs.

In addition, caregivers should be sensitive to the heightened sense of time that individuals with life-threatening illness sometimes experience. There is an exercise in which each student holds a lighted match as he or she relates the most important moments of his or her life. As the match burns down the person's pace sharply quickens. Individuals with life-threatening illness often respond in a similar way, but throughout their illness, not just in the few moments it takes for a match to burn. Time is the unknown. They feel well today, but tomorrow they may have a relapse. They may have little patience. There is much to do, to experience, and time is unsure. I mentioned in Chapter 7 a handout given to hospice volunteers on how they might handle dying persons' requests such as a desire for flowers, a need to talk, a wish to taste pizza. The correct response in each incident was "Do it now."

SENSITIVITY TO CULTURAL DIFFERENCES

In past decades there has been an increasing concern about the challenge posed while providing care to individuals from different cultural backgrounds (for example, Giger & Davidhizar, 1991; Sue & Sue, 2008). That concern arises from the central fact of caregiving that all good care is based on communication. For communication to be effective, both the caregiver and the individual cared for must be able to correctly interpret each other's verbal and nonverbal messages. This process can become very complicated when different cultural groups exhibit different nonverbal and verbal behaviors. It can be especially complicated when linguistic barriers further complicate the process. Even the use of interpreters can complicate interaction; for example, interpreters may seek to shield those for whom they interpret, changing the message to make it more palatable.

Counseling culturally different persons can be particularly difficult. The counseling process is rooted in Western and middle-class assumptions, such as the value of individualism and the importance of self-disclosure. Other cultural groups may not share these assumptions and may be mystified and threatened by counseling. Some groups may be uncomfortable with self-disclosure, particularly, with outsiders. Dillard (1983), for example, indicates that many Asian Americans have been taught to mask behavior and avoid eye contact. He also notes that many Asian females may be uncomfortable if left alone with a male. Leong (1986), in a comprehensive review of counseling with Asian Americans, also suggests that Asian Americans may not respond well to unstructured and ambiguous counseling contexts. More recent reviews have emphasized that Asian Americans, especially less acculturated populations, may be reluctant to discuss death or prepare advance directives, are more likely to prefer aggressive treatment, and often defer decisions to family members (Hsiung & Farrans, 2007; Braun & Nichols, 1997)

Providing care to individuals with life-threatening illness is also complicated by the fact that different cultural groups have different expectations, attitudes, beliefs, behaviors, and values concerning health, illness, pain, and death. Cultural groups may differ on definitions of illness as well as theories of etiology and treatment.

Western medicine often focuses on immediate (for example, virus, bacteria, trauma, and so forth) and underlying (for example, poor sanitation, poor nutrition, weakness due to drug abuse, and so forth) causes, whereas many other cultural systems will focus on ultimate causes (for example, God's will or sin). Caregivers also should be aware that cultural expectations could influence relationships with caregivers and expectations about the caregiver's role. Hispanics, for example, may expect that a relationship with a caregiver will be personal and marked by trust. Family involvement in care and consultation is expected, especially with elders. Standards of etiquette and modesty also differ. Hispanics may expect that caregivers will spend time chatting with their clients prior to taking care of business.

Moreover, each cultural group has distinct values and perspectives that may influence even choices and ethical decisions as individuals face treatment for life-threatening illness and even, possibly, the end of life (see Cohen, 2005; Tiano & Beyer, 2005; Braun, Pietsch, & Blanchette, 2000). Caregivers need to retain a sensitivity not to assume that others share similar ethical principles. For example, a basic principle of Western ethics is a major emphasis on individual autonomy that may not resonate with persons from more collectivist or familial-based cultures. Here there may be an expectation that decisions must be addressed within a larger group such as the family and individual interests would be subordinated to what the family considers best. Similarly, cultures that have experienced a history of discrimination and devaluation may distrust suggestions to discontinue care and allow death to occur. Naturally, caregivers should always be careful never to assume an individual's personal sense of identity or that individual's adherence to the perceived values of that group.

In preparing to care for culturally different persons, the caregiver needs to begin with a strong sense of self-awareness. Counselors need to be cognizant of their own values and biases, comfortable with cultural differences, and ready to refer their clients elsewhere if necessary. They may also need to recognize that some groups may perceive them as representatives or symbols of a repressive system and thus become targets of anger. Caregivers may have to spend considerable time in developing rapport and trust with members of other groups.

Caregivers should also familiarize themselves with the individual's cultural group. Taking such simple actions as placing culturally relevant magazines in the waiting area can facilitate care. Such an act sends a message to the members of the group that the caregiver is cognizant of and sensitive to their concerns. Sometimes members of that culture may be effective resources. In other cases the caregivers can assume a stance of "enlightened ignorance," asking the individual to inform them about the beliefs, traditions, or behaviors with which they are unfamiliar. Often simple questions, such as "Is there anything that you wish us to know about your culture that can assist our work together?" can be quite revealing.

If caregivers have frequent contact with members of other cultural groups, they should make the effort to learn more about these cultures, seeking out information about their historical experiences, customs, other components of the culture, and especially cultural factors that might facilitate caregiving and coping with life-threatening illness. Such sensitivity is particularly necessary at the very beginning of the caregiving process, because even the way one defines or describes a group may affect subsequent development of trust and rapport. Many Hispanic/Latino groups, for example, resent the label "Spanish," preferring either a generic term such as Hispanic or Latino or identification with a particular country or culture of origin such as Puerto Rican or Cuban American.

In studying a culture, caregivers must always remember the individual. Many cultures are quite diverse, encompassing many values, traditions, and practices. Individuals may have grown up in families that are blended, that is, in families that draw from a variety of cultures. Individuals may differ in the degree to which they identify with a culture. Some may have a strong cultural identity: they grew up in their country of origin or in a strong ethnic neighborhood, have lived in or returned to such areas, participate in traditional events, take pride in their native culture, and socialize primarily with other members of that culture. Other individuals may be at midpoints in the continuum of cultural identity. And for many others, cultural identification can be remote and distant.

Once a culture is understood, and an individual's level of cultural identification is assessed, caregivers can adapt their methods to that culture and draw on that culture's unique strengths. Dillard (1983), for example, suggests that cognitive approaches may work very well with Asians, because cognitive approaches are compatible with beliefs and behaviors about will power and self-control. Dillard also describes how holistic health approaches work very well with Native Americans because holistic practices are consistent with their beliefs and values. In other situations caregivers may be able to use strong family support systems. Even traditional beliefs and folk practitioners may have a role. In one of my cases I counseled a Haitian immigrant being treated for cancer who had a recurring dream she would die on a given date. Conventional counseling did little to change her perspective. At the suggestion of a nurse, I contacted a folk healer from her community. He was able to convince her, after a ritual, that the curse implied by the dream was now removed.

Descriptions of the illness and treatment can sometimes be cast in traditional terms. And cultural rituals, too, may provide comfort and support in crisis. Ryan (1993) tells of an elderly Chinese American who was dying and who requested that incense be allowed beside his hospital bed. Participating in this ritual seemed to ease his anxiety.

It is also important to recognize that culture is not defined solely by ethnicity. Cultural groups can be defined by a variety of variables such as degree of education, social class, religion, or shared behaviors. Each social class, for example, can be defined as a subgroup within the greater cultural group, with its own shared behaviors, values, and beliefs. Again, caregivers from one class may need special sensitivity in assisting members of other classes. Lower income groups, for example, may be highly suspicious of authority, may be fatalistic and resigned about their condition, and may face a variety of economic and social barriers that complicate their adjustment to illness. They may be isolated from both formal and informal social support. Lower income families may also be coping with many concurrent crises. In addition, they may lack personal physicians, receiving much of their care in emergency rooms, thus limiting any continuity of care. On the other hand, some lower income people have had to fight so hard to survive that they have a toughness that can be used as a significant coping skill. In short, illness will present unique issues to each social class. I once counseled a 35-year-old man from a wealthy and powerful family who was dying from cancer. Although his wealth and connections enabled him to receive the best medical care, including participation in some experimental protocols, he and his spouse became angry and depressed during the terminal phase. They had so much, so enjoyable a life, that death seemed particularly unfair. He was extraordinarily angry and distressed that, with all his resources, he could not surmount the present crisis as he had so easily surmounted other problems in the past.

Religion too can define cultural groups. Caregivers should be sensitive to the unique religious traditions, practices, rituals, and beliefs of individuals. In one case nurses decided to cheer a patient up by celebrating her birthday. They were unaware that Jehovah's Witnesses do not celebrate such occasions.

Even shared behaviors may define a cultural group. The AIDS epidemic has made many caregivers sensitive to gay and drug subcultures. In each subculture, responses, feelings, and coping behaviors may differ. Medical treatment and counseling interventions will have to be adapted to that culture. For example, in designing interventions for intravenous (IV) drug users, caregivers should be sensitive to the often-chaotic lifestyles of members of this population, as well as the fatalism and self-destructive behaviors evident in many of them. Many IV drug users have long tolerated poor health along with addiction and have continually faced the risk of death. Interventions may have to be designed that take into account the unique experiences, behaviors, and issues of each subculture.

Finally, caregivers too may face their own unique stresses in working with the culturally different customs and behaviors of different groups. Vachon (1987) offers an illustration of a group of nurses who were discomforted by deathbed rituals of a given ethnic group. Caregivers may find it hard to understand the values, therapies, and rituals of other cultural groups. Caregivers may experience their own bias, fears, and anxieties. For example, many caregivers may be uncomfortable dealing with homosexuals or drug users. Communication difficulties also can frustrate caregivers.

In summation, caregivers have to remember that with any population, special issues often arise. The sensitive caregiver should try his or her best to adapt to each individual's cultural heritage, situation, or culture. Cultural competence remains a key attribute of the sensitive caregiver. Although awareness of cultural differences is a part of cultural competence, cultural competence is less a body of knowledge than it is a spirit of inquiry. Ultimately it is an openness and willingness to allow patients to teach about their own way of life.

SENSITIVITY TO GOALS

Throughout the course of the illness, there may be different goals for treatment. In the acute and chronic phases of the illness the realistic goals may involve saving, or at least significantly prolonging, an individual's life. In the terminal phase the goal is palliative, to provide comfort.

The sensitive caregiver must always be cognizant of these larger treatment goals. Many times the issues that arise in the caregiving and counseling process will be affected by treatment goals. For example, I remember two cases that had a surface similarity. In both cases a hospitalized leukemia patient wanted to attend a significant family event. Given the fragile nature of the individual's health, attendance held considerable health risk. In one case, though, the man was in the initial phases of treatment. There was a realistic hope of significantly prolonging his life and even hope of possible cure. Here the counseling goal was to make him aware of the risk he faced by leaving the hospital, and then, later, to help him find an alternate way of being part of the family occasion. In the second situation the woman was clearly in the terminal phase. Although her attendance at the family function held risk, this medical risk was secondary to the tremendous psychological comfort of attending. The treatment goal here was comfort, and my first counseling goal was to help the client understand the risk she faced. When she remained committed to her desire to attend the family function, I changed roles to serve as her advocate and facilitator.

This discussion presumes that treatment goals are shared by all involved caregivers and are realistic. When that assumption is not met, caregivers may have to question implied treatment goals. For example, I once observed a scene between a physician and a nurse. The doctor was reluctant to increase pain medication for his patient, expressing concern about possible addiction and adverse effects upon survival. "But," the nurse reminded him, "I thought we believed the patient would not recover? Isn't our goal now palliative?" This question allowed the care team to openly discuss and clarify treatment goals, and then to deliver care based upon these realistic goals.

Sometimes, too, it is the ill individual or other family members who are unwilling to recognize that treatment goals have shifted. For example, in one case a man was deeply upset and offended by a physician's suggestion that he consider hospice care because, although staff and family recognized he was dying, he unrealistically held to the hope of another remission. In such cases caregivers should tread carefully. An ill person's hopes may be explored, but it should be up to that individual to set the pace. A person's sense of hope and his or her defenses should not to be assaulted to obtain unanimity on treatment goals. An individual's sense of hope, whether realistic or not, should not expire much before he or she does.

REFERENCES

Braun, K., & Nichols, R. (1997). Death and dying in four Asian American cultures: A descriptive study. *Death Studies, 21*, 327–360.

Braun, K, Pietsch, J., & Blanchette, P. (2000). *Cultural issues in end-of-life decision making*. Thousand Oaks, CA: Sage Publications.

Chandler, K. (1965). Three process of dying and their behavioral effects. *Journal of Consulting Psychology, 29*, 296–301.

Cohen, C. (2005). Religious, spiritual and ideological perspectives on ethics at the end-of-life. In K. Doka, B. Jennings, & C. Corr (Eds.), *Ethical dilemmas at the end-of-life* (pp. 19–40). Washington, DC: The Hospice Foundation of America.

Dillard, J. (1983). *Multicultural counseling*. Chicago: Nelson-Hall.

Doka, K. J. (2006). Social, cultural, spiritual, and psychological barriers to pain management. In K. Doka (Ed.), *Pain management at the end-of-life: Bridging the gap between knowledge and practice* (pp. 59–74). Washington, DC: The Hospice Foundation of America.

Edmondson, D. (2006). Policy barriers to pain control. In K. Doka (Ed.), *Pain management at the end-of-life: Bridging the gap between knowledge and practice* (pp. 213–227). Washington, DC: The Hospice Foundation of America.

Giger, J., & Davidhizar, R. (1991). *Transcultural nursing: Assessment and intervention.* St. Louis: Mosby.

Hogshead, H. (1976). The art of delivering bad news. *Journal of the Florida Medical Association, 63*, 807.

Hsiung, Y., & Farrans, C. (2007). Recognizing Chinese Americans' cultural preferences in making end-of-life treatment decisions. *Journal of Hospice and Palliative Nursing, 9*, 132–140.

Leong, F. (1986). Counseling and psychotherapy with Asian-Americans: Review of the literature. *Journal of Counseling Psychology, 33*, 196–206.

Puchalski, C. (2006). Spirituality in the care of the aging and the dying. In K. Doka (Ed.), *Pain management at the end-of-life: Bridging the gap between knowledge and practice* (pp. 39–56). Washington, DC: The Hospice Foundation of America.

Rosenbaum, E. (1978). Oncology/hematology and psychological support of the cancer patient. In C. Garfield (Ed.), *Psychological care of the dying patient* (pp. 169–189). New York: McGraw-Hill.

Ryan, D. (1993). Death: Eastern perspectives. In K. Doka and J. Morgan (Eds.), *Death and spirituality* (pp. 75–92). Amityville, NY: Baywood Publishing Co.

Shneidman, E. (1982, September). *Reflections on contemporary death.* Keynote presentation to the Forum for Death Education and Counseling, San Diego, California.

Siegel, B. (1986). *Love, medicine, and miracles.* New York: Harper & Row.

Sontag, S. (1978). *Illness as metaphor.* New York: McGraw-Hill.

Sontag, S. (1988). *AIDS and its metaphors.* New York: Farrar, Strauss and Giroux.

Sudnow, D. (1967). *Passing on: The social organization of dying.* Englewood Cliffs, NJ: Prentice-Hall.

Sue, D. W., & Sue, D. (2008). *Counseling the culturally diverse: Theory and practice* (5th ed.). New York: Wiley.

Tiano, N., & Beyer, E. (2005). Cultural and religious views on nonbeneficial treatment. In K. Doka, B. Jennings, & C. Corr (Eds.), *Ethical dilemmas at the end-of-life* (pp. 41–60). Washington, DC: The Hospice Foundation of America.

Vachon, M. (1987). *Occupational stress in the care of the critically ill, the dying, and the bereaved.* New York: Hemisphere.

4   The Skilled Counselor

Counselors working with families and individuals struggling with life-threatening illness need more than sensitivity—they need skills. These skills include not only an ability to work with individuals and families throughout the life cycle, but also a facility to carefully monitor their own roles and reactions while modeling effective self-care. These two sets of skills are highly interrelated. A failure to master both is a formula for compassion fatigue and burnout (Doka, 2006).

SKILL AS A COUNSELOR

Effective caregivers recognize the nature and limits of their roles. Caregivers can struggle for the individual only *with* the help of that individual and his or her family. Primarily counselors will help individuals and families to identify the issues they are dealing with, explore the dimensions of these issues, and find effective ways to cope with their concerns. Primary caregivers share many things in common with counselors. Many of the processes are still the same. One still needs to establish rapport. Varied approaches may be used, including cognitive approaches, as well as expressive therapies such as art, music, drama, play and dance, or even pet therapies. Although the content of counseling is determined by the individual's needs, and based upon the tasks raised at each phase of illness, communicative skills remain the same. Among the most important of these are:

1. *Open-ended questions* that allow more than a "yes" or "no" answer. These questions encourage the individual to share concerns.
2. *Active listening*, which includes
   a. using silence—so that the individual may fill in space.
   b. restating content—allows the counselor to assure others he or she is listening; crystallizes client's comments; checks counselor's perception. Generally, the caregiver paraphrases what was said by the individual.
   c. reflecting feelings—here the caregiver reflects on the feelings expressed.
   d. summarizing content—similar to restating but with more material.
   e. summarizing feelings—synthesis of the individual's effective response.
3. *Interpretation of an individual's nonverbal behaviors*—a tentative interpretation of nonverbal behaviors, for example, "You seem anxious." This is often a good technique to facilitate awareness of or expression of emotion. One has to be careful that one recognizes that the nonverbal behaviors are individually expressed and influenced by culture.
4. *Problem-solving skills*—a broad array of techniques that seek definition and analysis of problems and consideration and evaluation of options.
5. *Empathic statements*—summaries and interpretation from the individual's perspective that allow the counselor to gently confront underlying issues (for example, noting, "It's difficult to experience such disability. Often it makes you feel a little sorry for yourself.") These interpretations are based on prior content.
6. *Theme identification*—the caregiver identifies underlying themes (difficulty in dealing with loss, for example).

7. *Self-disclosure*—revealing your feelings and reactions to facilitate the other's sense of being understood. (Note: These should resemble the individual's feelings and be brief enough so as not to change focus from the individual under care.)

8. *Perception check*—attempts to tentatively check the caregiver's perception ("You seem very removed today; are you tired or bored?")

9. *Techniques that try to understand the meaning of a client's feelings, behaviors, and attitudes,* such as

   a. Clarification—simply seeks to facilitate client and counselor's understanding: "Are you angry today?"

   b. Confrontation—a delicate technique that must be well timed and sensitive to an individual's receptiveness. Confrontations may point to a person's discrepancies between verbal statements, between verbal and nonverbal messages, provide alternate frames of reference, or help individuals understand that they are evading issues or ignoring feedback.

   c. Immediacy—the caregiver responds with his reaction and interaction with the person. ("I'm finding it hard to stay tuned. We seem to be rehashing old material." "How are you feeling about our interactions?")

10. *Action strategies,* such as

    a. Desensitization—uses counterconditioning and relaxation techniques to reduce anxiety.

    b. Contract setting—agreement to modify behavior.

    c. Social modeling—allows the client opportunity to role-play varied situations with counselor feedback.

11. *Affirmation*—that the individual is valued and likable. Caregivers should remember that certain approaches such as exhortation, false optimism, or careless phrases ("We will all die sometime") are countertherapeutic, alienating individuals and inhibiting open and effective communication (based upon George & Christiani, 1981).

Although providing care to individuals with life-threatening illness shares similarities with a variety of counseling and caregiving situations, particularly to crisis contexts, some factors make it unique. Shneidman (1978) has identified several factors that make counseling the dying unique. Whereas Shneidman more narrowly stresses counseling the dying and focuses upon the terminal phases, his factors may have broader application in other phases of life-threatening illness. To Shneidman, counseling the dying is different because

1. **The Goals are Different.** Psychological comfort is the major objective. In such a context, defenses and coping mechanisms are respected and rarely challenged by the caregiver unless these defenses threaten the life of the ill individual or others.

I have already discussed the importance of allowing denial. Individuals are under no psychological mandate to "accept" their death. The coping mechanism of denial should not be challenged just because the caregiver or family members are uncomfortable with this attitude. And denial is not the only coping mechanism that must be accepted. I once worked with a young man who was dying of muscular dystrophy. He had constructed a vivid fantasy about the value and significance of his life. This distorted image provided critical psychological comfort. In another counseling context I might have tried to challenge that fantasy and then assist the individual in reconstructing a more authentic identity. Here, though, given the limits of time imposed by his life-threatening illness, I could not take that risk. This young man did not have the time to construct a new sustaining identity. Shneidman comments that "no one needs to die in a state of psychoanalytic grace." His wise words should be a reminder to all caregivers that there is no ideal way for every individual to face his or her own death.

2. **The Rules are Different.** Shneidman particularly notes that transference can be intense during this phase of illness. To Shneidman, the caregiver can become, and even desire to become, a significant other in the client's life. Thus the caregiver can often play an important role in helping that person validate his or her life or cope more effectively with the illness. For example, I once counseled an older woman who was dying and struggling with her perception of being a failed parent. One of her daughters died from a drug overdose. Her other child, a son, was estranged—homeless and dealing

with alcoholism and probably mental illness. As she faced the end of life, she obviously began to look at me—about the same age as her son—as a sort of surrogate son. Rather than analyze her reaction with her, I used it to validate her parenting.

3. Countertransference Can Be Intense. Whenever caregivers assist others in facing their mortality, they themselves can be reminded of their own mortality and losses. Fulton (1987) has described the Stockholm syndrome and applied it to caregivers. The Stockholm syndrome refers to a common process in hostage taking in which hostages often identify with their captors. Fulton argues that under extremely stressful situations, close relationships can be forged quickly. Thus, caregivers may identify with the individuals under their care and grieve about their illness and deaths. Counselors and other caregivers may not recognize their grief, or discuss it with peers, because they believe it violates professional norms of "overinvolvement." They may not receive support from friends who may negate such work-related cases. Their grief, then, although intense and real, can become disenfranchised; that is, neither they nor others around them recognize their real loss and grief.

4. The Process is Different. In counseling individuals with life-threatening illness, particularly as it moves into the terminal phase, one no longer needs to work toward reaching a terminal goal. Death itself provides termination.

5. The Caregiver Can Be More Active. Generally, caregivers seek to challenge individuals to resolve their own problems and difficulties. Given the frailties of life-threatening illness, and the limits of time, caregivers can take more active roles, serving as advocates and ombudsmen. For example, in one case an individual was reluctant to ask questions of her physician. In another life situation the counselor probably would have tried to help her explore her attitudes toward authority and assist her in developing assertive strategies. Here the counselor served as her advocate.

6. The Person Sets the Pace. In describing *middle knowledge,* Weisman (1972) notes that individuals often drift in and out of a confrontation with their own mortality—sometimes denying the illness and approaching death, other times confronting their problems. Counseling strategies should allow individuals to set the agenda and pace. Because of the nature of middle knowledge, it is not unusual for caregivers to have intense conversations with dying persons about anxieties and fears about illness and death one day that are not even alluded to the next day.

7. The Caregiver Must Also Work With Families and Other Survivors. Life-threatening illness is a family illness, deeply affecting all others in the family system. Working with families during the illness and after the death is critical.

SENSITIVITY TO FAMILIES

I emphasize throughout this book that an individual's life-threatening illness always affects the entire family. Sensitive counseling recognizes the familial context of an illness. Sensitive counselors understand that individuals may define "family" differently and that family interactions are highly unique, influenced by a variety of factors such as culture. Counselors then should help families examine the ways in which illness affects them as a family as well as the ways that they are coping with illness.

I have found two models particularly useful in assisting families in coping with life-threatening illness. The first, Herr and Weakland's (1979) model of the family problem-solving process, can be generally applied to many circumstances in which families must assess their own problem-solving process and resolve difficulties. The second, network intervention, can also be a very effective technique that can allow family units to effectively use larger systems, both informal and formal, to resolve particular problems. Both will be outlined here as examples of types of approaches to family counseling that caregivers may find helpful.

Herr and Weakland's (1979) Model

1. Build Rapport and Make an Initial Assessment.
2. Define the Problem.
The first step after developing rapport and beginning an initial assessment is to clearly define the problem. Herr and Weakland caution that often the "identified problem," that is,

the problem that the family recognizes, is not the real problem that families actually need to resolve. For example, the "identified problem" may be that the patient does not take his prescribed medication, whereas the underlying problem could involve such issues as denial, family power, or control. Ideally, by the end of this stage, Herr and Weakland suggest that the family has defined a problem in a way that avoids both negativism and scapegoating, and recognizes the problem as a family issue rather than solely a personal problem. Instead of, for example, a problem defined as "a family member not pulling their weight," the problem is recast as "a need to better coordinate and distribute caregiving."

3. **Determine Solutions Attempted Previously.** Herr and Weakland note that many times families have attempted various solutions prior to seeking help. Reviewing these attempts will help one to avoid suggesting already failed solutions, to find solutions that may have been abandoned prematurely, and to see "solutions" that may have complicated problems. This review can often illuminate family dynamics.

4. **Establish Goals.** Once problems have been defined and attempted solutions viewed, families are now ready to set goals. Herr and Weakland emphasize that goals should be both realistic and carefully defined.

5. **Comprehend the Family System.** Throughout these first four phases the counselor has observed much about family dynamics. Herr and Weakland suggest that now is an appropriate time for families and caregivers to review the family system and its problem-solving process.

6. **Mobilize the Family System.** In this stage caregivers assist families in developing strategies that will allow them to achieve their goals. Herr and Weakland emphasize that interventions and their rationales must be formed within perspectives the family can identify with and understand.

7. **Achieve a Successful Termination.** Herr and Weakland point out that the goal of all family counseling is termination, that is, helping family members reach the stage at which they can resolve difficulties by themselves and have learned enough about their own problem-solving process that they should not need further counseling. Herr and Weakland suggest that the counselor at termination should emphasize the family's role in resolving its own problems

and help the family to anticipate possible problems that may arise. In the constant crisis context of life-threatening illness, however, counselors need to recognize that families may need continued contact and help. In such situations a model that allows continued monitoring of the family and provides care mandated by the crisis may be a more suitable approach. Herr and Weakland, however, provide a warning about fostering an overdependence upon the counselor that impairs the family's coping capacity. Ultimately the counselor's role is to act as a facilitator—assisting the family as it copes with illness and possible death.

Network Intervention

This technique was originally designed for work with troubled and delinquent youths (see Thorman, 1982). It can sometimes be successfully applied to families coping with life-threatening illness. The goal of the approach is to mobilize a network to resolve a particular problem. This approach can work well when the problem is a tangible one open to a quick fix. While discussing this model, I will refer to a particular case in which network intervention was successfully used. In that case a woman residing with her spouse and adult child was in the late chronic phase of cancer. This family had no other children. Since the son worked long hours, the woman's care was mainly in the hands of her retired husband, who provided meals, supervised her medication, and took care of the house. The crisis was caused by the sudden death of the woman's husband from a heart attack.

Preparatory phase: The decision to use the network model should be made carefully, after an assessment by a counselor that network intervention has a reasonable chance to succeed. In the preparatory phase a counselor must assess the problem and determine the potential viability of the network to resolve the problem. Usually such networks consist of 20 to 40 people. The counselor may also need to put together a team to assist this process. After consultation with the family network, the counselor arranges a meeting of the support team—usually over a weekend and at the home, if possible, of the ill person. This time at the home allows the network to reconnect and work together, even in the arranging of such details as meal planning and preparation. It also allows the counselor to measure the level of initial commitment.

In this case, network intervention was considered viable. The family did have financial resources to pay for some services such as homemaker assistance. The primary problems identified, that is, providing for monitoring and supervision of medication, companionship, and meals, seemed tangible and open to intervention. Although the family system was quite small, consisting only of mother and son, the family was deeply involved in a small church that had a pastor and parishioners eager to help. A meeting was set for a Saturday and Sunday afternoon, and about 20 people attended.

Phases of Network Intervention

1. **Retribalization Phase:** In this phase people socialize and reconnect.

2. **Polarization Phase:** Here the family and the team present the problem and the group reviews possible solutions. Team leaders may facilitate the formation of small groups to discuss alternative solutions. Often sides can form when members commit to a given solution. In this case, one group investigated Meals on Wheels and other options such as restaurant delivery to ensure that the ill woman would have her meals while her son worked. Another group considered the possibility that church members could share some responsibility.

3. **Mobilization Phase:** The group begins to consider the tasks needed to find a solution. Often the group recognizes the extent of required commitment and the difficulty of the tasks.

4. **Depression Phase:** The group's initial optimism wanes when its members discover that there is no easy solution to the problem and become discouraged by its scope. Some members may be resentful that their ideas were not given a fair hearing. The team helps the group recognize and verbalize their frustration. Now the family may renew its request for help.

5. **Breakthrough Phase:** In response to this request for help, the group recommits, reaches a viable solution, and assigns tasks. In this

case the group recognized its limits for providing daily meals, since only 10 people were able to commit to regularly delivering a meal. Each of these 10 people promised to deliver a casserole-type meal that would provide two days' meals. The son resolved to provide meals on weekends and promised to purchase a microwave oven to make preparation of meals and reheating of casseroles easier. These solutions gave members a sense that all ideas were used and it limited the cooks' commitment to one day a month. Other members, here about 15 in number, agreed to serve as companions to the ill woman, visiting her on days when the cooks would not. A church secretary and another parishioner agreed to serve as coordinators for the whole intervention.

This intervention is just one example of the types of techniques that counselors may find useful. Other approaches may have similar value. The basic point is that counselors will need to develop sensitivity to the needs of the family as well as appropriate interventions to assist families as they cope with life-threatening illness.

SENSITIVITY TO DIFFERENT AGE GROUPS AND POPULATIONS

Earlier I discussed the ways that life-threatening illness is different for people at different phases in the life cycle because developmental issues can often complicate responses to life-threatening illness. Sensitive caregivers will recognize the unique issues that arise at any point in the life cycle. They will also recognize that populations that are developmentally impaired may have special difficulties in responding to the crisis of life-threatening illness. This section emphasizes the particular problem of three groups: children and adolescents, the developmentally disabled, and older persons.

Working with Children and Adolescents

Counseling children and adolescents with life-threatening illness can be very difficult. Counselors may find themselves emotionally drawn to the ill child and greatly affected by the child's illness and death.

Even beyond such intense emotional involvement, counseling children and adolescents creates other difficulties that complicate the counseling process.

One of the first complications is that counselor-child relationships are always triadic. Counselors must simultaneously deal with the child and the parents or guardians of that child. Since the needs of the child and the needs of the parents are not always identical, this can impair trust. Young clients may be reluctant to confide in their counselors because they are unsure of how much the counselor can be trusted.

Early in their work with children and adolescents, counselors should confront this issue. Counselors can affirm that the child's confidences will be respected. Depending on the needs of the parents or the child, counselors can indicate that they will periodically talk with the parents. But in each case the caregivers and the child together should discuss problems, develop a plan, and agree about what will be reported to the parents. Counselors may forewarn the child of exceptions to confidentiality, for example, when the child is engaged in actions that endanger his or her life or the life of others or the counselor is mandated to report any abuse. Counselors should make parents equally aware of this arrangement.

Another issue that often may be a significant one between parents and children involves communication and truthfulness. Many parents take a protective approach toward communication in which they attempt to shield the child from the nature or implications of the illness. Counselors need to respect these strategies, but they also need to help parents evaluate the implications of such strategies. Often these strategies are not effective since children have access to a wide range of information about the condition: internal health cues; external treatment cues; information from books, TV, and videos; input from ill peers; and more. Previous studies (Bluebond-Langner, 1978, 1987; Doka, 1982) indicate that regardless of parental disclosure decisions, children often know the nature and seriousness of their conditions. Such strategies can be costly, for they can impair trust at a critical time in the parent-child relationship, and they may also complicate compliance with medical regimens. In working with children under communicative restrictions, counselors can assume a nondirective approach, offering little information but allowing the child to freely discuss feelings, fears, and relationships. When confronted with requests for information, caregivers can help the child identify the people who can address the child's concerns. Counselors can also serve as quiet advocates for the child's concerns and his or her readiness to assimilate information. Again, it is important to share that approach with parents.

In communicating with children suffering from life-threatening illness, there are two critical points caregivers should recognize. First, it is important to understand what the child is really asking. "Am I going to die?" may not be a request for information but a call for reassurance. Only by asking the child to clarify such questions can the counselors understand and address underlying concerns.

In one case, for example, a 10-year-old boy asked whether his leukemia was fatal. The caregiver began by asking the child what he had heard about the disease. The child talked about a student at his high school, still honored by an annual award presented in her name, who had died of the disease some 20 years earlier. The conversation seemed to indicate that the child wanted reassurance. By honestly discussing the child's anxieties, and by responding to his needs by pointing out that treatment had advanced in the past two decades, the counselor was able to maintain open communication and hope.

Second, as in any communicative process, each counselor must be clear about his or her own role. Perhaps the caregiver may not be the person best suited to answer medical questions. His or her most critical role may be to help the child clarify underlying concerns and questions, identify appropriate resources, and examine the effects of responses on the child's feelings and behaviors.

Truthfulness is not the only thing that can complicate communication with children. Often communication can be complicated by the child's level of cognitive development. Children may not have the vocabulary or conceptual framework necessary to process the information they receive. They may exhibit magical thinking, finding it difficult to separate reality and fantasy. Counselors can facilitate communication in these situations by patiently providing sufficient time for the child to assimilate information and ask questions. The "report back," a technique in which children recount the information as they understand it, is often an effective way to gain insight into the child's intellectual level and vocabulary, to identify anxieties and feelings complicating the communicative process, and to clarify any misunderstandings. Visual aids appropriate to the age level, such as dolls, models (anatomical models of organs or systems, for example), books, diagrams, and videos, can facilitate this communicative process. One physician I know, to help prepare a child for surgery, actually drew the incisions with washable magic marker on the boy's abdomen. This allowed the child two days to get used to the idea of scars and to experiment with clothes could effectively mask the scarring.

Limits to the child's cognitive development can also impair the task of reviewing life. One of the key tasks in illness is to integrate the illness into one's life. Jarratt (1994) suggests that time lines can be an effective way for children to explore the ways that illness has affected their lives. Young children can use different crayon colors to represent periods of life (for example, the child may choose blue for the time before school, green for the time between school and illness, gray for the onset of illness, and so on). Older children can create linear time lines. Such time lines can become the basis for discussion about how they felt and coped during these times and how various changes in their lives affected them.

Dealing with feelings is another complicated problem for children and adolescents. They may have a difficult time identifying the many emotions they face, and they can find it hard to recognize and assimilate emotions such as anger or guilt. Again, Jarratt (1994) in her work with bereaved children has developed many techniques that can easily be applied to children with life-threatening illness. Among them are

1. Feeling Checks: This is a simple technique in which the child is asked to tell how much of a given emotion, he or she is experiencing. Younger children may show the emotion by using their hands (close together for little anger, far apart for great anger, and so forth). Older children may demonstrate their level of feeling by selecting a number on a scale. Often the counselor will prepare the child by talking about how some children can have such feelings, thus validating these emotions.

2. "Five-faces Techniques": These refer to a variety of techniques that use five faces (glad, sad, mad, scared, and lonely). These faces may be placed on cards and a number of games may be developed. Children may draw cards explaining when they felt that emotion and how they responded when they felt it. Or they may tell stories about someone who is feeling the emotion expressed on a given face.

3. "Show Me": Here the caregiver asks the child to "show me how you look sad, or angry, or whatever." This not only gives permission for the feeling but also opens discussion of these emotions.

4. Fables and Metaphors: In this projective technique in which the caregiver begins a "fable" such as "A child wakes up and says 'Oh, I am afraid.'" The child is then asked to complete the fable. Fables can be constructed to uncover any emotion or anxiety.

In addition to these techniques, counselors may wish to use other approaches. Often expressive therapies such as art, play, drama, or music can be useful with children. Jarratt also suggests that counselors should check out family rules about feelings and help children explore their coping by examining how they connect actions with feelings.

Life-threatening illness can often complicate the entire process of a child or adolescent's development. The process of development is a gradual move toward independence and autonomy. Life-threatening illness can reverse this process, generating greater dependence. Dependence can be complicated by parental overprotectiveness, a common response to a child's illness. Caregivers, children, and parents may need to address these issues, recognizing the child's need for independence and the parents' emotional needs and their deep desire to be involved in care. Often counselors can help families find mutually agreeable solutions. In one case, for example, parents felt that their adolescent daughter, dying of cancer, was rejecting them. The daughter felt that her fragile independence and dignity was threatened by her parents' response. When they shared their concerns, they were able to reach an agreement on appropriate involvements. It was all right for parents to change her dressing, because that was clearly related to her illness, and she clearly needed her parent's support and comfort. But she preferred to be dressed, bathed, and fed by the nursing staff because if her parents performed those tasks, it painfully reinforced her dependency. Such agreements are always tentative and may continually need to be reworked as the child's physical condition changes and the child's development continues.

Adherence issues, especially in the chronic phase, can often be a battleground between parents and children that reflects the struggle between the child's need for independence and autonomy and illness-induced dependency. Often by allowing the child full partnership in treatment; by fully informing the child about the need for adherence; by tailoring the regimen as much as possible to the child's schedule, needs, and lifestyle; and by soliciting the child's participation in discussions and decisions, such conflict can be mitigated. Children and adolescents should be given as many choices as possible during treatment including scheduling times, injection sites, and decisions on who should be present during treatment. Self-help networks, for both parents and children, can also assist both in expressing their feelings and fears and in developing successful coping strategies.

Counselors should monitor the effects of illness on family life. Because of the great stress of a child's life-threatening illness on the family and the developmental struggle it often creates, there can be deleterious effects upon the family. Although earlier observations of extensive marital disruption in families of terminally ill children have not been supported by subsequent research (see Stephenson, 1985), there still may be other negative effects. One study (Hawkins & Dunkin, 1985), for example, found that in families in which children face chronic health conditions there was an increased risk of physical abuse or neglect because of both the increased burden and the consequent stress. Although such situations are rare, monitoring family relationships can sensitize counselors to the ways that changes in the illness and the child's continued development are affecting family relationships and coping patterns.

It is often worthwhile to explore the family's initial response to the illness. The process of health seeking is complicated with children, since it can include an additional step in which the child, especially in the older years, must bring the symptom to the parents' attention and the parents then need to make a decision on seeking help. Exploring this process will often shed light on the family's coping styles and beliefs about illness. This exploration can also sensitize counselors to issues that might affect other family members and their responses to the illness. For example, parents who were slow to respond to the child's complaints may face considerable guilt throughout the illness.

This exploration might well include not just family but everyone within the child's circle. Everyone in that circle may be affected by the child's illness. Persons may respond by avoiding the child, or perhaps by overprotecting or overindulging the child. Other parents may prohibit their children from playing with the ill child. The illness may effectively remove the child from arenas for peer interaction, or the child may withdraw and be reluctant to participate in normal activities. Thus it is important to explore the ways that the illness has changed relationships with all those in the child's circle. When caregivers are working within institutions such as hospitals, they may develop support groups for friends and staff.

One important area to explore with school-age children is the response of schools to the illness. The child's experience of illness may be complicated by school life. Schools can vary in their willingness to accommodate a child's illness and regimen. Some schools will make great efforts to accommodate the child and facilitate adherence to the medical regimen, whereas others will be resistant to small modifications of routines or regulations. Some schools can be insensitive to a child's threatening illness, perhaps even perceiving education as an unnecessary bother since that child may not survive. Counselors can assist children and their families in identifying school-based barriers to adherence and help them to develop problem-solving strategies. Some strategies can be as simple as providing the child with privacy for medications or adjusting schedules to accommodate the child's regimen.

Counselors may also wish to educate schools about symptom control and crisis management. In one case, for example, a counselor arranged for a nurse and a physician to speak to teachers, a guidance counselor, and a school nurse of an entering high school freshman who had cystic fibrosis. This visit alleviated some fears and allowed the school to identify possible problems that the illness might pose to the child's daily schedule. Once these problems were identified, such as frequent trips to the bathroom, teachers felt more confident that they could handle the child. The guidance counselor appreciated information about the best times to schedule varied courses. Both the school nurse and the guidance counselor also felt relieved at the opportunity to discuss symptoms and their control and to develop crisis management plans. Everyone left the meeting with lists of problems they should watch out for, as well as actions (for example, call the parents; call the ambulance, then call the parents; and so forth) they could take and important emergency numbers. In many cases physicians and other medical personnel can provide information that will alleviate needless fears. In other situations counselors may choose to advocate.

Disclosure concerns can be another school-related issue for both children and parents. Parents may wish to clarify with principals just who would have access to sensitive information. Counselors may need to help children and parents in clarifying and exploring their concerns. Parents, children, and school staff may also want to develop and periodically review any necessary restriction or emergency and contingency plans. Teachers will need continuous, appropriate, and educationally related information. This information will need to be updated throughout the course of illness. The child's education will be facilitated when teachers and school nurses are incorporated as part of the caregiving team.

Other school-related problems can also develop, particularly during the chronic phase. It is not unusual that the disruptions caused by the disease, the effects of medication and treatment, and the child's responses to the illness can affect cognitive and social development. Caregivers may need to assess such effects with children and their parents, perhaps assisting them to reevaluate their expectations. One young girl suffering from leukemia was deeply distressed that her grades declined and she was no longer able to participate in volleyball. Sensitive to the latter concern, the coach made her his timekeeper when she was able to take this role. Although the school also provided access to tutoring, she had to redefine her expectations, recognizing that the maintenance of health was now her highest priority. However, there may be times that the schools suggest inappropriate placement, placing the child unnecessarily and unsuitably in special education classes or imposing needless restrictions on the child that may run counter to treatment. For example, one school excused a child from physical education despite that the doctor felt no such need and suggested exercise. In such cases caregivers can be very effective advocates.

Working with Persons with Developmental Disabilities

One special population that counselors may come into contact with more frequently is persons with developmental disabilities. In the past three decades more persons with developmental disabilities have survived early childhood and are living a longer life span. They are less likely to be living that life within institutions. During the course of that extended life, persons with developmental disabilities will experience illnesses in the manner of their nondisabled peers and will be treated for those illnesses within the same facilities and by the same staff. Yet this is a population that will require special sensitivities and approaches from those who care for them.

It is important to remember that the persons with developmental disabilities are not homogeneous. They share the same differences in terms of background as other groups. Levels of cognitive disability can vary from mild to severe. Living conditions can also vary: some may live independently, others with their families or in group homes, still others in institutions. Levels of social and psychological impairments can also differ, and may not neatly correspond to cognitive impairments. Thus an impaired person's age may not be predictive of developmental level or behavior.

Lavin (2002) describes certain characteristics typical of persons with developmental disabilities. They often have an external locus of control, lack confidence in their own ability to solve problems, find it difficult to think abstractly, have limited ability to transfer skills from one level to another, and have poor short-term memory skills.

Because of these limitations, persons with developmental disabilities may have a very difficult time coping with abstract concepts such as "disease," "dying," or "death." Some research has suggested that these concepts may be easier for persons with developmental disabilities to master as they age. Chronological age, rather than cognitive level, may be a factor, since it provides a rough index of the level of experience with dying and death of the person with developmental disabilities. Often family and staff may exacerbate these conceptual difficulties if they try to overprotect the client with developmental disabilities, effectively disenfranchising the client from any role in the treatment.

In discussing grief counseling with persons with developmental disabilities, Lavin (2002) makes several points that can be applied to counseling persons with developmental disabilities in any crisis. First, she emphasizes the need for caregivers to be patient and clear with their clients. Comfort and continued reassurance may be particularly important throughout the crisis. Second, Lavin emphasizes that caregivers will have to teach coping skills throughout the crisis. This begins by analyzing what behaviors and skills will be necessary at each phase. Lavin then suggests that a four-step process can facilitate learning:

1. **Preparation:** Here the goal is to prepare the person with developmental disabilities to be exposed to the experience. Counselors may wish to begin by talking about the individual's previous experiences with illness. This will provide an opportunity to draw upon these experiences in later times.

2. **Direct Instruction:** The counselor can teach skills that may be useful to the person, providing constant reassurance and reinforcement. For example, he or she may have to go over circumstances in which the individual should notify an appropriate caregiver about changes in health, carefully explaining the symptoms the person might monitor.

3. **Modeling:** In this approach someone models the expected behavior for the individual. The counselor may help to interpret the event (for example, "He is going to tell the nurse what's bothering him"). The person with developmental disabilities can then attempt to copy the behavior with the encouragement and support of the caregiver.

4. **Emotional Support:** Throughout the crisis, persons with developmental disabilities may have to be helped to understand and express their emotions. Directive questions such as "Are you scared?" or "How do you feel when you are scared?" may help such individuals to recognize their emotions. Counselors may need to provide considerable support throughout the crisis of illness. Nonverbal behaviors such as reassuring touch may provide that needed and welcome presence.

Counselors may find that counseling individuals with developmental disabilities requires considerable flexibility in approach. Depending on the level of disability, the present crisis, and the person's previous experiences, caregivers may have to continually adapt approaches to each person. But these clients still share the same needs as other nondisabled individuals, including the need for autonomy, control, and respect.

Working with the Older Persons

Though two thirds of dying persons in the United States are 65 years old or older, comparatively little attention has been paid to their unique concerns and issues. Many health-care workers, like other segments of the population, prefer to work with younger clients, often because they have been influenced by negative stereotypes of older persons. Thus, older persons who are ill may face a double burden.

Three basic understandings are fundamental. First, counselors must realize that older persons are not a homogeneous group. They differ, as does any age group, on any number of variables such as ethnicity, culture, class, educational level, coping skills, family, and informal and formal support systems.

Second, counselors must have a basic understanding of the aging process. This includes an ability to distinguish between changes due to normal aging and those that are pathological and/or illness related. For example, confusion and disorientation are not part of the normal aging process but rather symptoms of underlying disorders that can be either acute and reversible or chronic and irreversible. Should such symptoms become evident during treatment, the individual should be assessed. In some cases disorientation may be caused by dietary changes, medication, or other facts of a treatment program; in other cases disorientation may be a manifestation of the illness or a sign of another condition. These symptoms should not be readily dismissed as evidence of aging. In fact, any caregiver should view any symptom, pain, or discomfort experienced by older individuals with the same seriousness as a complaint by someone younger.

Third, counselors must examine their own beliefs and feelings about the aging process and older persons. Are older persons being treated with respect? Are their needs for independence and autonomy being considered? Are their psychological and social needs, including sexual needs, being recognized?

Five issues may complicate older persons' attempts to cope with life-threatening illness and/or their efforts to engage in the counseling process.

1.   Resistance to Counseling: Many older persons may be resistant to engaging in the counseling process. The reason may be historical. Older persons may not have the same familiarity with counseling services as younger people. In addition, older persons may associate use of mental health services with stigma. Older individuals may be reluctant to engage in an activity that they perceive as challenging their autonomy or privacy. Thus it is important for counselors and other caregivers to be sensitive to such resistance. Counselors and caregivers should try to present the option of counseling in a manner that both explains and normalizes the counseling process. They should not assume that older persons have a clear image of what counseling entails. They should be open to questions and should respectfully examine the misperceptions and anxieties that the elderly may have about the counseling process. For example, one elderly man diagnosed with cancer was reluctant to have a psychological and social work assessment since he feared that the process would inevitably lead to his institutionalization in a nursing home. Naturally, the older person's right to reject participation in counseling should be respected. In such cases the counselor should reassure the person that the option remains open. Even if an older person does agree to counseling, there may be times within the counseling process when the issue of resistance must be addressed.

2.   Stereotypes of Aging may Inhibit Health Seeking: A second issue that may arise with the counseling process concerns health-seeking behavior. Successful coping with life-threatening illness entails constant monitoring of one's bodily state. Whereas some older individuals may exhibit obsessive hypochondrias, other elderly people may ignore, dismiss, or discount symptoms. Elderly individuals are just as likely to be deluded by aging stereotypes as their families and others; often they may dismiss symptoms of mental or physical decline as evidence of the aging process. This tendency can be identified when counselors explore the initial process of health seeking. Here they may find that an elderly client chose self-medication or delayed seeking medical help for a considerable, perhaps even fatal, interval. Once identified, the danger of such strategies can be explored and elderly individuals can be taught more effective strategies for monitoring and supporting health. In some cases these discussions will uncover feelings of fatalism and resignation. For example, one older woman delayed seeking treatment for skin cancer. Questioned as to why she had waited so long, she replied that at age 84 something was bound to kill you. This can arise too in counseling since an older person may feel considerable guilt about delayed treatment.

Sometimes other dynamics may be apparent. Physicians and family members may share stereotypes of health and may not take the complaints of older persons seriously. If older persons are suffering from confusion or dementia, family caregivers may feel guilty that they did not recognize symptoms of life-threatening illness.

3. Social Support May Be Limited: Although the issue of social support is not unique to the older persons, it is more likely to be a problem with the older individuals than with other age groups. Older clients may well have outlived other family members, or surviving family members—wife or husband, siblings, even children— may be too old themselves to be able to help. Thus it is essential for counselors to ascertain both the size and the nature of any possible support system as well as its ability to provide care. Once the support system is identified, counselors can assess barriers to its effective use, for example, the client's reluctance to request assistance. Counselors can assist elderly individuals in identifying additional sources of support. Local offices of aging may be particularly helpful in assisting with needs assessments as well as with identifying, providing, and monitoring supplementary services. Such exploration can uncover significant information about the client's perceptions and misperceptions concerning social support. One 87-year-old woman, for example, was intensely angry because she thought her only daughter should be providing more help. But the daughter herself was near 70 and taking care of an ailing husband. Lack of support can accentuate feelings of loneliness, complicate adjustment to life-threatening illness, and even limit access to varied programs such as hospice that may require the presence of a family caregiver.

4. Other Physical and Cognitive Impairments: Older persons with life-threatening illness may suffer other cognitive and physical impairments. Although such impairments are not an inherent part of the aging process, they become more common as persons age. Naturally, the presence of such impairments must be considered when developing regimens and when assisting individuals in meeting the tasks necessitated by life-threatening illness. Moreover, the effects and complications of these other conditions and impairments must be monitored throughout all the phases of illness.

5. Problems with Life Review: Finally, older persons may have particular concerns connected with the life-review process. Whereas this process is common to all experiencing a sense of finitude, older persons may have unique concerns. At this point in their lives they may see the unfolding of events that cause them special pain. One elderly man, for example, was distressed to recognize that none of his grandchildren would carry on the family name. In counseling he was able to redefine his concept of family continuity in ways that provided psychological comfort. In similar ways elderly individuals may be deeply distressed about the plight of their survivors, concerned about the ability of spouses, or even adult children, to function without them. One elderly woman, for example, was deeply concerned about the effect of her death upon her husband, who was both physically impaired and showing signs of confusion. Another woman was troubled by the fact that she was leaving a son with developmental disabilities. In both cases contingency planning with a caregiver and other relatives eased anxiety.

With older persons (and, in fact, with any individual struggling with an awareness of finitude), life review and reminiscence offers a potent therapeutic approach. It can affirm continuity of identity—often threatened both in later life and with illness; allow older persons to retain self-esteem and create a sense of parity with caregiving staff; and confirm an ability to cope as persons draw comfort from the knowledge that they coped successfully with earlier crises (Magee, 1988, 2007). The techniques for reminiscence and life-review therapies can vary considerably since any of the senses stimulate memories. Certainly music and photographs, but even foods and smells, can be usefully employed to engage remembrance.

Counselors also need to understand that caregivers may experience their special stresses as they deal with older clients. Caregivers can be troubled by the loneliness of older individuals or the plight of survivors. Problems may arise about the appropriateness of care. Given the age and probable continued suffering of an older individual, caregivers may be resistant to any form of extraordinary care, creating a sense of moral distress.

SENSITIVITY TO SELF

Giving care to persons who have life-threatening illness can be stressful and emotionally draining. Whenever one cares for someone struggling with life-threatening illness, one risks having to confront the death of the client, a consequent sense of loss, and fears associated with one's own mortality, all of which can be profound stresses. Sensitive counselors should realize that unless they address their own needs, they have little left to give to others. They have an important role in modeling effective self-care to the caregiving community as a whole.

Professionals often find it difficult to realize and admit how the losses others experience can affect oneself. One of the most destructive myths about professionalism is that the mark of the professional is to remain emotionally unattached and uninvolved. In fact, caregivers often forge very close relationships with ill individuals and their families. Naturally, crisis points in an illness will affect caregivers, and deaths can be devastating. Moreover, even though a caregiver may feel an intense loss when a special client dies, that sense of loss may not be recognized and validated by others. Even the caregiver himself or herself may not recognize or admit deep feelings of grief. Such grief is real but effectively disenfranchised because the caregiver recognizes no perceived right to mourn. As Katz and Johnson (2006) acknowledge, it is natural to have feelings toward a client. The key issue is to retain a sense of self-awareness that inhibits a destructive sense of countertransference, in which the counselor seeks to work through his or her own conflicts through the patient.

Caregivers may experience this sense of loss even before families have recognized the extent of their loss. Kastenbaum (1987) describes the phenomenon of "vicarious grief" among older individuals. He points out that older persons often experience grief vicariously when they hear of the losses of younger persons. Kastenbaum suggests that the elderly person, having experience in grief, may empathize more with the newly bereaved, because the elderly person understands the pain and turmoil the newly bereaved are likely to face. Perhaps caregivers undergo a similar experience. Even in the early and more hopeful periods of an individual's illness, caregivers may have the background and experience to anticipate and grieve vicariously for the pain and difficulty persons are likely to face.

The death of a client may cause a caregiver to confront his or her own mortality. Usually by midlife one develops a true awareness of one's own mortality. The deaths of others, particularly when they are close to our own age, may sharpen that awareness of mortality. One grieves not only the loss of another, but also a recognized eventual loss of self.

Caregivers may also find it stressful to cope with the choices that individuals make in the course of their illness. For example, many caregivers are personally offended when clients seek alternative treatments and therapies. Rather than understanding this choice for what it is, the decision to explore any path that offers hope, caregivers may experience it as rejection. In such situations caregivers should accept the client's right to choose, and instead of offering dire predictions or condemning the client's decision, the caretaker should make it clear that the welcome mat will always be out. Even at later points in the illness caregivers can be troubled by an individual's choices, particularly by decisions to end treatment. As caregivers confront the disparity between their preferred choices and what the ill individuals actually choose, the caregiver's own sense of stress can increase.

Jameton (1984) defines *moral distress* as the inner conflicts that health-care professionals may experience as they care for patients in life-threatening illness. This moral distress results when a caregiver experiences personal, professional, spiritual, or ethical dilemmas that may arise from conflicts between his or her values, the institutional values and policies, and the wishes of the patient and the family. Sources of moral distress can include beliefs that the current treatment is futile, disagreements to forgo or withdraw treatment, beliefs that the treatment is causing harm, beliefs that the patient and/or family has not been given truly informed consent, thoughts that the patient's wishes are being ignored, or thoughts that the patient has had inadequate pain management. In such circumstances caregivers feel torn because they perceive that they are not giving the best care they can offer or feel that they are offering care contrary to their beliefs. For example, several years ago, I was involved in ethical grand rounds that followed the death of a patient with dementia. The patient had lived in the nursing home for many years. In her confused mind, she believed that all who cared for her were her children. She treated each staff member with a wonderful sense of kindness, touching their cheek and telling them what a good son or daughter the person was. Her adult children were actively involved in her care as well. Over time she developed a serious infection. Her wishes (prior to admission) were clear, and her children concurred with a decision not to offer further treatment. The staff, however, was outraged at her death. As we reviewed the decisions to withhold, one nurse objected, "if it is so ethical, why do I feel so damn bad?" (Doka, 1994).

Studies (Vachon 1987, 2007; Papadatou, 2000) have revealed other factors that can contribute to caregiver stress. For example, children and adolescents with life-threatening illness often create unique stress. Individuals with whom caregivers identify, preexisting family problems that complicate an individual's coping, factors related to the particular illness such as its symptoms or trajectory, and a variety of other factors can affect the caregiver's experience of stress and grief. In addition, caregivers may now lose a relation with family members. Caregivers may experience a sense of past or future losses or feel that they still had goals for the patient that were yet unmet. Papadatou (2000) acknowledges the significant balancing act that is essential to resilience. Caregivers must oscillate between both experiencing and containing grief.

The work environment often exacerbates caregiver stress. In fact, for many caregivers work difficulties such as communication problems, inadequate resources and support, or structural and role difficulties add greatly to their stress.

Caregivers need to be sensitive to the effects that working with the seriously ill and the dying have on them. Stress and grief may manifest itself physically in minor and major illness. It may emerge in behaviors evident at home or at work, in steep disturbances, for example, or in psychological reactions such as depression, guilt, anger, irritability, frustration, anxiety, or a sense of hopelessness. It can affect caregiver's cognitive processes, causing errors in judgment or magical thinking. Caregiver grief can impair work relationships, lower morale, and increase absenteeism and staff turnover.

Caregivers need to be sensitive to their own feelings and must develop effective coping strategies. Some of these may be structural. Provision for formal support and sharing, both in a group and in an individual context, can be helpful. Ongoing education can provide caregivers with new insights and techniques that enable them to function better. Work flexibility that allows caregivers opportunity to distance themselves and find periodic respite can minimize stress and facilitate grief. Attending funerals or finding other ways to memorialize significant clients may provide a final opportunity to share thoughts or memories with family.

I once led a session for social work staff of two different agencies. Staffs at both agencies were dealing with foster children who were HIV positive. Often children in their care died. The staff in one agency seemed to be coping noticeably better than the staff in the other agency. A critical factor in this difference was the work environment. In the former agency staff had developed a team approach, with weekly support meetings. In the latter agency staff were expected to function autonomously. In the first agency the director set a tone that was very responsive to the emotional needs of staff. She often suggested that staff should go home after they experienced a death, perhaps taking a day or two off. In the other agency the director was concerned that staff not take unanticipated days off, reminding her social workers that they knew the nature of the job when they accepted it. I asked each worker to write down the average number of hours each worked. It was the same for each agency. The flexibility in the first agency did not diminish the amount of work accomplished. It did, however, allow staff space and time to meet their own emotional needs. As Papadatou (2000) notes, the work unit itself can significantly mitigate or exacerbate caregiver stress.

Whereas structural modifications may help caregivers deal more effectively with their own feelings and reactions, caregivers also need to examine their own personal coping mechanisms.

Weisman (1979) uses a concept that he calls the "least possible contribution" as a way that caregivers can effectively cope with their own stress and sense of powerlessness. Weisman suggests that if caregivers can do something just a bit extra, for example, bake cookies for a person or bring someone a special tape or book, such simple little acts can later help to assuage feelings of grief and loss. The idea is not to do as little as possible, but to try to do something, however small, that will make a difference to a person's life. Studies (Vachon, 1987, 2007) have identified some other factors that may mitigate stress and facilitate grief. One of the most important factors is that caregivers and counselors should develop effective ways to manage their own lifestyles. Proper rest, good nutrition, exercise, and opportunities for respite, relaxation, diversion, and renewal are all important aspects of lifestyle management. Informal social support can also be a critical factor, especially when support is not available within a professional or work context.

A personal philosophy that allows one a perspective on the suffering and unfairness evident in life-threatening illness and that defines a professional role in ways that permit a sense of competency and control may also assist coping. In my training of clergy and chaplains, for example, I often talk of a "theology of the unknown" and a "ministry of presence." By the former I mean that clergy have to accept that they cannot explain every act: illness and death are mysteries beyond comprehension. The ministry of presence refers to a role in which clergy and chaplains define themselves as supportive presences, providing comfort and contact rather than resolution. Caregivers must explore and develop their own philosophies and perspectives on roles that provide them with succor in grief and stress.

Caregivers have a unique role to play in an individual's struggle with life-threatening illness. That role might be compared to a candle. A candle can help illuminate an experience, provide a path in the darkness, and give courage to explore. Caregivers, at their best, can provide that light. That light can accompany individuals as they negotiate a sometimes treacherous and scary path. The journey will still be dark, but the light can make it less terrifying.

REFERENCES

Bluebond-Langner, M. (1978). *The private worlds of dying children.* Princeton, NJ: Princeton University Press.

Bluebond-Langner, M. (1987). Worlds of dying children and their well siblings. *Death Studies, 11,* 279–295.

Doka, K. (2006, Autumn). Caring for the carer: The lessons of research. *Grief Matters: The Australian Journal of Grief and Bereavement, 9,* 4–7.

Doka, K. (1994, August). Caregiver distress: If it is so ethical, why does it feel so bad? *AACN Clinical Issues: Critical Care Nursing, 5,* 346–352.

Doka, K. J. (1982). Staff interaction with the dying child. In E. Pacholski & C. Corr (Eds.), *Priorities in death education and counseling* (pp. 231–246). Arlington, VA: Forum for Death Education and Counseling.

Fulton, R. (1987). Unanticipated grief. In C. Corr & R. Pacholski (Eds.), *Death: Completion and discovery* (pp. 49–60). Lakewood, OH: Association for Death Education and Counseling.

George, R. L., & Cristiani, T. S. (1981). *Theory, methods, and processes of counseling and psychotherapy.* Englewood Cliffs, NJ: Prentice-Hall.

Hawkins, W., & Dunkan. D. (1985). Children's illnesses as risk factors for child abuse. *Psychological Reports, 56,* 638.

Herr, J., & Weakland, J. (1979). *Counseling elders and their families.* New York: Springer.

Jameton, A. (1984). *Nursing practice: The ethical issues.* Englewood Cliffs, NJ: Prentice Hall.

Jarratt, C. J. (1994). *Helping children cope with separation and loss.* Harvard, MA: Harvard and Common Press.

Kastenbaum, R. (1987). Vicarious grief: An intergenerational phenomenon. *Death Studies, 11,* 447–453.

Katz. R., & Johnson, T. (Eds.) (2006). *When professionals weep: Emotional and countertransference issues in end-of-life care.* New York: Routledge.

Lavin, C. (2002). Disenfranchised grief and individuals with developmental disabilities. In K. Doka (Ed.), *Disenfranchised grief: New directions, challenges and strategies for practice* (pp. 307–322). Champaign, IL: Research Press.

Magee, J. (1988). *A professional guide to older adults life review: Releasing the peace within.* Lexington, MA: Lexington Books.

Magee, J. (2007). Life review, paradox, and self-esteem. In K. Doka (Ed.), *Living with grief: Before and after death* (pp. 27–44). Washington, DC: The Hospice Foundation of America.

Papadatou, D. (2000). A proposed model of health professionals' grieving process. *Omega: The Journal of Death and Dying, 41,* 59–77.

Shneidman, E. (1978). Some aspects of psychotherapy with dying persons. In C. Garfield (Ed.), *Psychosocial care of the dying patient* (pp. 201–218). New York: McGraw-Hill.

Stephenson, J. (1985). *Death, grief, and mourning: Individuals and social realities.* New York: Free Press.

Thormen, G. (1982). *Helping troubled families: A social work perspective.* Chicago: Aldine.

Vachon, M. (1987). *Occupational stress in the care of the critically ill, the dying, and the bereaved.* New York: Hemisphere.

Vachon, M. (2007). Caring for the professional caregivers: Before and after the death. In K. Doka (Ed.), *Living with grief: Before and after death* (pp. 27–44). Washington, DC: The Hospice Foundation of America.

Weisman, A. (1972). *On dying and denying: A psychiatric study of terminality.* New York: St. Martins Press.

Weisman, A. (1979). *Coping with cancer.* New York: McGraw-Hill.

5 Responses to Life-Threatening Illness

Rob and John share a room in a hospital. Both are dying of cancer. Beyond their illness they have little in common. Rob is a 49-year-old man who works as a bank manager. Always taught to be polite, he is a model of graciousness to the staff. Brought up into a strong Baptist faith, he faces early death with some quiet anxiety but also with a sense of faith. John is a 67-year-old retired steamfitter. Always a brawler with a fearsome temper, he is still angry, constantly lashing out at family and staff.

These two men illustrate an important point. Each individual will die much as that person lived. The ways by which one currently responds to everyday crises often give clues as to how a client will respond to the crisis of illness or death. Thus it is useful to explore the ways clients and patients have responded to crisis in the past.

Each individual has his or her own vision of what is an appropriate death. To some it may mean peacefully accepting death. To others it may mean fighting death bitterly to the end. Still others might choose to die quickly or opt for heavy sedation. *Each* person has his or her own definition of a "good death."

Researchers and clinicians also stress that the ways we respond and react to the crisis of death are also highly individual and varied.

Shneidman (1978), a pioneer in death studies, has characterized dying persons as exhibiting a "hive of affect." By that, Shneidman meant that dying persons could rarely be characterized in terms of a single emotional response such as "anger" at any given point in the illness. Rather, they may experience a range of many—sometimes contradictory—emotions simultaneously. Think, for example, of a minor life crisis such as an adolescent who has not returned at curfew. Parents experiencing this minor crisis may be experiencing anger, guilt, anxiety, disappointment, and sadness, all at the same time. Responses to life-threatening illness are not only experienced on the emotional level but on physical, behavioral, cognitive, and even spiritual levels as well. This chapter describes the many and major types of responses that individuals can have as they cope with personal or familial crises of life-threatening illness and death.

PHYSICAL RESPONSES

Physical Manifestations of Stress

The diagnosis of life-threatening illness is an extraordinarily stressful event. This intense crisis begins with the diagnosis itself. Although the sense of crisis may recede during the chronic phase, new stressors including treatment, accommodating the demands of life as the illness continues, and often a continued uncertainty will arise. Stress itself can become chronic at this time. In the terminal phase dying itself is an irresolvable crisis. This too creates acute stress.

Many individuals will manifest this continuing stress physically. The range of physical reactions to stress can include insomnia, headaches, dizziness, fatigue, nausea, tingling sensations, and a variety of other physical ills. One should alert one's physician if experiencing any of these reactions, because physical responses, particularly changes in eating and sleeping patterns, may also result from the effects of the disease and treatments.

Preoccupation with Health

In life-threatening illness many people begin to shift their focus inward. A natural result of the trauma of diagnosis is that one can become extremely aware of and sensitive to one's body. Given this heightened anxiety and a preoccupation with oneself, minor symptoms and sensations, once ignored or quickly dismissed, may become the focus of considerable attention and concern. It is also normal during serious illness to become particularly sensitive to certain physical reactions that one fears may indicate particular dangers, such as relapse, metastasis, or reoccurrence. For example, one woman recovering from breast cancer became extremely concerned about back pain. Investigation revealed that a dying woman she had met in the hospital who described such pain as the first symptom that her breast cancer had metastasized instigated her concern. This preoccupation with health can affect anyone who is ill; indeed, a concern with health is heightened whenever one faces illness, even the illness of another. Illness tends to remind one of one's own vulnerability. One takes chest pains much more seriously when a friend has had a heart attack.

Counselors should encourage clients to report any symptoms to a physician. This is critical in order for the physician to monitor the illness and treatment. Within this context though, counselors can validate that these physical responses to disease are normal responses to the illness experience.

COGNITIVE RESPONSES

Shock

Often one's initial response to life-threatening illness is a profound sense of shock. Just as humans will respond to severe physical trauma by going into shock, a person can respond to the psychological trauma of a serious diagnosis with a similar reaction. This may be evident in high levels of stress, as well as confusion, disorientation, and numbness.

Denial

One of the most common and complex responses to life-threatening illness is denial. However, as Weisman (1972) indicates, there are a number of different levels of denial. For example, as discussed in

Chapter 3, Weisman defined "first-order denial" as a denial of the facts. Here one denies the symptoms of the illness: "This is not really a lump or, if it is, it is a result of an earlier injury." In "second-order denial" one admits the symptoms and diagnosis but refuses to acknowledge the implications of that diagnosis. One often focuses on each symptom, crisis, or event as an isolated item. A person with cancer, for example, may focus on an impending operation, giving little attention to the long-term implications of the disease. "Third-order denial" occurs when one recognizes an incurable disease but still views the illness as indefinitely prolonged. In other words, one denies the possibility of death.

Denial is also made more complex by the fact that what seems like denial can, in fact, be many other things. One of the key issues of life-threatening illness, especially in its early phases, is managing information about that illness. One needs to make decisions about whom to tell, when to share that information, and what to say about the disease. Work, promotions, relationships, even self-esteem may be affected by these decisions. It is not unusual to guard this information carefully, perhaps by emphasizing the most optimistic scenarios or even by using evasion and deception. These (mis)communications may shed little light on the person's own awareness of illness. Also, one can consciously choose to suppress the fact of illness, remaining aware of the disease and its implications but concentrating on less traumatic issues.

There may be a very thin line between public acknowledgment and private awareness of illness. Again, as noted in an earlier chapter, Weisman (1972) used the term *middle knowledge* to express the complex reality of awareness and denial. Dying people may drift in and out of awareness of death. At some points they may acknowledge, selectively to given individuals, the seriousness of their illness, whereas at other times they may seemingly ignore such issues.

Denial in the early phases of illness is not only common but also understandable. Many serious life-threatening illnesses, for example, such as HIV infection or chronic lymphocytic leukemia, are asymptomatic in the early stages and typically include extended periods of remission. For many life-threatening diseases prognosis is uncertain. It is certainly natural to avoid the possible implications of threatened survival.

Denial may also be functional. It is not always negative. Sometimes it helps people adjust to illness. A degree of denial allows us to continue to plan for the future, maintain social relationships, and even participate in treatment. After all, it makes little sense to submit to painful treatment if there is no possibility of ultimate beneficial effect.

Denial may be adaptive when recognition will not alter the situation. It may be very useful early in the illness as a way of mitigating the threat. There is even research (Weisman and Worden, 1975) that indicates denial is associated with longer survival. In all of these circumstances, denial may have a useful role to play and should not be condemned by outsiders.

Denial should be challenged only when it constitutes a threat to the health of a person or to the health of others. For example, a person who denies the seriousness of his illness or who maintains an irrational delusion of health so that it affects participation in or adherence to treatment may need to be questioned. This problem often occurs during periods of remission when the ill person, encouraged by recovered health, denies an initially accepted diagnosis. Signs of such denial may be evidenced by relaxed adherence to treatment or even its total suspension. In one case a man who had suffered from heart failure experienced a significant gain in health after initial treatment. He then became convinced that the original diagnosis was a mistake, a result of mixed test results, and he stopped taking his medication and visiting the outpatient clinic. The unfortunate result was that his health rapidly deteriorated.

Similarly, a counselor may need to confront a person who endangers the health of others, such as a person who is HIV positive but who denies infection and continues to participate in behaviors that have a high risk of transmitting the virus to others. Here, counterproductive denial jeopardizes the welfare of others. In other cases, denial should be recognized for what it is—a psychological defense. This defense buffers an individual from encountering a severe psychological threat in the circumstances that the person may be unable to handle.

It is always valuable to allow the client to honestly explore, at his or her own pace, any concerns that may develop. Given the reality of "middle knowledge," people will at times address issues of illness, physical deterioration, or dying and at other moments they will entertain hopes for eventual recovery. But in an understanding and accepting context, the person may, at times, choose to let down the defense of denial.

Egocentricity and Constriction of Interests

At the time of diagnosis one may turn inward. One can become egocentric, severely limiting all outside interests. There are many reasons for this. Physiological factors focus attention on bodily sensations: one becomes tuned in to one's own body during illness. Psychologically, the crisis of diagnosis centers all attention on the illness, the source of the stress. In addition, interactions with others may be limited by hospitalization, the attention of family and friends, and the attempt to spare them further stress or to exempt them from role responsibilities. Even family members caught in the crisis may experience that same sense of egocentricity.

Generally, as one moves from the crisis of the diagnostic phase into the chronic phase, egocentricity tends to diminish. Here hope for continued existence may strongly reemerge. In addition, the challenges, diversion, and stimulation of resumed roles tend to refocus attention outward. Both the ill person and other family members have gone back to work or school and family life, and a degree of normalcy returns. In many cases, though, some egocentricity and constriction of interests may still be observed during the chronic phase. Treatment and symptoms are constant reminders of disease. Fears of deterioration, relapse, or recurrence place constraints on any future planning. The fact of illness, the demands of treatment, lessened energy levels, and even decisions on priorities may diminish or end involvement in certain activities and roles.

As health begins to deteriorate, especially in the terminal phase, egocentricity and constriction of interests are likely to reemerge. Often, disengagement of the dying individual from others is a clear sign of impending death. The dying person seems to withdraw from others and lacks interest in any outside needs. This disengagement may be a manifestation of underlying depression and grief, a psychological reaction to irresolvable crisis, a response to the withdrawal of others, or a reflective struggle as the person focuses attention on inward spiritual needs.

Bargaining

Bargaining too has been identified as a common response to a life-threatening illness. Bargaining is a feeling that by omitting or committing certain actions one can avoid or forestall further illness or death. It is often expressed through explicit or implicit "deals" with some figure of authority. For example, bargaining may revolve around lifestyle and adherence issues. One may promise to amend certain lifestyle practices that contributed to the illness or may agree to accept medical treatment.

One may exhibit an almost magical thinking about adherence to the medical regimen. "If only I watch my diet, take my medication, and do everything I am told, I will achieve continued remission or cure." Sometimes this can have an initial positive aspect in encouraging adherence to the medical regimen, but later in the course of the disease the impact can be negative when the individual feels disenchantment and discouragement as the illness proceeds. Thus it is important for caregivers to provide hopeful yet realistic messages about what adherence to the medical regimen is likely to achieve.

Sometimes clients may even perceive that a change in lifestyle will ensure health. A gay client with AIDS once stated, "I became sick because I engaged in promiscuous and unsafe sex. If I stop doing what made me sick, I will stay well." A person with heart disease promised God he would attend church regularly if the operation was successful. The turning toward religion that has often been observed in persons diagnosed with life-threatening illness may be, at least in part, a manifestation of the "bargaining" response to illness.

The nature of bargains often strongly reflects the person's experience of illness. Early on in the illness bargains may emphasize cures or significant remission. Later, as the individual begins to experience deterioration, bargains may focus on living to enjoy certain significant events or milestones (such as birthdays, anniversaries, a daughter's wedding, and so on), living pain free, or even living on in an afterlife.

Bargaining can have both constructive and destructive aspects. In some cases it can facilitate life-enhancing behaviors. In others, however, it can lead to feelings that may inhibit adaptation. In the chronic phase of illness, such bargains may continue to encourage adherence. Individuals may believe that as long as they participate in treatment, that will forestall continued decline. However, should deterioration continue, individuals may feel discouraged and angry that the "bargain" was not kept, losing motivation for adherence to treatment.

Changes in Body Image and Self-Esteem

Every culture values its own image of physical vitality and attractiveness. The combination of disease and treatment can cause effects that undermine a person's sense of physical attractiveness, thereby impairing body image. Because body image is so interwoven with sexuality, gender identity, self-concept, and self-esteem, the effects on body image can be highly significant.

Goffman, in his book *Stigma* (1963), described the impacts of stigma or impaired body image on self-concept. To Goffman, stigma creates a discrepancy between actual and virtual social identity; that is, there is a difference between the way someone would like others to view him or her and the way others perceive that person. Often this stigma affects both interaction and identity. The following cases illustrate the stigma that chronic illness creates:

> Barbara is an attractive 49-year-old woman with cancer. She had an operation that left scarring on her abdomen. She also received chemotherapy that sometimes made her appear bloated. Although a very attractive woman, she is very sensitive about the scars on her body, even though they are relatively minor.
>
> She feels much less attractive since surgery. A divorcee, involved in a serious relationship with a man, she has not been able to have sex since her first surgery. She worries that eventually her boyfriend will leave her and she will live on as a "lonely old, ugly woman."

Changes in body image caused by disease and treatment can affect other aspects of identity and self-esteem. It is important to note that body image has a subjective reality. One's body image may plummet when objective changes seem only minor.

"Near-Death" and Other Extraordinary Experiences

Since the publication of Moody's *Life after Life* in 1975, there has been considerable interest in "near-death experiences" or "altered consciousness experiences." As Moody describes it, persons near death often experience a common sequence of events in which they experience their body moving through a dark tunnel, glimpsing the spirits of others who have died. To Moody these experiences were warm and positive and often left survivors with a lessened fear of death.

In addition to these experiences, clients might report other forms of extraordinary experiences akin to what LaGrand (1997) found in bereaved individuals. Individuals with illness may experience "visitation" dreams or other extraordinary experiences that have relevance to the illness. For example, one client reported that he had a dream in which his father, long dead, reassured him that he would recover. In another case, a woman reported feeling the comforting presence of her dead grandmother as she was wheeled into surgery. In other circumstances, coincidental experiences can take on great symbolic importance. One man reported that when he was awaiting surgery, he could hear the radio in the operating room playing "Hang On, Sloopy"—a song his father would sing to him in rough times.

Near-death and other extraordinary experiences are not uncommon in life-threatening illness. But they do not seem to be universal or uniform. Nor are they always comforting and positive. Some researchers (Kastenbaum, 1979) have found that many individuals have experienced frightening episodes involving terrifying images.

Further, such experiences may have many possible explanations. Whereas some (eg. Moody, 1975) feel that they may represent proof of an afterlife, others (Kastenbaum, 1979) hold that they may be a reaction to drugs or internal chemical changes. The key issue is how the individual who has this experience interprets it, and whether he or she finds it comforting. Counselors should ask individuals if they have had any such experiences and then allow them to recount and interpret that experience.

Other Dreams and Sleep Disturbances

During a life-threatening illness sleep disturbances are common. Stress and uncertainty may lead to bouts of insomnia. An individual may be troubled by dreams that reflect preoperative anxieties, anxieties associated with illness or treatment, or fears of death. One man facing amputation dreamed he was in a butcher shop with limbs and body parts hanging from meat hooks. In another case a woman newly diagnosed with multiple sclerosis (MS) dreamed she was invisible as she frantically tried to receive help from family and friends, thereby reflecting her fears of abandonment and death.

Dreams may sometimes reflect spiritual anxieties, especially during the acute and terminal phase. For example, one woman who was facing surgery was deeply troubled by her decision to bring up her children in a faith different from the one in which she had been raised. She began to have recurrent dreams in which she saw a poker table covered with pennies. (Penny poker was her major form of recreation.) Each penny had a different face. A large finger, which she assumed was "the hand of God," was separating the pennies into different piles. She would always wake up when the finger was placed upon her face.

Dreams do not always have to be fearful. One adolescent, soon after his diagnosis of a brain tumor, had a dream about a "peaceful warrior." This warrior was able to surmount numerous obstacles to resolve his quest and prove his manhood. The dream became a metaphor, providing inner strength for the youth's struggle with his illness. Dreams, then, are an effective way to reflect upon a person's underlying concern. Again, caregivers do well to ask people what they have dreamed, to note the images, thoughts and feelings associated with the dream, and to encourage them to explore and interpret these dreams.

EXISTENTIAL PLIGHT, REASSESSMENT OF LIFE, AND MORTALITY

Confronting life-threatening illness often leads to an intensified awareness of one's own mortality. Facing death often causes both the individual and the family members to review and make sense of their past lives, and to assess the present and future as well. One may reassess one's values, beliefs, and priorities. This struggle can sometimes intensify feelings of anger, anxiety, and guilt. An individual may feel bitter or guilty about missed opportunities, prior choices, or unfinished business. One may ponder what he or she has done to deserve this disease or fall into despair over the meaning of his or her own existence.

There may be positive reactions too. Often an individual will make decisions that will enhance the quality of life. It is not unusual for persons who experience life-threatening illness to speak of the illness as a turning point in their lives—because of their illness they have reordered their priorities, thereby enriching the quality of whatever time remains. Some people are able to construct systems of thought that allow them to integrate and interpret their experience of illness in ways that enhance self-esteem. One man struggling with a crippling disease found comfort in the fact that it caused him to think more about his family. He was able to reinterpret the time he was forced to stay at home as an opportunity to reconnect with his children. The knowledge of mortality may give present life new vitality, even turning mundane tasks into pleasurable achievements.

Cognitive Impairments and Psychiatric Disturbances

The tremendous stress of life-threatening illness, the anticipatory grief that it may engender, and the effects of both the disease and its treatment may manifest themselves in cognitive impairments and psychiatric disturbance. Cognitive impairments such as forgetfulness, confusion, inability to concentrate, and poor concentration may be evident. Illness may reactivate earlier unresolved difficulties and may create such stress that the person's coping abilities are overwhelmed.

Psychiatric disturbances are also far more common in life among persons with life-threatening illness. One study (Hobbs, Perrin, and Irays, 1985), for example, found that children with life-threatening illness are seven times more at risk for psychiatric disturbances than their well peers. Similarly, another study (Cyntryn, Van Moore, and Robinson, 1973) found that 59% of a sample of cystic fibrosis patients had at least some degree of mental disturbance. Studies of persons who tested HIV positive (Buhrich, 1986; Winiarski, 1991) have identified a series of AIDS-related psychiatric syndromes such as dysphonia, phobias, anxiety disorders, and immobilization that follow diagnosis.

Suicidal Thoughts

The diagnosis of life-threatening illness, because it causes heightened anxiety for the survival and well-being of self and others, may well cause suicidal thoughts. If death is likely, an individual may reason, why not experience it now and avoid expected personal deterioration as well as the negative effects on family? Since suicidal wishes can be self-fulfilling, they should be resolved prior to surgery or other forms of treatment. The threat of suicide usually recedes in the early chronic phase after the crisis of diagnosis but may return with continued deterioration in the later chronic and terminal phases.

Hope

Hope usually exists throughout the experience of life-threatening illness. Many believe that hope can enhance coping skills and even influence survival. For example, Siegel (1986) emphasizes the importance of maintaining positive outlooks, believing that negative perceptions can become self-fulfilling. For Siegel the body and mind are inexorably intertwined; hope, strengthened through active imagining of the most positive outcomes, becomes a catalyst in achieving those desired results.

Throughout the course of the illness the focus of hope may change. In the prediagnostic phase, hope usually centers on the symptoms either disappearing or having no serious significance. During the diagnostic or acute phase, hope may center on the most optimistic outcomes—that the diagnosis will not be life-threatening, for example, or that treatment will lead to cure or significant remission. Hope of cure or remission may continue throughout the chronic phase. In the latter periods of that phase, hope may center on a slowed rate of deterioration or on a lessening of pain. In the terminal phase, hope may center on surviving beyond significant milestones or events, or on the abatement of symptoms or pain.

Throughout periods of decline the time frame of hope will diminish. In the early phases of illness hope is likely to be expressed in years. In later periods that time frame may decline to days. "I hope to live to 70 years" may become "I hope to live to my birthday on Friday." In the early phases of illness hope is important because it encourages treatment and preserves self-identity and social relationships. In the terminal phase, hope may focus on the afterlife or other modes of symbolic immortality, such as living on in the lives of descendants and a community, or in one's creations and accomplishments.

EMOTIONAL RESPONSES

Guilt and Shame

Guilt and shame are common reactions to life-threatening illness. There may be *causation guilt,* in which the individual feels guilty over personal behaviors or a lifestyle that may have contributed to the disease. For example, in one case an older man who had been diagnosed with throat cancer blamed his pipe smoking for the disease and felt very guilty that he continued to smoke despite previous warnings. Given the fact that many life-threatening diseases have behavioral components, this is not an unusual response.

There may also be *moral guilt.* Here the individual perceives the disease as a punishment for some moral or character offense. Religious or spiritual issues are often intertwined in moral guilt. Here the individual believes that the illness is a punishment from God or a sign of cosmic karma. Moral guilt can result from other factors, however, as well. Many life-threatening diseases are often publicly perceived not only as lifestyle related but also as character related. A smoker with lung cancer may feel guilt both because he knows that his smoking contributed to the disease and because he has internalized social attitudes that smokers lack willpower. In other cases even the person's basic personality may be blamed for the disease. For example, explosive personalities may be seen as contributing to heart disease, and those who find it difficult to express emotion may be blamed for causing their own cancer. Counselors need to be sensitive to the reality that one unfortunate by-product of theory and research on the psychological correlates of disease is that disease victims may incorrectly internalize blame for their own illness. One study (Bennett and Bennett, 1984, p. 561) emphasized that "excessive belief in the power of human influence over painful afflictions always carries a destructive potential."

In addition to moral and causation guilt, individuals may also exhibit a sense of *role guilt*. Here the focus of guilt is upon opportunities wasted and the limited time remaining. For example, an ill husband may feel guilty about past behavior to his wife. These feelings may even be exacerbated by the wife's support during the crisis. And he may feel guilty over the ways that his illness and perhaps death will affect his spouse's life. Role guilt can also be expressed as guilt over being a burden. Particularly in the chronic and terminal phases of illness, when one may require the intensive help of others, individuals may feel guilty about the demands they are making upon others and the ways in whch their illness is affecting the lives of others.

ANGER

Anger is another common response to life-threatening illness. An individual is naturally angry that the illness is troubling his or her daily existence, complicating life and threatening possible death.

This anger may be directed at God. The individual feels outraged and cheated by the illness. There may be a sense of deep unfairness. "Why me?" is often an angry theme that emerges as persons cope with illness. For example, one young woman with cancer felt tremendous anger over the unfairness of the illness. She had two young children. She considered herself a moral person who had made great efforts to have a healthy lifestyle. The questions of "why me?" and "why now?" loomed large.

In other cases the anger may be directed at other individuals who can be blamed for the condition. In one case a worker blamed his employers for exposing him to hazardous chemicals that he believed were responsible for his cancer. In another case a woman who had contracted lung cancer was angry with her brother, who had introduced her to smoking when they were both teenagers.

Sometimes anger may be directed at caregivers. One phenomenon that counselors must be aware of is "splitting." Here an individual's anger is turned toward one caregiver while others are excused from blame. Such scapegoating often exacerbates tensions among caregivers. Often the individual's false perception reinforces caregivers' self-concepts that they are just a bit more sensitive and skilled than others. It is important to recognize that client complaints, even when focused upon one person, may be a manifestation of an individual's anger over the illness.

Targets of anger can also include family and friends. An individual may become angry with his or her family, often because these targets are both closest and safest. Again, it is not unusual that one or two family members are scapegoated. One man with MS constantly focused his anger on his young teenage son. In counseling, it became clear that his anger tended to focus on the boy since he resented his son's growing vitality and emerging athletic powers just as his own mobility and physical state were so rapidly declining.

Friends too may become a focal point of anger and hostility. An individual may feel that friends are insensitive or unsupportive. Although in some cases this may be true, in other situations friends are merely uncomfortable with or unable to respond effectively to the ill person's new, ambiguous status. The friend may also be receiving mixed messages about what the ill individual wants, needs, and expects.

Anger should be seriously evaluated and explored, because sometimes it has a legitimate cause. Counselors should beware of too readily dismissing anger. I once knew a chaplain who listened to a nurse's story about a patient who always complained about cold potatoes. The nurse suggested that this complaint really reflected the patient's anger at his illness. The chaplain asked the nurse whether she ever put her finger on the potatoes!

Although anger is a natural response, it can generate interpersonal tension, which both exacerbates stress and alienates crucial support. An individual's anger at the illness may cause him to strike out repeatedly at others in the immediate environment, often those very same people who are most needed to help in the struggle with disease.

JEALOUSY AND ENVY

Jealousy and envy are common human emotions, so common that two of the Ten Commandments address them. Persons with life-threatening illness may experience jealousy and envy. An individual may be jealous of the good health of others. In some cases he or she may feel resentment of those who do not seem to appreciate their health, who misuse their time, or who lead lives perceived to be destructive. An individual may be jealous of other persons who seem to be responding better to treatment, coping more effectively with illness, or seemingly receiving more support. Family members may feel envious of other families untouched by illness, or by families that seem to be coping better. Because jealousy and envy are defined negatively, an individual or family may experience guilt over these emotions. Counselors should recognize that these concerns are normal, and they can help by encouraging individuals to review the ways in which these emotions are influencing responses to illness and relationships.

FEAR AND ANXIETY

The crisis of diagnosis produces fear and anxiety. Fears can include fears of the unknown, of loneliness, of extinction, of loss of family and friends, of the loss of body or mental functions, of loss of control, and of pain and suffering. In some cases fears will focus on what the disease and treatments may do to an individual's roles and identity. For example, an operation that mars the face may well cause anxiety about appearance and attractiveness that will, in turn, challenge identity. There may be fears the disease and its treatment will impair performance or make it impossible to maintain a career. Fears can focus on the operation or subsequent treatments; indeed, fear can be especially high prior to and immediately following surgery. Preoperative anxieties may focus on the fear of anesthesia, the loss of consciousness, or the effect of the operation (for example, causing additional damage, loss of organ and function, negative findings). Fears about postoperative care and life can focus on ability to function, employability, attractiveness, and finances. Postoperative anxieties may concern prospects for recovery. It is not unusual for anxious individuals to scrutinize carefully the remarks of physicians, nurses, and family for clues to their condition. There may be fears related to various therapies and their side effects. An individual may have fears that chemotherapy or radiation will cause sickness or sterility, leave him unable to function, or even create new cancer. Additional fears may focus on the fear of the dying process or on the ability of others to cope with the illness and possible death.

Fears and anxieties are likely to ebb and flow throughout the chronic phase. Often there is a persistent level of anxiety. During crisis points this anxiety can be intense. Even small events, such as the onset of a minor ailment such as a cold, can create great anxiety. Levels of fear and anxiety can continue even in cases of full recovery, often intensifying when illness or new symptoms threaten recurrence or perhaps when acquaintances suffer relapse or die of the disease. As the person approaches the terminal phase, anxieties may center on the process of dying (for example, the pain, dependence, indignity, loneliness); the loss of life (for example, separation, incompleteness, loss of mastery); the after-death (for example, fate of the body, judgment, the unknown); and the well-being of survivors.

Although specific fears and generalized anxieties are natural and understandable responses to life-threatening illness, they can be both destructive and disabling. In some cases anxiety may inhibit patients from sharing information with their health-care providers if they are fearful that the information portents bad news that they would rather not know. In other cases, the level of anxiety may be so high as to inhibit the client from functioning in other roles. Clients also might use dysfunctional strategies such as alcohol abuse to alleviate anxiety. Counselors should continually assess clients' levels of anxiety, the ways that anxiety is affecting their ability to cope both with the illness and life in general, and the strategies they use to deal with their anxiety. If the level of anxiety is highly disabling, psychotropic medications may be prescribed.

GRIEF, SADNESS, AND DEPRESSION

Learning of life-threatening illness often generates feelings of grief, sadness, and depression. Sociologist Robert Fulton (1987) has described what he calls *anticipatory grief*. Grief, he points out, is not only a response to losses one has experienced but also to those one *expects* to experience. More recently, Rando (2000) has described anticipatory grief as a "useful misnomer." Rando notes that anticipatory grief, or as she prefers the more inclusive term *anticipatory mourning*, refers to the range of reactions that persons cope with in the course of an illness. Rando's redefinition reminds readers that it is not only the expectation of anticipated loss that persons experience but even more critically, the ongoing losses that are inevitable throughout the experience of illness. Counselors, to review, then validate and address the issue of loss as clients continue to adapt to illness. For example, one client, a 50-year-old man suffering from amyotrophic lateral sclerosis (ALS) indicated that, on hearing his diagnosis of this progressive terminal disease that would likely end his life within a few years, the first loss that he experienced was his dream of a mountain retirement home with his wife. Later in the course of the illness, he dealt with a variety of losses as the disease progressed and he continued to lose physical functions and had to give up his career and other meaningful activities.

Whereas grief and other reactions such as sadness and regret are common in life-threatening illness, they should be differentiated from depression. Depression is a diagnostic category—a manifestation of a mental illness—that may be manifested in several ways including constant sadness, fatigue, loss of energy, diminished interest in activity, insomnia or hypersomnia, and feelings of worthlessness. Although depression is an understandable response to life-threatening illness, it should be viewed seriously. Depression can sap energy for treatment, impair the quality of life, lead to suicidal acts, and perhaps even hasten death. Depressions that last more than two weeks should be evaluated professionally and treated. Often antidepressants or therapy can be useful in mitigating depression.

Resignation

Kübler-Ross identified acceptance as a common response to life-threatening illness, particularly in the terminal phase. Here the individual recognizes the inevitability of death and ceases to fight death. According to Kübler-Ross (1969, p. 113), "Acceptance should not be mistaken for a happy stage. It is almost void of feelings. It is as if the pain had gone, the struggle is over, and there comes a time for the 'new final rest before the long journey.'"

Acceptance can be a very complicated response. In some cases it may reflect the resignation that Kübler-Ross describes, whereas in others it may simply define an emotional collapse. Roberts (1988), basing her work on crisis theory, suggests that people unable to surmount the crisis of death experience a collapse of any remaining defenses. In still other cases death is anticipated, that is, looked forward to, either as a release from pain and/or dependency or as an entry into a better and continued form of existence. And sometimes individuals actively acquiesce in death, even taking actions such as poor compliance to a medical regimen, refusing treatment, or even committing suicide. In summary, there are a variety of responses that may be identified as "acceptance" ranging from resignation to acquiescence.

It should also be noted that acceptance is not necessarily a desired state for all people. Such a position ignores the individual ways one faces death. Each individual has a different perspective on what constitutes a good death. Some may choose to struggle continuously against death, whereas others will almost rush to accept it. Sometimes acceptance can be premature. An acceptance response, particularly in the early phases of illness, may inhibit treatment and complicate any hopes for recovery.

OTHER EMOTIONAL RESPONSES

Since illness and dying are processes of life, all the emotions experienced in life may be evidenced in life-threatening illness. There will still be moments of joy, happiness, and love. Sometimes such reactions can be experienced as part of the response to illness. Once a woman in the chronic phase of illness shared with me her joy and zest about being able to continue mundane household work tasks that she had feared she might never be able to do again. Another client, faced with a continued decline, expressed his "unspeakable joy" at experiencing family moments and events.

Emotional responses, or any other pattern of responses, do not follow any order. And in any human situation, particularly a crisis, there may be considerable mood swings. Clients may feel sadness in the morning and seem much better by lunch. Journaling can be an effective way for clients to monitor feelings and reactions throughout the course of an illness, and such a technique can assist counselors in assessing factors that generate patterns of responses.

BEHAVIORAL RESPONSES

Hypersensitivity

Persons with life-threatening illness may become hypersensitive. An individual often becomes extremely conscious of how others—family, friends, and medical staff—respond to him or her. He or she may exhibit great sensitivity to verbal and nonverbal behaviors of others. One woman, recovering from cancer surgery, for example, was convinced that her neighbor's use of paper plates at a casual barbecue indicated her fear of "catching" cancer from the woman who had cancer. An individual may scrutinize even casual remarks, especially those made by doctors and other caregivers, for clues about his or her condition, perhaps because he or she is suspicious that he or she has not been told the whole truth.

Humor

Humor is one of our most basic coping mechanisms, one that can be very effective in times of crisis since it can release tension, ease stress, and strengthen social relationships. Sometimes it can even mitigate the shock of bad news, allowing individuals to regain their sense of control. Claire Kowalski, a dear colleague, composed this limerick at a time when she had heard some bad news:

> A doctor I talked to this noon
>   Forecast some dire symptoms quite soon.
>   So I'll seek my own cure,
>   And succeed to be sure,
>   And that doctor can sing a new tune.

Another limerick illustrates the way that humor allowed her to maintain hope and continue a positive outlook even in the middle of treatment.

> This dear body on which I depend
>   Is becoming my very best friend.
>   So I'll treat it just right,
>   Loving care day and night,
>   And I know I am now on the mend.

Another colleague facing ovarian surgery remembered that her last words to the doctor as she went under anesthesia were "keep the playpen." Norman Cousins, in his book *The Anatomy of an Illness* (1979), expressed his strong belief that his positive attitude and therapeutic use of laughter not only eased his adjustment to his illness, but also was the key to his recovery.

Disengagement

Clinicians and researchers have long recognized that people often respond to life-threatening illness with disengagement, behavior in which they withdraw from others. Disengagement is often seen in the acute phase and also quite often in the latter period of the terminal phase.

The causes of disengagement can be quite diverse. In some cases it may be a manifestation of intense anxiety, pain, and egocentricity, all of which can cause people to withdraw from social interaction and focus on the self. In other cases it may be a symptom of underlying depression. In still other cases it may result from an intense involvement with inner issues and struggles. Finally, it may be a response to the isolation experienced when significant others—especially family and friends—withdraw from the ill individual.

Mastery and Control Behaviors

Someone who experiences life-threatening illness may have a strong feeling that his or her life is no longer in control. Not only are clients facing an uncertain future, but they may be forced into a dependent role or they may anticipate future dependency. One way to respond to this loss of control is by trying to assert control even more strongly and attempting to master this experience.

These attempts at mastery and control can be expressed in a number of ways. Clients may try to learn as much as possible about his disease. The ease of information on the Internet then can be both helpful and problematic. It can make clients better informed and thus partners in the treatment of the disease. It may even offer options for online support. However, because the Internet is unregulated, clients also may receive false or even exploitive information. Counselors should continue to assess whether and how clients are using the Internet.

Other clients may assert mastery and control in different ways. Clients may plunge into physical fitness activities; use cognitive modes of control by intellectualizing the threat; be very sensitive about maintaining personal control, for example, by carefully checking emotional expression; resist attempts by family, friends, and professionals to intrude on treatment decisions or by asserting control in the disclosure process. For example, an older man insisted that his wife keep the diagnosis from his four adult children, but over the next two days he individually shared that information with each child, swearing each one to secrecy.

Individuals may become assertive about their rights. For example, one researcher (Gustafson, 1972) found that nursing home patients were insistent over issues such as new glasses or clothes, since these struggles gave them a sense that they were still alive. In some cases people can become exceedingly manipulative, using their illness to obtain secondary gains. For example, in one case a young man attempted to use the fact that he had leukemia to maintain and control his relationship with his girlfriend. Whenever they had problems, he would insist it was because she could not deal with his disease, and he always added that a breakup would surely result in his relapse.

As with any response, these behaviors can be both appropriate and inappropriate. In some cases they can lead people to assume realistic responsibility for treatment. In other cases they can have negative implications, such as causing individuals to reject any dependent relationship, even one that might facilitate subsequent treatment.

Other problematic reactions include compulsive behaviors or counterphobic reactions in which the person asserts control through rejection of expert advice. Examples of compulsive behaviors include obsessions with health or adherence to particular rituals that an individual believes are associated with health. A diabetic adolescent who defiantly eats junk food and drinks beer would be an example of a counterphobic reaction.

Regression and Dependent Behaviors

Regression and dependent behaviors are another response to the loss of control inherent in life-threatening illness. A person may respond to partial loss of control brought on by illness by surrendering additional control. Some psychologists suggest that persons typically respond to loss of control by making renewed efforts to exert control. Feeling that they are losing control, they try even harder to maintain it. However, if these efforts seem to fail, they may give up completely, allowing others to take even greater control of their lives than is necessary.

Overwhelmed by the diagnosis or decline, some people regress and become dependent. This dependency can have other implications.

Earlier conflicts over dependency, autonomy, and authority can reemerge. One older man, for example, who was struggling with diabetes, began to become very dependent upon his wife, asking her to monitor his diet, control his portions, and cook appropriate meals. At the same time, however, he would sneak snacks and eat forbidden candies. In counseling, he recognized a similar pattern from his adolescence. As an overweight teenager he had expected his mother to help him adhere to his diet. But he also resented her efforts and frequently sabotaged them. He realized he had transferred many of his unresolved feelings and behaviors from this earlier life experience to his current situation.

It is important for counselors and other caregivers, including both family members and medical staff, to try to emphasize, whenever possible, the autonomy of the ill person. Although it is often easier for caregivers to do something for the ill person instead of leaving him or her to do it, each act may reinforce the person's own dependencies and lessened abilities. Often the line is difficult to draw, but individuals should be encouraged to do as much as possible.

Acting-Out and Resisting Behaviors

An individual may also respond to life-threatening illness by acting-out and resisting behaviors. Displaced anger and hypersensitivity can lead to acting-out behaviors and increased interpersonal conflicts. People who are ill may be short-tempered and have frequent angry outbursts. Resisting behaviors, rooted perhaps in anger and denial, may be evident here as well, and may be manifested in such things as missed appointments, poor adherence to treatment, and counterphobic behaviors.

SPIRITUAL RESPONSES

Changes in Spiritual Behaviors

Life-threatening illness may very well provoke an existential or spiritual crisis, causing clients to question the nature of their faith, the quality of their lives, and even the fairness of the world. For some, there may a renewed interest in religion. They may begin or intensify religious and spiritual activity such as attending church and praying. They may seek to complete or even repeat religious rituals. A formerly nonobservant Jewish man decided, for example, to have a bar mitzvah, even though he was 57. In another case a nonpracticing Roman Catholic began to attend church once more and even insisted upon a new baptism. Such behaviors may reflect renewed interest and appreciation of spiritual and philosophical concerns, brought to the fore by people's struggles with their own mortality.

It is important, however, that caregivers recognize that even though illness may awaken or intensify spiritual interests in some people, others may have a faith crisis. This may be observed as anger with God or a falling away from former spiritual practices. For some, the very fact of the illness may create a crisis of faith. Counselors should always assess any changes in spiritual and religious beliefs, practices, or rituals.

Seeking a Miracle

For some persons, the crisis of a life-threatening illness may lead to a quest for a miracle, particularly when medicine has little to offer beyond palliative care. They may attempt various modes of spiritual healing, from visiting shrines to laying-on of hands to New Age techniques such as healing crystals.

Counselors and other health caregivers have to walk a thin line here between allowing a client to maintain hope, respecting the client's religious beliefs, and at least alerting clients to the possibilities of fraud. Two principles may be helpful. The first is that spiritual practices that complement any existing medical therapies and do no harm can certainly be used. A second principle is to assist clients in evaluating practices and promises that do not seem evidence based or spiritually centered and allow for the possibility that unscrupulous persons are preying on vulnerable patients.

A case might illustrate these differences. A young client with ALS began to search for faith-based programs as he realized traditional medicine had little to offer. He found two programs that he attended. One was a church, in a faith tradition similar to his own, that had a monthly healing service where the congregation joined in prayer for healing. People flocked to these services. The minister reminded the congregation that healing was a mysterious process. He truly believed that some were healed by this service yet he made no claims that all would be healed, at least physically. The congregation did have a free will offering, but he scrupulously reminded the congregants that although they were free to offer any gift, healing could not be purchased.

The second healer was far different. He promised that he could cure the disease given enough treatments. The sessions were costly, and only cash was accepted—no receipts were given. As we worked together he decided to continue to visit the church but ceased seeing the healer. Evidently the healer was arrested and convicted of tax evasion.

Transcendent Behaviors

Concerns about the meaning of life may encourage people to take actions that will use their remaining time to fulfill goals even if the activity exacerbates risk. For example, a woman with MS chose to have a child, even at the risk of further deterioration of her health, because being pregnant fulfilled a life goal and enhanced her sense of biological survival through an offspring. In another case a man diagnosed with Parkinson's disease decided to intensify his efforts to complete a doctorate. Thereafter, medical decisions and procedures took second place to his educational concerns.

In some cases individuals focus on assisting others. When one older man, for example, learned that he had a life-threatening disease, he became concerned about his wife's survival. She had a number of controlled chronic conditions that required a complicated medical regimen. He spent considerable energy on teaching his wife to be medically self-sufficient.

CONCLUSION

In recent years, there has been a move away from seeing responses to a life-threatening illness or a loss as a series of stages to understanding the wide range of responses, the very individual pathways, of how persons respond to crises. Counselors have a role in assisting clients to recognize the very many ways—physically, cognitively, emotionally, behaviorally, and spiritually—in which they are responding to the crisis of illness.

There is more than mere recognition. The ways that clients respond to life-threatening illness are often reflective of underlying adaptive styles or the process whereby individuals attempt to manage situations that place intense demands upon their intrapsychic and interpsychic resources.

In short, there are many different ways that clients may adapt to a life-threatening illness. Counselors can assist clients in understanding the ways in which their adaptations may help and hinder them at times. For example, a certain degree of dependency can facilitate adjustment, allowing one to accept help. However, too much dependency can sabotage one's rehabilitation at times when one may be expected to do more things for oneself. Similarly, adaptive styles that emphasize fighting and resisting disease may, many believe, increase survival time. But they can also create difficulties such as resisting needed help. There is also the risk of emotional collapse when these responses no longer seem to forestall deterioration or death (Roberts, 1988).

It is important, then, to examine the ways in which clients adapt to the crisis of life-threatening illness. Are their adaptations allowing clients to confront the crisis, offering flexibility as the course of the illness shifts or conditions and information change—or are the adaptive patterns, such as continued denial or failing to adhere to treatment, hastening death? As mentioned earlier, reviewing the client's responses to prior crises in life can pinpoint strengths and forewarn counselors—and clients—of possible problems.

When clients really understand their responses, they are empowered to assess the ways in which their reactions and adaptation styles affect their sense of self, influence relationships with others, and complicate or facilitate the struggle with life-threatening illness. This may not only influence the quantity of life, it may even change its quality.

REFERENCES

Bennett, M. I., & Bennett, M. S. (1984). The uses of hopelessness. *American Journal of Psychiatry, 141,* 559–562.

Buhrich, N. (1986). Psychiatric aspects of AIDS and related conditions. *Mental Health in Australia, 1,* 5–7.

Cousins, N. (1979). *Anatomy of an illness.* New York: Norton.

Cytryn, L., Van Moore, P., & Robinson, M. (1973). Psychological adjustment of children with cystic fibrosis. In G. J. Anthony & C. Koupernik (Eds.), *The child in his family: The impact of disease and death* (pp. 37–48). New York: Wiley and Son.

Fulton, R. (1987). Unanticipated grief. In C. Corr and R. Pacholski (Eds.), *Death: Completion and discovery* (pp. 49–60). Lakewood, OH: Association for Death Education and Counseling.

Goffman, E. (1963). *Stigma: Notes on the management of spoiled identity.* Englewood Cliffs. NJ: Prentice-Hall.

Gustafson, E. (1972). Dying: The career of the nursing home patient. *Journal of Health and Social Behavior, 13,* 226–235.

Hobbs, N., Perrin, J. & Irays, H. (1985). *Chronically ill children and their families.* San Francisco: Jossey-Bass.

Kastenbaum, R. (1979). *Between life and death.* New York: Springer.

Kübler-Ross, E. (1969). *On death and dying.* New York: Macmillan.

LaGrand, L. (1997). *After death communication: Final farewell.* St. Paul, MN: Llewellyn Worldwide.

Moody, R. (1975). *Life after life.* New York: Bantam Books.

Rando, T. A. (Ed.) (2000). *Clinical dimensions of anticipatory mourning: Theory and practice in working with the dying, their loved ones, and their caregivers.* Champaign, IL: Research Press.

Roberts, M. (1988, April). Imminent death as crisis. Paper presented at the annual conference of the Association for Death Education and Counseling, Orlando, Florida.

Shneidman, E. (1978). Some aspects of psychotherapy with dying persons. In C. Garfield (Ed.), *Psychosocial care of the dying patient* (pp. 201–218). New York: McGraw-Hill.

Siegel, B. S. (1986). *Love, medicine, and miracles.* New York: Harper and Row.

Weisman, A. (1972). *On dying and denying: A psychiatric study of terminality.* New York: St. Martins Press.

Weisman, A., and Worden, J. W. (1975). Psychological analysis of cancer deaths. *Omega: Journal of Death and Dying, 6,* 61–75.

Winiarski, M. (1991). *AIDS-related psychotherapy.* New York: St. Martins Press.

6 Understanding the Illness Experience

INTRODUCTION

Death has been called "the great leveler." In many ways it is. We will all die: rich or poor, black or white, death is the common certainty. Nevertheless, life-threatening illness is affected by many factors. Our heredity, gender, social class, environment, culture, and lifestyle will influence how long we live, the illnesses we develop, the treatment we receive, and the ways we respond and react to the threat of illness.

Not only are the causes and course of life-threatening illness influenced by many factors, but also the experience of illness is also very different for each person. Each illness is distinct, affected by the nature of the disease, the time in life when it strikes, and the circumstances that surround it. It is important to explore the unique experience of an illness, for such exploration enables each person, whatever his or her role—the person struggling with disease, a family member, a friend, or a caregiver or counselor—to understand and empathize with the very individual problems and issues that the illness brings. This inhibits one from making unhelpful comparisons with how other individuals or family members dealt with illness. "Why can't she deal with it like Dad?" "How come I don't seem to have the attitude that served me so well before?" By recognizing the unique, personal experience of any encounter with life-threatening illness, counselors become better able to understand each person's response.

This chapter highlights three critical factors. First, every life-threatening disease or condition creates special concerns for the individuals it strikes and their families. Second, the time in the life cycle when a disease strikes also affects the experience of that disease. Third, an individual's lifestyle and personality influence his or her response to illness.

DISEASE-RELATED FACTORS: WHAT ARE THE PARTICULAR ISSUES RAISED BY THE ILLNESS?

The Nature of the Disease

Where and how a disease manifests itself is often significant. Breast cancer, by its very nature, threatens sexuality and identity in ways that lung cancer does not. Breast cancer raises fears of possible death, but also can undermine a woman's self-esteem, impair her sense of sexuality and attractiveness, and thereby affect her relationship with a spouse or a lover.

Any form of cancer can also leave strong fears about metastasis or recurrence, such that any subsequent symptom or pain will cause great anxiety. Any future cancer, even one that strikes years later and is unconnected to the first episode, may create a sense of hopelessness.

Other diseases raise their own particular issues. Many heart attack patients are left, even after recovery, with a heightened sense of vulnerability and anxiety that can permeate every activity and relationship. A client who suffered a heart attack now literally fears for his life whenever he faces serious stress. Similarly, those individuals who have experienced stroke may experience a reactive depression to any remaining physical or intellectual impairments.

Predictability of the Disease Course

Another factor that is important is the predictability of the disease. For some diseases both the prognosis and the probable course of the disease, including its timing are known, within certain limits. People with that disease are likely to have a specific life expectancy. In other cases, prognosis, course, or timing may be uncertain. An example of the latter kind of disease is multiple sclerosis (MS), which is characterized by great unpredictability. Some individuals with MS may decline rapidly, whereas others will continue to function at high levels for decades.

Often the less predictable the disease is, the more difficult it is to cope with it. When illnesses are reasonably predictable, everyone, including the ill individual, the family, and other caregivers, has clear expectations. Some kind of planning, however awful, can be done. When the disease has an unpredictable course, even this manner of coping is denied.

Symptoms

Different symptoms will also influence the experience of life-threatening illness. In some illnesses pain will be a constant, unwelcome companion, often affecting relationships and seriously impairing the quality of life. Diseases characterized by a persistent or disruptive set of symptoms can also create difficulties. For example, the constant coughing and wheezing and the foul-smelling stools characteristic of cystic fibrosis can lead to increasing isolation for its sufferers. Similarly, symptoms that are more visible, such as visible lesions, can create a greater sense of stigmatization for those who are ill, because they feel more set off from the healthy than those whose diseases do not include such obvious signs.

Psychological Effects

Manifestations of the disease can also differ in the psychological discomfort they can create for individuals. Threats to identity (for example, involving sexual organs or the face), colostomies, threats to mobility, loss of cerebral function, and specific critical incapacities (for example, loss of a leg for an active person) can be particularly distressing (Rosenblatt, 2004; Amir & Ramati, 2002).

Diseases have different meanings to different individuals. Because of past experiences or prior knowledge some individuals may have strong fears about a particular type of death. For some, cancer is the great fear, whereas others may fear a different disease (Doka, 1997).

Even the site of the disease not only creates a unique physical effect but a psychological one as well. Breast or testicular cancer, for example, is inevitably intertwined with sexuality and self-image. Other sites may generate other complicating meanings depending on the culture or the experiences of the individual.

Social Consequences

Different diseases also have different social consequences. Tuberculosis and cancer were once greatly feared. A few decades ago, AIDS generated such intense fear that persons with the disease were often isolated, stigmatized, and ostracized.

Disease Trajectory

Another important aspect of a disease is its trajectory or pattern. Glaser and Strauss (1968) describe the special issues each pattern has for individuals and their families. For example, a trajectory characterized by progressive deterioration and decline may cause different concerns than one characterized by remissions and relapses. The following trajectories create very different illness experiences:

The Gradual Slant: In this trajectory one experiences a long, slow decline. Here the chronic phase may be quite long, often lasting years. Throughout this time the individual may continue to receive treatment, perhaps to retard gradual, progressive deterioration. The predictability often found in this pattern tends to create less anxiety, and the evident gradualism tends to facilitate adjustment. However, the very length of the trajectory, particularly during the terminal phase, can create considerable stress for individuals and families. Often they may describe the illness as "going on too long."

The Downward Slope: In this pattern the decline is rapid, the chronic phase short or nonexistent, and medical treatment aggressive. Here the person must cope with rapid deterioration and the likelihood of death. Families must learn to cope with relatively sudden loss.

Peaks and Valleys: In this trajectory, exemplified by diseases such as AIDS or leukemia, there are alternating patterns of remission, relapse, and recovery. This pattern is characterized by considerable anxiety and constant stress, because often the timing of the relapses and remissions is unclear. Individuals and their families may not know how long a remission will last, how total recovery will be, or whether any given relapse will signal a final decline into death. Families may also experience the Lazarus syndrome, where, because they expect the death of a person, they fail to adjust to that person's recovery and the continued repetition of the cycle.

Descending Plateaus: This pattern is characteristic of diseases such as MS. Here the person experiences declines, an indeterminate period of stabilization at that diminished level, then further decline and new stabilization. Like the pattern of peaks and valleys, this pattern is characterized by considerable uncertainty. One may not know how long a period of stabilization will last or when a decline is likely to begin or how deep it will be. Unlike the peaks-and-valley pattern, however, declines tend to be irreversible, necessitating adjustment to a new level of disability.

Presentiment: This pattern characterizes persons who recover from sudden heart attacks or strokes. Here the recovery may be total, but the individuals and their families are very aware of their vulnerability to both subsequent reoccurrences and death.

Treatment Differences

Not only are the trajectory, nature, and symptoms of various diseases different, but their treatments differ as well. Treatment will have a significant effect upon the individual's experience of life-threatening illness. Three factors regarding treatment are important: the type of treatment, the nature of the treatment regimen, and the side effects and aftereffects.

Rando (1984) has described the psychological effects of different treatment modalities. For example, she noted that many people have considerable misconceptions and fears about surgery. Fears may be associated with the use of anesthesia and loss of consciousness, pain after the operation, or the visible scars resulting from surgery. Persons may be anxious about the extent of the surgery and the degree of dependence it may create in both the immediate postoperative period and later. They may also worry about the outcome of surgery, perhaps fearing that the surgery will not improve or may even harm their condition. In some cases surgery can even arouse other psychological issues such as feelings about guilt and punishment.

If long periods of bed rest following surgery or other special treatments are required, this rest may also have negative effects. Prolonged bed rest can adversely affect all the body's systems and create psychological difficulties, such as depression, decreases in problem-solving abilities, lessened motivation, and negative changes in body image.

Radiation may be feared because it is believed to be dangerous, perhaps even causing cancer, sterility, and other difficult side effects. Chemotherapy can raise similar fears.

The side effects and aftereffects of treatment will also influence the experience of illness. Whereas in some cases side effects are minimal and barely disruptive, in other cases the side effects of treatment can be more devastating than the disease itself. Aftereffects too may vary. In some conditions the aftereffects of treatment are limited. Soon after the treatment stops patients can resume normal activities with little reminder of their ordeal. In other cases, though, the aftereffects can be lasting. Regimens too may range from simple self-monitoring of health to heavy, extensive, and burdensome regimens evident in diseases such as cystic fibrosis.

Individuals experience different reactions to treatments. Some people may be angry over the treatment or the resulting complications. Others may experience depression. In any case, every disease and every treatment creates different issues. The first step in understanding one's own or someone else's reaction is to consider the particular problems caused by this disease.

WHEN DOES DISEASE STRIKE? THE IMPORTANCE OF THE LIFE CYCLE

Although the characteristics of any given disease influence the experience of life-threatening illness, the experience is also affected by the time in life when that disease strikes. Illness is a different experience for adolescents than it is for older persons—not necessarily easier, but certainly different. At any point in life a disease brings up different issues as individuals respond both to the disease itself and to the different expectations and tasks of that phase of the life cycle.

Infancy and Early Childhood

There are a number of ways that life-threatening illness affects the young child. The intermittent periods of separation, the ever-changing environment, as well as painful and (to the very young) incomprehensible procedures may impair both the child's bonding and his or her development of trust. Periods of hospitalization can be particularly frightening since a young child may feel abandoned to strangers who cause pain. Many hospital programs now allow unlimited visitation by parents, including overnight stays, and encourage full parental participation in care and medication. This often mitigates some of the separation anxiety and isolation that children may experience during hospitalization. Parents may wish to ask about or even to suggest such programs if their infant or young child needs to be hospitalized.

Communication can be another major issue. Often parents of a young child are reluctant to inform the child about the disease or treatment. Their concern here is to protect the child and limit his or her distress. But often these attempts are counterproductive. Even young children will often be aware of the seriousness of their condition. This awareness can result from self-monitoring of their own condition, parental cues and responses, and comments from hospitalized peers. It is often less anxiety provoking to honestly answer a child's questions. Children will also find it comforting if they are prepared beforehand for any surgical or treatment procedures. Honest and open communication between parents and their children is effective in building and maintaining trust.

As the child continues to age and develop, the physical limitations caused by the disease and its treatments, and also by parental restrictions, may limit his or her ability to explore the world and develop autonomy. In addition, parental attempts to set limits and provide discipline, so critical at this stage, may be compromised by concern about the illness. Parents may be anxious and overly restrictive, sympathetically lenient, or seemingly inconsistent and arbitrary (based upon an assessment of the child's condition at that time). The result is that the child's developmental tasks of both exploring the environment and finding and recognizing limits are impaired.

Although the child's ability to understand the reality of death or of life-threatening illness is a topic debated by many professionals (Kenyon, 2001), the differences between the parents' and the child's understanding of the situation as well as the anxiety generated in parents and children by the illness can complicate communication between parents and children. Parents may have considerable uncertainty about how, how much, and when to respond to their child's questions. The young child too may have considerable misunderstanding of the nature, cause, and treatment of the illness. Children often assume that illness is punishment for some offense. A five-year-old girl once told me that she thought she had cancer because she had left the gate open, allowing her mother's dog to escape to the street, where it was run over by a car. She was convinced that her illness was a punishment for her act and her later lies about it.

At any stage in their child's life, but particularly early in development, parents may also have intense anxiety about the long-term effects of both the disease and its treatment on subsequent development. They may worry that their child will have physical, social, psychological, or intellectual scars that may haunt the child's later life.

The School-Age Child

Life-threatening illness poses special issues for the school-age child. The child will need to learn to manage the illness within a school environment, which will cause him or her many problems. First, intermittent absences and the side effects of treatment can impair academic performance. Second, teachers sometimes assume that illness and treatment retard intellectual development, particularly if side effects include lethargy or confusion. Third, the treatment regimen may be difficult to manage within the classroom environment. Teachers may be resistant to interruptions posed by the need for medication or other aspects of treatment. School authorities may pressure parents to place their child in special education classes, which is an inappropriate classification for a child who can maintain academic performance because such a reassignment can increase the child's sense of stigma and isolation, impair self-concept, and inhibit intellectual development.

Schools thrust the ill child into interaction with healthy peers, which can create other issues. The stigma of the illness, limitations on activity, lack of self-confidence, and low self-esteem are but a few of the problems that can arise. In some cases other parents, afraid of the disease and overly protective of their own children, may discourage or prohibit their children from playing with the ill child. One study of children with cancer (Spinetta and Deasy-Spinetta, 1981) found that they were more reluctant to participate in activities than their well peers. This in turn impaired subsequent growth and development. Although teasing is a normal part of children's interactions with one another, such teasing can exacerbate the ill child's sense of being different—thus inhibiting interaction, and lowering self-esteem, especially since many ill children are already very sensitive and anxious about their disease.

Friends can share information that upsets the child. In fact, interaction with peers, either well peers or others with the same illness, in addition to increased access to both print and nonprint media (especially through the Internet) that occurs at this age, make it highly unlikely that parents or other adults can successfully control the child's understanding of the nature or implications of his or her disease. Many of these problems can be mitigated by means of honest and open communication with the child and through the education of teachers and peers.

Illness complicates the struggles for mastery and independence typical of this age. Parents may be reluctant to allow their child necessary autonomy, thereby breeding overdependence. The child's own ability to master his or her environment may be affected either by the direct limitations of the disease or by an impaired self-concept. On the other hand, this natural desire for mastery can be put to good use, particularly within the chronic phase, by encouraging the child's increased responsibility and participation in treatment and treatment decisions.

The school-age child does face illness with two particular strengths. First, the child is often able to reach out for and to accept the help of supportive adults, something the adolescent may be more reluctant to do. Second, the child often firmly believes in his or her philosophy and faith, deriving comfort and strengths from those beliefs. The school-age child is more likely to ask "What is heaven like?" than to ask "Is there a heaven?" William Easson in his book *The Dying Child* (1970, p. 45) summarizes these strengths well:

> The grade school child has the emotional ability to face the prospect of his death and to reach out to his parents and his family for comfort and understanding.
>
> Yea though I walk through the valley of the shadow of death . . . thy rod and thy staff comfort me. This verse was written by a believer. These words could have been said by a grade school child.

Adolescence

The key developmental issues of adolescence are often called the three I's: identity, independence, and intimacy. Life-threatening illness poses unique threats to each of these issues.

The adolescent's identity can be impaired in a number of ways. First, the physical deformities resulting from treatment of the disease may impair body image and self-concept. Second, these physical effects, associated limitations on activity, and periods of hospitalization can cause isolation from and rejection by peers, hampering self-esteem.

These same effects can also affect intimacy. The adolescent may be limited in his or her ability to establish ties with a peer group. As Easson (1988) notes, the limitations and disabilities caused by the illness may limit participation in and acceptance by more socially or athletically oriented peer groups. Or treatment and illness may retard academic progress, thereby limiting association with and acceptance by more intellectually inclined groups. These same factors, he adds, limit the seriously ill adolescent's sexual outlets.

Illness is likely to complicate independence. If the illness begins in adolescence, the adolescent is forced into a more dependent role just at the time in the life cycle when he or she is trying to achieve a degree of independence. If the illness extends from childhood into adolescence, the adolescent may have already experienced a history of overprotectiveness that may result in a lack of early maturing experiences that increase passivity and impair the assumption of a more independent role. In both cases the uncertainty of the disease may limit and complicate planning for later adulthood.

The disease may face other difficulties as well. Although adolescent conflict with parents is exaggerated, relationships with parents are often characterized by considerable ambivalence. This ambivalence, as well as the adolescent's quest for independence, may complicate the adolescent's ability to seek or to accept support from parents and other adults. Sometimes adherence issues can become a battleground between adolescents and their caregivers, reflecting the adolescent's need for independence and control. Allowing the adolescent to become a full partner in treatment by informing him or her about the need for adherence, tailoring the regimen to the adolescent's lifestyle, and soliciting the adolescent's participation in discussions and decisions can reduce that conflict.

In addition, adolescence is often a time of questioning beliefs. Thus beliefs about God and the afterlife that can be very comforting to the school-age child may provide less support to the adolescent.

The adolescent struggling with life-threatening illness also brings certain strengths to his or her struggle. Often the adolescent's resiliency and beliefs about personal indestructibility can provide significant hope. Cognitive abilities and coping skills are more developed at this age.

Many of the negative affects of illness can be mitigated if those around the adolescent support the adolescent's individuality and independence. Recognizing that the normal needs of adolescence for autonomy and bonding with peers, as well as adolescent concerns about body image, are often expressed in concerns about clothes and appearance can help provide a sense of normalcy.

The Young Adult

Young adulthood is a time of looking outward, of beginning families and a career. Illness forces attention inward. As with the adolescent, then, illness during young adulthood can seriously affect the completion of tasks in the life cycle. It may impair independence and affect the development of relationships. It may introduce uncertainty to marriage and family plans. Disease may disturb the developing equilibrium between spouses, perhaps creating less balanced relationships. It may have deep adverse effects on a career, impairing performance, limiting career mobility, and perhaps even affecting employability and insurability. It may also influence financial planning and increase financial insecurity. Possible problems with insurance, the uncertain costs of illness, and unpredictable effects on future earnings may severely limit options at all stages of the life cycle. The thought of a limited life span may create deep anxiety and intense affect, and these issues may be intensified because everything the young adult has strived to achieve is now threatened.

The Middle-Aged Adult

Many of the same problems that plague young adults afflicted with life-threatening illness also trouble middle-aged adults. In some respects, life may have a more settled quality for those in middle adulthood. Jobs, careers, family, and friendship networks have probably stabilized. Yet life-threatening illness can unsettle all of these patterns. Relationships can undergo profound change. Career and financial stability may be jeopardized. Because financial and familial responsibilities may be at an apex in midlife, life-threatening illness can create great anxiety. And, as in early adulthood, it may also generate a strong sense of anger that one is being cheated so close to the prize.

It may also intensify normal developmental struggles. Midlife adults often develop an awareness of mortality, realizing that death is inevitable but still expecting it to occur decades in the future (Doka, 2008). This awareness, however, does intensify a desire to leave a mark, to pass on something to a younger generation. The psychologist Erik Erikson characterizes the challenge of midlife as "generativity versus stagnation." Life-threatening illness means that the awareness of mortality is not only future and abstract, but also present and real. The man or woman whose illness threatens life may frenetically strive to accomplish all life goals even while struggling with disease. For example, in one case a teacher suffering from brain cancer insisted upon completing a master's degree and securing a job even though these goals added additional stress to an already stressful life. It was critically important for her to achieve these lifelong goals, delayed by the pressures of beginning a family, prior to her death.

The Older Adult

If the middle-aged adult is aware of mortality, older persons are often described as aware of their own finitude. The older adult realizes the nearness of death, yet this awareness coexists with a continued sense of a personal future. Although older persons recognize that they are approaching the end of their life span, they still may not envision their own personal death. Indeed, life-threatening illness may still come as a psychic shock.

Older individuals have their own unique problems as they cope with life-threatening illness. First, this illness may come at a time when they are already coping with other chronic, although not life-threatening, illnesses. Thus their ability to surmount this illness may be threatened by their frailty. Second, their support systems may have been weakened by death or disability. They may lack able and appropriate caregivers. And they may worry about spouses or others dependent upon them. Illness may threaten their own caregiving responsibilities and heighten their fears for another's health, happiness, or survival should they become incapacitated or die. Third, many elderly people may ignore or discount serious symptoms because they believe that aches and pains are to be expected as part of the aging process.

Finally, there may be developmental difficulties as well. Developmental psychologists recognize that older persons often undergo a life-review process, assessing their goals and accomplishments. Those who can say that their life had value, that they have accomplished much, can be said to have reached a state of ego integrity. Often this state makes it easier to face death. Perhaps the appeal of Frank Sinatra's song *My Way* is that it expresses that sense of having had a worthwhile life. In contrast, the person who feels that he or she has wasted life often spends his or her last days in despair.

This process of life review seems more related to a sense that death is near than to simple chronological age. For example, most dying persons will review their life as they become aware of death. Still, older persons may sometimes face unique issues that complicate this process. For example, the failures of children or the fact that they are the last of a name or line may be apparent only in later life, complicating life review.

SOCIAL AND PSYCHOLOGICAL FACTORS

As stated earlier, our response to and experience of illness is influenced by a variety of social and psychological factors. Among them are:

Characteristics Such as Gender, Race, Ethnicity and Culture, Social Class, and Income

Social class and income level often affect the experience of illness. For example, persons of high social class have considerably more resources and therefore more options when coping with illness. Such access to health care may not only increase survival time; it also may offer comfort that all possible options are being considered and reinforce a sense of control and empowerment at a critical time.

Gender and ethnicity also can influence the experience of illness. Longevity, causes of deaths, as well as responses to dying, death, and grief differ between sexes and ethnic groups. Even responses to caregivers and treatment may be influenced by these factors (Stillion, 1985; Martin & Doka, 2000).

Intellectual Ability, Knowledge, Education, and Prior Experience

An individual's prior experience with disease as well as his or her knowledge, education, and intellectual ability can affect the experience of life-threatening illness. Previous experience with the disease, even if that experience is of limited relevance in the present context, can greatly influence the ways in which one perceives and responds to an illness. For example, a client who had suffered a heart attack at a relatively young age had considerable misconceptions and anxiety about heart disease, all rooted in his experience of his grandfather's disabling heart condition. In other cases, the experience with the disease may help us maintain more optimistic perceptions. A client who had breast cancer, for example, was deeply encouraged by two acquaintances' successful treatment.

Knowledge, education, and intellectual ability can have similar mixed effects. Individuals with higher levels of knowledge, education, and intellectual ability may be better able to relate to caregivers and take more participatory roles in treatment. But there may be negative factors too. One nurse, for example, was aware of symptoms that she could associate with recurrence of cancer. Hence any such symptoms, even when these symptoms had clear alternate explanations, created intense anxiety for this nurse.

The Meaning of Illness, Life, and Death: Religious, Spiritual, and Philosophical Systems

Life-threatening illness is a crisis that has spiritual and philosophical dimensions since it raises questions about the reasons for illness, the role of suffering, and the meaning of life and death. Religious and philosophical beliefs and rituals can facilitate or complicate the spiritual struggle often associated with life-threatening illness. For some individuals, their religious or philosophical beliefs can be a source of great comfort. Belief in an afterlife may be a source of comfort and hope. Rituals too can be helpful. Prayer can be a highly therapeutic tool, allowing individuals opportunities to think about and share concerns. But in other cases effects can be negative. Sometimes religious rituals can inhibit meaningful exchanges or convey unintended meanings to participants. One Italian Catholic mother was enraged that her priest administered the sacrament of the Anointing of the Sick to her son, newly diagnosed with leukemia, because she thought of it as the "Last Rites" associated with imminent death, although since the 1960s the Catholic Church has encouraged wider use of it in cases of sickness in general. Some beliefs may also complicate the illness experience. A young gay man with AIDS was deeply troubled by his fundamentalist background, because his childhood beliefs equated homosexuality with sin, punishment, and death.

Personality, Coping Skills, and Will to Live

In recent years considerable attention has been paid to the fact that personality, coping skills, and attitude are significant factors that affect not only the experience of illness but perhaps even survival time and survival rates (Carmel, Baron-Epel, & Shemy, 2007). And although some question claims of longer survival, it seems evident that stress-resistant personalities, personalities that allow one to seek and accept help, better coping skills, and positive attitude can mitigate the great stress associated with life-threatening illness. It is also evident that medical staff responds differently to clients whom they perceive as having a "will to live," often intensifying their own involvement and efforts.

One's self-concept too is a critical factor in how one handles life-threatening illness. Self-concept can also affect a person's ability to seek or accept help. One whose self-perception emphasizes independence and self-reliance may be unable to easily accept aid.

Informal Support: The Importance of Family, Friends, and Confidantes

Another critical set of variables influencing how we experience and respond to illness is the level of support we receive from family and friends. Supportive others can mitigate the stress of life-threatening illness in many ways, providing emotional support; assistance in daily living, particularly during the chronic phase; help in adhering to medical regimens; and other aid. Strong support from family and friends can help prevent a sense of hopelessness that may increase biological vulnerability and shorten survival time. Because the period of life-threatening illness can be long, and the care demands at times heavy, supportive networks that are both extensive (i.e., drawing from a larger number of family and friends) and intensive (i.e., having members that are strongly tied to the patient) are best able to provide support. Not only are the quantity and quality of relationships important, but also the ways that family and friends relate. Relationships characterized by openness and honesty provide most support for individuals coping with life-threatening illness.

Formal Support

Formal support, or support from medical staff and other professionals, is another factor affecting how a person responds to and experiences life-threatening illness. Access to quality medical and nursing care can certainly affect survival time. But other forms of care such as social, psychological, and spiritual care can also influence both the quality of life and the life length. For example, one study (Spiegel, Kraemer, Bloom, & Gortheil, 1989) found that persons with metastasized breast cancer who attended weekly support groups lived longer than a control group that did not.

Concurrent Crises

Life-threatening illness is both extraordinarily stressful and self-absorbing. When this crisis is compounded by other crises, it may affect one's responses, strain coping resources, and inhibit support. For example, a woman with MS found her life greatly complicated when her husband had a car accident. Now he too needed care, just when her mobility was limited. Many IV drug users with AIDS may also have chaotic and crisis-ridden lifestyles that inhibit their ability to deal with their condition. Any ability to seek care and follow a complicated regimen is affected not only by low income, limited social support, and cognitive impairments associated with long-term drug use, but also by such crises as homelessness and arrests.

CONCLUSION

In short, anyone's experience of life-threatening illness and his or her response to it is highly unique and individual. It is affected not only by the distinct nature of the disease itself and by the time in the life cycle it strikes, but also by a range of psychological and social variables. A key concern of counselors is to examine these factors to understand how they complicate or mitigate the experience of illness.

REFERENCES

Amir, M., & Ramati, A. (2002). Post-traumatic symptoms, emotional distress, and quality of life in long-term survivors of breast cancer: A preliminary research. *Journal of Anxiety Disorders, 16,* 191–206.

Carmel, S., Baron-Epel, O., & Shemy, G. (2007). The will-to-live and survival in old age: Gender differences. *Social Science & Medicine, 65,* 518–523.

Doka, K. (1997). *AIDS, fear, and society: Challenging the dreaded disease.* Washington, DC: Taylor & Francis.

Doka, K. (2008). Completing the picture: Adult perspectives on death—Implications for children and adolescents. In K. Doka & A. Tucci (Eds.), *Living with grief: Children and adolescents* (pp. 43–56). Washington, DC: The Hospice Foundation of America.

Easson, W. (1970). *The dying child: The management of the child or adolescent who is dying.* Springfield, IL: Charles C. Thomas.

Easson, W. (1988). The ill or dying adolescent: Special needs and challenges. *Postgraduate Medicine, 8,* 183–189.

Glaser, B., & Strauss, A. (1968). *Time for dying.* Chicago: Aldine.

Kenyon, B. (2001). Current research on children's conceptions of death: A critical review. *Omega: The Journal of Death and Dying, 43,* 63–91.

Martin, T., & Doka, K. (2000). *Men don't cry, women do: Transcending gender stereotypes of grief.* Philadelphia: Brunner/Mazel.

Rando, T. A. (1984). *Grief, dying, and death: Clinical interventions for caregivers.* Champaign, IL: Research Press.

Rosenblatt, M. (2004). No apology. *Ostomy, 41*(4), 39.

Spiegel, D., Kraemer, H., Bloom, J., & Gortheil, E. (1989). Effects of psychological treatment of survival of patients with metastatic breast cancer. *Lancet, 10*(14), 888–891.

Spinetta, J., & Deasy-Spinetta, P. (1981). *Living with childhood cancer.* St. Louis: Mosby.

Stillion, J. (1985). *Death and the sexes: An examination of differential longevity, attitudes, behaviors, and coping skills.* Washington, DC: Hemisphere.

The Prediagnostic Phase: Understanding the Road Before

INTRODUCTION

One's confrontation with life-threatening illness or death can develop in several different ways. Often it may result after one seeks medical advice and treatment in response to the appearance of a troubling sign such as a lump in a breast or blood in the urine. In other cases it may result from the confirmation of a positive test result, such as an HIV antibodies test or a tuberculin test. A person may have sought such tests, even though the person was asymptomatic, because he or she engaged in risky behaviors, suspected exposure, or simply sought reassurance. In still other cases the encounter with illness may be sudden, such as the experience of a heart attack or stroke. Finally, the encounter may come about as an unexpected result of a routine physical examination or test that reveals an unsuspected serious illness.

One often considers the beginning phase of illness to start with the diagnosis of illness. In reality, the encounter with life-threatening illness often predates the diagnosis. No matter what the circumstance of the encounter, there may well be a period prior to one's certain knowledge of illness during which one struggles with suspicion of illness or knowledge, at some level, of risk—*a prediagnostic phase.* Whatever the circumstances that lead one to the fateful moment of diagnosis, it is useful to understand the client's behavior in the process that preceded it. Making decisions to seek medical help— "health seeking" as it is sometimes called—is a complex process that can often tell much about how the client will respond to the crisis of illness.

Tom's case illustrates this point. Tom, a man in his 50s, has been having problems with urination for a few months. For a long time he simply ignored these problems, even neglecting to mention them to his physician during a routine visit. After a while he began to tell some friends about his problems, and they had the wisdom to advise him to seek medical help. When he did, tests indicated a growth on his prostate gland. His delayed health seeking almost cost him his life!

Understanding the process of how clients seek medical help should provide opportunities for growth rather than guilt or blame. Reviewing behavior prior to diagnosis can reveal the client's fears and anxieties, coping mechanisms, and sources of support. Tom, for example, recognized after the fact that he had suspected cancer all along. He knew, based on his own previous experiences with his father's death from cancer, how much that possible diagnosis frightened him. His new experience with disease taught him that he had a strong tendency to deny and avoid things that made him anxious. Realizing this characteristic helped him and his physician throughout the course of Tom's successful treatment. As a result of his illness, Tom also could identify the friends and family members with whom he was comfortable discussing his illness. He found, much to his surprise, that he had tried to shield and protect his wife, but that he was comfortable discussing his anxieties with a few close friends.

There is much value in understanding the ways one behaves prior to diagnosis. Each person may follow a different path to that diagnosis. In each case, though, it is worthwhile to review the context and circumstances that led to this moment of crisis.

One of the most common contexts, and certainly one of the most researched, is when a person learns of a life-threatening illness while seeking medical attention for a troubling symptom. Medical sociologists have long recognized that seeking such treatment is a complex process influenced by many factors. This process provides a model for the factors that characterize health seeking even in other situations.

Symptoms of illness, especially at their onset, are rarely so dramatic or unambiguous as to mandate immediate attention. Moreover, fear and anxiety can inhibit action. One may very well decide to wait rather than risk the possibility of confronting bad news. Thus there is often a period of delay during which these symptoms and their implications are interpreted and evaluated by the person so afflicted. In some cases this period of delay can be so long as to imperil any opportunity for successful treatment.

The evaluation of symptoms is likely to be influenced by four sets of factors: *symptom-related factors, physical and psychological factors, situational factors,* and *social factors* (Bloom, 1965; Coe, 1970; Davis, 1972; Dingwall, 1976; Harowski, 1987; Spector, 1985; Mechanic, 1968, 1980).

SYMPTOM RELATED FACTORS

Often the very nature of the symptom will be a major factor affecting the person's decision to seek assistance. Symptom-related variables include the following:

How Apparent, Recognizable, and Serious are Symptoms?

Symptoms that are more apparent, such as sharp pains, fever, or rashes, are more likely to command attention than those that are less apparent, such as a general malaise. Similarly, symptoms that are more recognizable and considered serious by most people, such as blood in the urine or stool or a lump in the breast, are apt to receive more consideration than vague feelings of fatigue or soreness.

The more a symptom is considered to be a sign of future danger, the more likely action will be taken. Although a lump in the breast can be symptom of several conditions, many of which are harmless, most women recognize such a lump as a possible sign of cancer. On the other hand, a backache can also foretell serious illness, but is often perceived as far less worrisome.

How Disruptive are the Symptoms?

The more a symptom disrupts family life, work, or other social activities, the earlier action is likely to be taken. A persistently painful toothache demands a quick trip to the dentist. A less disruptive symptom that does not impinge on one's personal or social life may not be as pressing.

How Frequent and Persistent are the Symptoms?

Symptoms that are perceived as both less persistent and routine may not receive the same concern as those that are persistent and/or recurring. In the former cases, it is easy to wait out the symptoms, hoping they will not recur.

Possible Alternative Interpretations

When an alternate explanation exists for a symptom it is often less worrisome than when an appropriate explanation is not available. A lump that follows trauma is often perceived as less frightening than one that simply appears "on its own." Similarly, fatigue or aches after vigorous activity are perceived as less troubling than those that lack explanation. When one can rationally account for symptoms, one typically feels less concern.

Part of the evaluation of explanations also includes a strong sense of personal biography. "Am I a person who is vulnerable to this disease?" is often part of the interpretive process. For example, a man with a family history of coronary disease may well perceive chest pain differently from one who has no such history. An IV drug user may respond with panic to a night sweat, a possible indicator of AIDS, whereas someone not at risk might consider the symptom of little consequence. A person who has recovered from cancer may be far more sensitive to signs or symptoms that might suggest possible relapse.

PHYSICAL AND PSYCHOLOGICAL FACTORS

In addition to the nature of symptoms, other factors such as physical and psychological states affect both the evaluation of symptoms and the decision whether to seek medical help. Among these are

Tolerance Thresholds

Individuals vary in their assessment and toleration of pain and discomfort. Sometimes our cultural background affects our experience of pain. One study (Mechanic, 1980) found that persons of Irish and English extraction tended to have higher levels of pain toleration than a sample of Jews and Italians. Men are less likely to complain of pain than women. Individuals also may differ in their pain thresholds. The point is that for a variety of physiological, cultural, and gender-related reasons, others may tolerate pain or symptoms that may send one person for medical attention (Doka, 2006).

Basic Beliefs and Knowledge

Another variable that affects health seeking is a person's basic belief systems. Basic to seeking medical attention are the beliefs that one is susceptible to disease and that disease states are harmful, that intervention can help, and that assistance is therefore worth seeking. But not everyone accepts the modern scientific theories that underlie disease diagnosis and treatment.

Social and cultural beliefs about the type of treatment that is suitable can also affect the health-seeking process. Every culture has beliefs about illness causation, treatment, and referral. For example, in a cultural system dominated by folk beliefs, an ill person will probably turn to folk practitioners before seeing a physician. In other cultures, outside treatment may always be sought within the medical system.

Knowledge too is a variable. Individuals may differ in the degree to which they recognize the significance of symptoms. This may affect the process of seeking treatment. A person who recognizes that numbness is a sign of multiple sclerosis will be more likely to seek help for that symptom than one who does not have that knowledge.

Anxiety Level

The level of anxiety produced by the symptom is also a factor in seeking assistance. Any symptom can generate considerable anxiety. The anxiety may result from several concerns including the nature, difficulty, and process of diagnosis and/or treatment; the humiliation, embarrassment, or stigma associated with the symptoms or suspected disease; and fears related to coping with the treatment such as anxieties about surgery, concerns about child care or work, or worry about finances. Maria, for example, an older Italian woman, delayed seeking attention for a lump in her breast because of embarrassment; and Mark, a 30-year-old businessman, neglected chest pains because he feared hospitalization would affect his work schedule.

Not only are levels and sources of anxiety likely to differ among individuals, but ways of coping with anxiety may vary as well. In some cases anxiety can distort the perceptual process of evaluation. For example, the level of anxiety may be so great that an individual like Tom will deny the symptoms. Behavioral responses may differ too. The anxiety experienced by some individuals inhibits them from seeking medical attention, whereas the anxiety felt by other individuals actually compels them to seek help.

Personality Characteristics

Other personality characteristics, such as one's willingness to disclose information about oneself, or how extroverted or trusting one is, are among the factors affecting the health-seeking process. Seeking medical assistance is often a later step in a process that involves both self-appraisal and discussions with family and friends. Although this process will be described in greater detail later; it is important to note that varied personality characteristics, such as low self-esteem, introversion, introspection, and a lack of trust and/or self-disclosure, may inhibit or distort this process. For example, people who are very private about their affairs may find it hard to consult others, whether professionals or their intimates, about troubling symptoms. Similarly, persons who are highly introspective are more likely to be aware of bodily sensations and physical symptoms than those who focus their attention outward.

Childhood Experiences

Developmental experiences also seem to play a role in the evaluation of symptoms. Early experiences with illness may make us more sensitive to symptoms and more acutely aware of bodily sensations. An adult who experienced rheumatic fever as a child may recognize a vulnerability to heart disease and therefore be more attentive to suspected heart-related symptoms. These experiences may be indirect as well. Persons who have witnessed the illness of a significant other may be more aware, attentive, and anxious regarding similar symptoms in themselves.

Parenting styles too may affect health-seeking behaviors. A study of young adults (Mechanic, 1980) found that those who had experienced abusive parenting tended to report and to monitor physical symptoms more closely, suggesting that this attitude may have resulted from additional stress or more introspection, which this early abuse seems to engender. As stated earlier, this introspection often leads to greater attention to one's physical state.

SITUATIONAL FACTORS

Social Context

Individuals' evaluations of their physical states are also influenced by the larger social context. For example, health campaigns or portrayals of illness in the mass media can make the public more aware of certain diseases and thus more attentive regarding their symptoms. Epidemics can sensitize people both to the significance of symptoms and to the likelihood of possible infection. For illustration, one study (Davis, 1972) showed that during a polio epidemic, parents were much more likely to call a doctor even though they believed their child only had a cold. Since they were aware of polio cases in their area, they were more sensitive to their child's potential vulnerability to polio. Similarly, as the AIDS crisis unfolded, many gay men were far more attentive to rashes and other symptoms than they had been before. Some, in fact, searched their bodies daily for evidence of rash.

Competing Needs

At times when many needs compete for one's attention, only the most sustained and serious symptoms will get attention. There are several reasons for this. First, one's attention is generally focused outward; therefore, physical sensations are likely to get less attention. One tends to focus on inner states only when the distractions from the external environment are minimal, or conversely when internal physical symptoms are so overwhelming that one is no longer able to function. Second, several symptoms such as fatigue, headaches, or soreness can be attributed to the press of external circumstances and therefore discounted. Third, seeking medical evaluation and treatment often has a lower priority than immediate pressing problems.

Availability of Help

Ease of seeking assistance can also be a factor. This has two elements. People are likely to seek out family and friends first. They may want to discuss and to compare symptoms with others whom they know and trust. This process will also be facilitated when they perceive the people available to consult as being similar to them. Thus, access to others to whom one is close can sometimes facilitate the health-seeking process.

Second, the accessibility of formal medical assistance will also be a factor. Easy access to appropriate medical help, unrestricted by financial, linguistic, class, or geographic barriers, will make it more likely that a person will seek such help. Persons without health insurance, for example, may be far more reluctant to seek help—especially early in the process when symptoms are not intrusive—than someone who has good coverage and easy access to care.

SOCIAL FACTORS

The previous discussion should make clear the importance of other social, intervening variables such as culture, social class, gender, age, and education. All have direct as well as indirect impacts on health seeking.

Culture

One's behavior is always influenced by culture. Culture frames one's entire belief system about the nature and cause of illness, the efficacy of treatment, even the process of seeking outside assistance. For example, in some cultures traditional healers may be consulted instead of or prior to turning to the medical establishment. In addition, linguistic or cultural barriers may inhibit both the process of health seeking and subsequent treatment.

Social Class

Social class too can have a significant impact on health seeking. For example, some observers believe that low-income persons are often fatalistic and present-oriented (Lewis, 1966). Low-income persons may feel that they have little control over the future; in any case, the problems of the present are so overwhelming that the individual has no energy left to address the future. In one case a lower-class woman with a family history of cancer who had a lump in her breast was urged to see a physician. She resisted, claiming, "It wouldn't make any difference." Even when convinced that medical care could help her, she repeatedly missed appointments both to take the cancer test and then to discuss the results, each time claiming a sudden family crisis or lack of funds. When the test results proved to be positive, she responded, "I was born under an unlucky star," and the pattern of missed appointments continued thereafter throughout her treatment.

Similarly, low-income people may have ambivalent attitudes toward authority figures, who are likely to differ from them in terms of educational levels or language. This problem can affect doctor-patient interaction, limiting the person's disclosure of illness and complicating a health professional's understanding of a client's description of symptoms.

Even more critical is that social class will also have a direct impact on the accessibility of medical care. There is considerable research that emphasizes that disparities in American health care between social classes persist from the time of diagnosis through palliative care and affect the entire course of treatment, including pain management, hospice admissions, and survival (Byrd & Clayton, 2002; Doka, 2006.)

Educational Level

A person's level of education has a clear relationship to his or her understanding of symptoms and sources of help. Disparities between the educational level of the patient and that of health professionals may inhibit the communication process.

Gender Roles

Gender roles also seem to be a significant variable in health seeking. First, there are differences between the sexes in both longevity and causes of death. These differences may affect the way an individual perceives risk and responds to symptoms. Second, as part of the traditional male role, males are taught to minimize and to ignore minor physical symptoms. There is also evidence that male doctors may not perceive certain female symptoms, such as morning sickness or menstrual cramps, as serious.

Age

Age also affects the evaluation of medical symptoms. First, standards of health differ by age. An acceptable blood pressure for someone 50 years old is far different from one for someone five years old. Second, the perceptions of both health professionals and patients themselves may be influenced by the age of the patient. For example, an elderly person may be more likely than a younger person to ignore symptoms by attributing them to age; of course, this attitude delays diagnosis. Similarly, health professionals may also discount the symptoms of an elderly person.

Other Social Roles and Behaviors

Other roles can influence perception and evaluation of symptoms. For example, even prior to the AIDS epidemic, promiscuous homosexuals were aware of their vulnerability to several sexually transmitted diseases. Certain occupational groups, such as coal miners, are often aware of potential occupational diseases and may be especially attentive to symptoms. As stated earlier, such attentiveness may be particularly acute when media attention or personal and group experiences cause one to focus on a particular illness. Religious beliefs too have been identified as influencing health seeking. For example, religious beliefs might influence attitudes about the illness and treatment (God's will) that inhibit health seeking, or they might suggest alternate treatment, such as prayer, pilgrimages, religious healers, and the like.

THE PROCESS OF HEALTH SEEKING

In summary, the process of seeking attention for a troubling symptom is complex, multifaceted, and influenced by many things. One can use Gestalt psychology to illustrate this process. A basic Gestalt premise is that one often ignores the ground and focuses on the "figure." In health seeking this means that one tends to ignore internal states until conditions force one to respond to them, either because the internal stimulus, such as pain, becomes so intense that it mandates a response or because circumstances in the external environment continually redirect one's attention to that internal state. In short, then, one's attention is normally directed outward, but some conditions will cause one to pay attention to bodily sensations and symptoms. Once that attention is redirected, it can create a great deal of anxiety and concern.

At that point, the person experiencing these symptoms may have to formulate both an evaluation of the symptoms and a response. People may interpret a symptom as normal and ignore it, or they may determine that information is incomplete so they decide to wait and see. Or they may judge the symptoms as abnormal. Even in that case the responses can be different; possible responses include ignoring the symptom, treating it oneself, or seeking some form of assistance. This process of evaluating symptoms and responses is ongoing. Evaluating symptoms is a constant process of hypothesis testing. One's tentative diagnosis is constantly evaluated in the light of new evidence. Fred Davis (1972), in his account of the polio epidemic, offers such an illustration. Some parents initially perceived the symptoms of polio as a cold. When their child failed to get well, the parents wanted to believe that the child was malingering. But when the child contin-ued to get sicker, their earlier hypotheses no longer held and parents were forced to recognize the possibility of polio. So, for example, a lump or a bruise may first be defined as normal. However, if it grows, or does not heal within a certain time frame, or if it changes in some way (such as becoming more painful), a new tentative hypothesis may be drawn and the individual may finally decide to seek medical care.

This process is also likely to involve consultation with others. A person experiencing a symptom may ask family members and friends for their evaluation of the symptoms, and also ask for their advice about treatment. In situations in which the symptoms are visible, or when they impinge upon behavior, family, friends, and others may offer unsolicited advice. Thus there may be cycles of assessment, reassessment, and treatment that only after time may culminate in a decision to seek medical treatment.

HEALTH SEEKING IN OTHER CONTEXTS

Not everyone finds out that they have a life-threatening illness when he or she seeks evaluation of a troubling symptom. Some may learn of the illness even though they have no symptoms. This may occur when an individual decides to take a diagnostic or genetic test or even in the course of a normal physical examination. Still, the previous dis-cussion of health seeking is relevant here too, because a process may precede either activity.

Often someone has elected to take a diagnostic test, even though he or she is asymptomatic, because he or she fears exposure to the disease. Individuals often take genetic tests because of family history or other risk factors. Given these contexts, clinicians may believe that a positive result would not be a complete surprise to the event.

Yet limited research on the HIV antibodies test or genetic tests casts doubt upon this assumption (Flowers, Duncan, & Knussen, 2003; Barnoy, 2007). A person's motivation for taking the test as well as his or her perception of risk can vary considerably. In some cases there is a high perception of risk, whereas in other cases there is no real expectation of a positive result. For example, people may take the HIV test because they are beginning a relationship, recovering from addiction, ending an infidelity, having a routine insurance physical, or making a political statement (for example, supporting an ex-addict or gay organization's call for testing). Such people may have every expectation that the result will be negative.

Even in these situations it is helpful to explore such issues as the individual's assumptions, motivations, anxieties, and expectations about the test; their knowledge, beliefs, and experiences about the disease and treatment; and their process of deciding to seek both the test and the results. Although this counseling has become relatively common with HIV and genetic testing, it is not common with other tests for life-threatening disease.

Evidence of life-threatening illness can also be found by means of routine tests and procedures. For example, a blood test may indicate possible chronic lymphocytic leukemia or prostate cancer or suspicion of another serious illness even though the person is asymptomatic. In these cases, the shock of life-threatening illness is compounded by the individual's lack of perception of risk.

Nonetheless, it is valuable to explore the motivations, behaviors, and anxieties preceding even these tests and examinations. Was this simply a routine physical, continued monitoring of a prior recovery, or was there a suspicion of illness? How often and under what circumstances does the person normally get examined? What was the process preceding this physical? For example, delaying and resisting or missing appointments preceding the physical may indicate anxiety and/or denial and may be a cause of subsequent guilt. What are one's feelings prior to a physical in general, and toward this physical in particular? Some may approach a physical with a sense of anxiety while others have no such feeling.

There are cases in which one encounters life-threatening illness that do not seem to involve any conscious decision on one's part to seek help. In these cases, one is suddenly and dramatically thrust into the situation. With a heart attack or a stroke, for example, one is quickly and unexpectedly made aware of one's own fragility and vulnerability.

But even in these cases, it may be worthwhile to consider prediagnostic behaviors and attitudes. Was there any suspicion or evidence of problems? Was there any expectation of risk? Could one, and did one, at some time perceive a risk (for example, high blood pressure, obesity, or the like)? What was prediagnostic behavior? Had friends and family expressed concerns?

Understanding the road before is critical. Whether one realizes it or not, the client has completed three tasks. First, the client recognized, at some level, a possible danger or risk. Second, the client began to cope with all the anxiety and uncertainty inherent in that danger. Third, the client developed a plan of action to deal with that concern. By reviewing and exploring that process, a person—whether the ill individual or a family member—not only knows where he or she has been but how he or she got there. Counselors can assist the client to understand and to use the strengths uncovered and compensate for the weaknesses discovered. The client can then use that knowledge to meet the challenge of other tasks throughout all the remaining phases of life-threatening illness.

REFERENCES

Barnoy, S. (2007). Genetic testing for late-onset disease: Effect of disease controllability, test productivity, and gender n the decision to take the test. *Genetic Testing, 11*, 187–192.

Bloom, S. W. (1965). *The doctor and his patient.* New York: Free Press.

Byrd, M., & Clayton, L. (2002). *An American health dilemma: Race, medicine, and healthcare in the United States, 1900–2000.* New York: Routledge.

Coe, R. (1970). *Sociology of medicine.* New York: McGraw-Hill.

Davis, F. (1972). *Illness, interaction, and the self.* Belmont, CA: Wadsworth.

Dingwall, R. (1976). *Aspects of illness.* New York: St. Martins Press.

Doka, K. J. (2006). *Pain management at the end-of-life: Bridging the gap between knowledge and practice.* Washington, DC: Hospice Foundation of America.

Flowers, P., Duncan, B., & Knessen, C. (2003). Re-appraising HIV testing: An exploration of the psychosocial costs and benefits with learning one's HIV status in a purposeful sample of Scottish gay men. *British Journal of Health Psychology, 8,* 179–194.

Harowski, K. J. (1987). The worried well: Maximizing coping in the face of death. *Journal of Homosexuality, 14,* 299–306.

Lewis, O. (1966, October). The culture of poverty. *Scientific American, 215,* 19–25.

Mechanic, D. (1968). *Medical sociology: A selective view.* New York: Free Press.

Mechanic, D. (1980). The experience and reporting of common physical complaints. *Journal of Health and Social Behavior, 21,* 146–155.

Spector, R. (1985). *Cultural diversity in health and illness.* Norwalk, CN: Appelton-Century-Crofts.

8 Counseling Clients Through Crisis of Diagnosis

THE DIAGNOSTIC DIVIDE: THE ACUTE PHASE

Whatever symptoms or suspicions may exist in the prediagnostic period, whatever fears are entertained, the diagnosis of life-threatening illness always comes as a shock. Anthony Ferrara, a psychologist who later died of AIDS, captured the moment well. Although he suspected the spots on his skin were Kaposi's sarcoma, an almost sure sign of AIDS, he was still stunned and overwhelmed at the actual diagnosis: "All of my mental preparation was insufficient to thwart the tidal wave of emotion that swept over me as I received what at the time I regarded as a death sentence" (1984, p. 1285).

Until the actual diagnosis, no matter what the expectation, suspicion, or fear, there is always a chance that the client's self-diagnosis might be mistaken. The lump may yet turn out to be a benign cyst, the rash to be only a minor problem. However, this changes at the moment when a diagnosis is rendered. Here the client's worst fears may be realized, and the person is forced to recognize that he or she is now in either a struggle for life or an inexorable slide toward death.

The time of the diagnosis is often described as a turning point, a time of crisis when one's whole orientation toward life changes. According to Weisman (1986), this confrontation with possible death overwhelms people, creating the shock and numbness that he terms "impact vulnerability." For Weisman, diagnosis is a time of "existential plight" during which one must cope with the crisis of possible death. Many psychologists emphasize that a diagnosis of life-threatening illness is second in causing stress only to knowledge of dying itself (Weisman, 1986; Patterson, 1969).

It should be recognized that the time of diagnosis is often not a simple moment, although it may culminate in that moment when the diagnosis is spoken. Rather, it is a process unfolding over time in which a person experiences various tests or procedures during which different hypotheses of illness are advanced and sometimes discarded. The counselor's role during this period is often to assist clients as they struggle with uncertainty, anxiety, and ambiguity.

The process of determining a diagnosis is often very difficult. During this time people may have to cope not only with a multiplicity of medical tests and procedures but also with a great deal of uncertainty. During this period an individual may be asked to take numerous diagnostic tests.

It is important to remember that many of these tests are part of *a process of diagnosis;* any one test may not be definitive in and of itself. For example, if physicians suspect a tumor, they may wish to perform a variety of tests such as a blood test, a CT scan, an MRI, and other tests to locate and assess the nature of the tumor. But only a biopsy will tell them whether the tumor is cancerous. Subsequent tests, called staging tests, may be required to see how advanced the cancerous condition is. In short, the time of diagnosis is a process during which physicians test their hypotheses, when varied explorations are evaluated against emerging information. Throughout this period the individual being tested will experience wide mood swings as a continuing flow of information changes both the possible diagnosis and the prognosis. For example, in my father's case, the initial symptom was blood in the urine. Although this physical fact stimulated great concern, we recognized that numerous conditions, some of which were minor, could account for the blood.

Subsequent examinations led to the suspicion of a mass on both the kidney and the pancreas. More tests pinpointed the growth on the gallbladder and kidney. Surgery successfully removed both tumors; one was encapsulated, but the other was unrelated and benign. During the course of the week when the testing and surgery took place, my father's prognosis changed from uncertain to poor to hopeful to excellent. The moods and reactions of my father, our family, and even the physician changed in tandem with the emerging diagnosis.

One always has to remember that diagnosis is as much an art as a science. Most life-threatening diseases have some degree of uncertainty. Many diagnostic tests really do no more than point to the *probability* of a certain result. At each successive level of testing, however, the diagnosis may become more certain. But even then the course of the disease—how the disease will unfold and develop—still may be uncertain.

Not only is the diagnosis characterized by at least some degree of uncertainty; the prognosis often has considerable uncertainty as well. Assuming that the diagnosis is as accurate as the process allows, numerous other variables can affect prognosis. Diseases themselves may differ in the degree that prognosis is clear. Moreover an individual's health, attitude, and adherence to the medical regimen as well as the effectiveness of varied therapies; the stage at which the disease was discovered; the impact of subsequent medical progress—all these factors can influence prognosis. It is important to remember that any prediction is at best a statistically grounded estimate, perhaps only loosely based upon relevant variables and the current state of ever-changing medical knowledge and treatment. For many clients, these predictions can be useful. They may allow all those concerned to envision a sense of time that will facilitate planning and assist individuals and families in evaluating different options. But no prediction should ever be considered certain. Almost every family can offer anecdotes about family members who not only outlived predictions but also, sometimes, even the physicians who made them.

The diagnosis of life-threatening illness creates an intense crisis filled with anxiety, strong emotional reactions, and many personal and interpersonal issues. Tensions and anxieties mount. Individuals must either learn effective ways of coping or experience personal disorganization and intense anxiety. The very knowledge of life-threatening illness results in intense crisis for newly diagnosed persons and their families. The fact of illness is beyond one's control. Yet the diagnosis of illness affects the whole family: all family member goals, all family member roles, and all family member relationships. Despite this crisis of uncertain nature, everyone in the family must make a series of initial decisions that well may radically affect the quality, nature, and even duration of a loved one's life. Life-threatening illness has ramifications that affect every aspect of life: relationships with families and friends, financial decisions, work, and school. In fact, virtually all plans will need to be reevaluated in the new context of diagnosed illness.

Throughout this period several issues are raised for the person who is coping with the diagnosis. These may be viewed as tasks that the person must consider. These tasks include

1. understanding the disease
2. examining and maximizing health and lifestyle
3. maximizing one's coping strengths and limiting weaknesses
4. developing strategies to deal with issues created by disease
5. exploring the effect of illness on one's sense of self and relationships with others
6. ventilating feelings and fears
7. incorporating the present reality of the diagnosis into one's sense of past and future

UNDERSTANDING THE DISEASE

The client's perceptions of the disease may be far different from a professional understanding of the disease. The meaning that someone gives to the diagnosis may be inaccurate and may affect him or her in negative ways. Some people may read the diagnosis as a death sentence, thereby extinguishing any hope and consequently impairing subsequent treatment. Others may take the diagnosis too lightly, failing to change their lifestyle or develop the kinds of behaviors that will enhance health.

One of the first tasks for individuals and families is to try to understand the disease at issue. This not only means discovering an accurate and realistic understanding of the disease, but also of learning to cope in a way that allows continued hope, a sense of control, and lower levels of anxiety.

This process begins by exploring the client's understanding of the disease. Often this is best done with a medical professional who can provide opportunities to probe any misunderstandings and to gently question misperceptions. During this process it is usually helpful to explore the sources of one's own information as well as the validity accorded each source. This is especially critical due to the emergence of the Internet as a source of information. Many clients, or their families and friends, will go there first. The difficulty here is twofold. First, the Internet will often include a range of information that varies from the accurate to the fanciful. Second, the Internet also can be a source of quack treatments and fraudulent claims of cure. Counselors do well to assess the degree to which the client is receiving information online as well as the types of information they are receiving.

It is also important to assess factors that may be blocking the client's comprehension. In some cases the barriers can be social. Sometimes the social status and authority of the physician or other medical personnel may intimidate the client. As a result, the client is hesitant to ask questions. There may be educational barriers because of which the ill person has a difficult time understanding the information offered and is reluctant to acknowledge that difficulty. These barriers often reinforce one another. The ill person may not understand the physician's language and may be too embarrassed or intimidated to ask questions.

If this could be a problem, counselors can suggest that clients ask to have another family member, friend, or some trusted intermediary such as a clergyman present when they hear the results or at subsequent visits. It may also help the client to write down any questions that he or she may have. Open communication is critical, but it is important to realize, especially in this early period, that not all questions will have definitive answers. Sometimes counselors can even role-play with the client so that clients are comfortable in confronting medical personnel. In an ideal world, physicians should be sensitive enough to present information and to provide access to information in language the person can understand. Offering a trusting, unhurried, respectful, and nonjudgmental context in which people may ask questions, repeating and reviewing what they know, will help this information process. Linking people with other persons of similar backgrounds who have the disease, informally and in self-help groups, is also quite useful. Not only can such information facilitate understanding, it can also offer coping strategies and provide hope. When communication is poor, someone should inform the caregiver.

There may be psychological barriers too. Serious anxiety can make it difficult to absorb and understand information about the disease. One client shared that she became so nervous once she heard the word "cancer" that she was frozen in fear, unable to hear, respond, or question. Sometimes talking over these fears with others can alleviate anxiety. Or returning at a later time when the level of anxiety has lessened, perhaps supported by a friend, may provide a better opportunity to question and to discuss the illness and its treatment. It also may help to explore the sources of anxiety. Becoming anxious may result from several sources: misinformation, prior poor experiences, or a generally pessimistic attitude about life. Negative perceptions due to misinformation or past experiences can generally be handled in the same way as any learning process. In a trusting context, earlier information can be explored, sources evaluated, and new information provided.

It is important to remember that many major life-threatening illnesses lumped together under such categories such as "cancer" or "heart disease" are really many different, related diseases. An individual's earlier experiences or the experiences of others with cancer or heart disease may tell very little about a similar but different condition. For example, a friend's or relative's experience with pancreatic cancer will not be all that relevant for someone who has prostate cancer. Each disease has its own treatment, symptoms, and prognosis. Moreover, the pace of progress of science is not only amazing but also constantly accelerating. In 1971 I worked in the pediatric ward of a major cancer center. Most of the children who died of cancer in the past could be successfully treated by today's methods. Even people diagnosed with AIDS today can expect to live considerably longer lives than those diagnosed a decade ago. Again, self-help groups or persons who have the disease may be very useful both in providing the most current information and in reinforcing hope.

Sometimes family members will be worried that the ill individual seems too optimistic. I usually do not find such an optimistic state to be troubling. Overly optimistic perceptions of disease are less problematic at this early stage of illness. Often such optimism will encourage adherence to the medical regimen. Beyond the serious obligation of physicians to provide patients with accurate information about their disease and the risks of treatment, these optimistic perceptions should not be challenged unless they impair adherence with treatment or endanger the lives of others.

EXAMINING AND MAXIMIZING HEALTH AND LIFESTYLE

Life-threatening illness can often be influenced by the client's lifestyle. In some cases lifestyle can be a significant contributor to the disease. In other cases lifestyle factors may have an effect on treatment, course, or recurrence of the illness. In any case, good health practices will contribute to reducing stress and facilitating adaptation. Thus it is worthwhile to examine the ways in which the client's current lifestyle affects health, as well as the ways by which one may modify lifestyle practices to enhance health. Suitable exercises, good nutrition, adequate sleep, and effective stress management are more important when one is seriously ill than ever before. It is important, of course, to encourage the client to discuss any major lifestyle modification, such as diet or exercise, with his or her physician. In addition to improving health, such actions can reaffirm in the client a renewed sense of control over one's life that may have been threatened by the diagnosis.

MAXIMIZING ONE'S COPING STRENGTHS AND LIMITING WEAKNESSES

In any crisis—and the diagnosis of life-threatening illness is certainly a crisis—individuals and their families face certain challenges. If clients want to focus on the illness in such a way as to maximize chances for successful outcome, they will need to marshal their resources effectively and limit time, energy, and other kinds of losses to problems that might intrude upon this central struggle.

Here again, a good way to begin is by examining the client's coping styles and strategies. Often an effective way to start that exploration is to focus on the ways that the client has reacted to previous crises in his or her life. This method can reveal coping styles and strategies that might be useful now, in this current crisis. For example, if the client's previous tendency has been to get angry, such a response in the current crisis should come as no surprise. If in past crises the client was prone to make rash decisions or to panic, client awareness of that tendency may guard against that kind of reaction now.

Focusing on past strategies often helps clients to become aware of styles and patterns that may help or hinder current responses. Once a client has reviewed past coping strategies, he or she can consider what strategies can best be adapted to the present crisis. The client can also consider which styles work and which styles do not work. For example, anger can be a powerful motivational tool if it is focused against the disease. But if anger is directed toward family and friends, that same response may drive people away just at the time when they are most needed. Similarly, if a client has a tendency to carefully weigh decisions and is usually reluctant to choose until all the information is in, this characteristic can be helpful in avoiding rash actions, but it can also inhibit fast responses to a crisis. Examining coping styles early in the illness process allows the client to draw upon obvious strengths and also helps a client to become aware of weaknesses, perhaps to better overcome them.

Moreover, the very examination of how clients handle crises has a latent but critical function at this early crises point in the illness. It reinforces hope—reminding clients, in a chaotic and difficult time, that they have surmounted prior crises in their lives.

I should add that continuity in styles and reactions is not always present. Sometimes clients have changed so much that previous ways of coping are no longer indicative of present responses. But sometimes this lack of continuity can be a cause for concern. For example, it might show that the person is in a sustained destructive denial or an immobilizing panic. I always suggest to counselors and other caregivers that if this continuity is absent, they should explore reasons that might account for these new ways of coping.

A second area to consider is social support. To whom can one turn for help? In what ways can the people you know best help? What are one's own feelings about asking for or accepting different kinds of help?

Many times sources of support may be underestimated. Once family and friends are identified and approached, they can surprise one with their willingness to help, each in their own way. During counseling I ask my clients, "Whom can you turn to in crisis?" Often they name only a few people, but when I probe deeper, asking them questions about whom they have told and who has offered help, they discover that their network is larger than they had realized. In some cases they may recognize that their own inhibitions limit help options. For example, a 30-year-old man diagnosed with MS was surprised at the help offered by his formerly estranged brother.

I find a simple exercise to be helpful. I ask clients to come with a list of all the persons they know who have promised or are likely to offer support. As we examine the list, we are likely to expand it. I often ask questions here such as: "Is there anyone else we should include such as people at work, in your faith communities, or other neighbors or friends?" Once the list is complete, and clients are often both reassured and surprised at how extensive the list is, I ask clients to put an L next to all the persons on the list who are good listeners. Next, I request that they put a D next to the names of doers—people they really can count on to complete a chore or errand. Finally, an R goes to people who offer respite. These are people who may never ask how the client is doing and seem to avoid any discussion of the illness. Nonetheless, they often can provide "respite or time away from the disease"—laughter and distraction. This exercise, which can be used at any point in the illness, even with family caregivers, reaffirms three issues. First, it often reassures clients that they have extensive informal support. Second, it allows clients to assess whether or not they are using their support systems effectively—asking the doers to do and the listeners to listen. Third, it validates both the idea of respite and the role that such persons offer in their support.

Although this exercise may seem simplistic, it does emphasize a key point: different people are comfortable helping in different ways.

For example, a daughter I know was very uncomfortable with changing her father's medical dressing, but she was happy to cook food for him and to feed him. Another woman became tense when asked to drive her friend to the doctor's office. She deeply wanted to help, but found the particular request painful and often made excuses not to go. After she shared her true feelings she found other ways to help, such as babysitting her friend's children; she thus met her desire to help and fulfilled a real need for her friend.

Naturally, counselors need to determine that an informal support system does function prior to using such an exercise. Not every client has such support.

When support is not forthcoming, it is often valuable to explore the reasons why. Sometimes possible networks simply do not exist. This is often the case with many elderly people. They may have outlived spouses, family, and friends, or those who remain may be too frail or too ill themselves to offer assistance. Here formal systems may need to compensate.

In other cases, client expectations for help may be unrealistic. One client of mine, for example, was outraged that her daughter did not quit her job to care for her. The daughter was more than willing to help when she was not working and to coordinate her mother's care. Her mother's expectations, though, ignored the constraints imposed on her daughter by her own life needs.

Perhaps potential helpers are receiving mixed or ambivalent messages. In one case a man with cancer was annoyed that his adult children did not make themselves more available to help him. Yet whenever they asked what they could do, he put them off. An offer to drive him to the doctor's office would be met by the response, "No thanks, I've called a cab." They felt they were respecting his independence; he believed they should have insisted upon driving. This example indicates the importance of clients clearly communicating their needs and desires, and not expecting others to guess what help they need and expect.

Sometimes clients have to recognize that family or friends can be destructive if they encourage negative behaviors such as non-adherence to a regimen or substance abuse. For example, an adolescent client with leukemia had a friend who thought the cure for every moment of anxiety or depression was a can of beer. Family and friends whose own needs or behaviors are so extreme that they sap strength rather than providing support do more harm than good. Verbally or physically abusive persons, people whose lives are so chaotic that they constantly involve others in their own crises, or people who are so self-absorbed that even when the client is in a crisis they still look to the client to meet *their* needs will make your problems worse. Such individuals attack self-confidence, self-esteem, and hope. One client coping with his father's cancer told me of a friend with whom he bicycled. The friend would tell constant stories of people he knew who had cancer, often stressing negative outcomes! "For example," this client indicated, "One time when I was discussing my father's chemotherapy, he told a long story about someone's long struggle with chemotherapy. I was waiting for a punch line like 'She's doing well now.' Instead, he told me she died six months later."

There are three ways for clients to deal with other people's destructive behaviors. Some clients can just ignore them, attributing that behavior to misguided attempts to help, the destructive individual's own needs and problems, or lack of effective coping abilities. In other cases, it may be necessary to avoid or discontinue a destructive relationship. Or the client may choose to confront the person, explaining that these behaviors are not helpful and perhaps offering concrete suggestions on how they can help better.

Clients should not neglect formal sources of support. Many services, including transportation, nursing, home care, support groups, meals, counseling, even financial help, may be available. These can often supplement help from family and friends. Often hospital social workers or agencies such as the American Cancer Society can provide information on what services are available in different communities and how one applies for their help. Finding available help, even as early as the time of the diagnosis when this help may not be necessary, can alleviate anxiety, avoid the difficulties associated with trying to find help at a time when it is critically necessary, and reaffirm the client's own abilities to cope.

Part of limiting weaknesses is placing other problems in perspective. It is difficult to cope with the crisis of diagnosis when it is just one of the problems a person is considering. For example, it is doubly devastating to learn that one has AIDS when one is struggling with the psychological crisis of sexual identity or drug use. It is difficult enough to cope with cancer or heart attack, but more so when the crisis follows divorce or career reverses. In these cases clients need to prioritize concerns. Focusing on the illness first, and leaving other concerns for later, is one way to avoid being overwhelmed.

DEVELOPING STRATEGIES TO DEAL WITH ISSUES CREATED BY DISEASE

A diagnosis of life-threatening illness creates immediate practical issues that must be resolved. Some of the most pressing of these issues are discussed in the following sections.

Whom to Tell

Clients need to make decisions about how much information to reveal and whom to confide in. Given uncertainty about the client's fate, clients will be very concerned about how much information to share with family and friends, and how that information should be presented. The issue of disclosure is critical for several reasons. Among family and friends, disclosure can be an important factor in the ability to mobilize social support throughout the course of illness. If clients choose to keep a diagnosis secret, their intimates may be deprived of opportunities to share information and offer support. One friend told me an illustrative story. He had made an appointment for tests but decided not to share this news with his brother and sister, because he did not wish to upset them. For a week he and his wife struggled with their anxiety. At his physician's office he learned that the condition was minor and easily treated. When he shared his joy at this news with his siblings, they told him they both had the same problem. Had he shared news about his health problem earlier, he and his wife would have been spared an anxious week. Disclosing news about disease to others can be a positive experience. Many ill people find that family and friends are far more supportive and helpful than they had expected. Disclosure allows others to show concern and offer support.

Sometimes the issue of disclosure or how much to communicate comes up just in deciding how to answer the question "How are you?" A colleague with leukemia struggled with the problem of how to respond to this common question and finally decided to respond, "I'm doing very well, thank you, though I do have a serious disease."

Sometimes individuals find it useful to rehearse ways to disclose the disease with a confidante. Others ask a family member or confidante to share news about the diagnosis with other family and friends. As one woman explained, "It got us past the 'awkward moment' and it allowed friends to respond as they wanted. Most called and were very supportive."

Although friends and family generally are supportive, it often takes a little time for relationships to return to normalcy. One woman mentioned that it took her friends about two weeks before they would talk about their own problems again.

Clients diagnosed with a serious disease may be very secretive about their problems for several reasons. They may not have come to terms with the diagnosis themselves. Secretiveness can be a form of control; if an individual feels that he or she cannot control the disease, the individual might take some comfort from knowing that he or she can control who else knows and what they know. One adolescent diagnosed with leukemia, for example, swore school officials to secrecy. She later told her classmates the diagnosis, in turn swearing each one to secrecy. Some people may wish to protect others or they may wish to protect themselves. They may be anxious, perhaps realistically so, that disclosure will affect their relationships with others, their plans, and their careers. The pressure to keep things secret is particularly strong whenever the disease is highly stigmatizing, such as with AIDS or Alzheimer's disease, or potentially embarrassing, such as colon cancer.

Ill individuals need to remember that attempts to jealously guard information can be counterproductive. Family and friends can often sense an intimate's anxiety. Coworkers will attempt to make sense of frequent absences, changes in behavior, and changes in appearance. Given the relative medical sophistication of many people in our society, they will evaluate the information they receive from the evidence they observe. Inconsistent accounts made to different individuals can create confusion and rumors. Insurance claims, visits to medical personnel, and other such factors may yield significant clues to the diagnosis. In short, clients must be reminded that their ability to actually control information is probably quite limited—especially as time goes on. Secretiveness may backfire, because rumors about the diagnosis can often be far more damaging than the truth. Moreover, excessive secretiveness can harm relationships by undermining trust.

It is important to remember that disclosure decisions do not have to be put in all-or-nothing terms. Decisions need not be cast in the form, "Whom do I choose to tell or not to tell?" Instead, the question can be posed as, "What information do I need to share with which others, at what point?"

Coping with Medical Professionals

Clients may need assistance in coping with medical professionals. During the diagnostic phase clients have many important concerns about what course of action to pursue. Should they seek a second opinion? Are clients comfortable with their physicians and specialists? If further testing or exploratory surgery is contemplated, are they satisfied with the medical facility?

Feelings about professionals need to be explored. In some cases discomfort or ambivalence may be a result of anxiety over the diagnosis or anger at a physician for delivering bad news. But in other cases ambivalence or discomfort may reflect realistic concerns. Not every physician is the perfect physician, nor is every hospital or specialized medical facility equally good as a place of treatment.

While reviewing these feelings with clients, it helps to remember that a second opinion may be a good idea; another doctor may well offer valuable medical advice and alternatives for treatment. He or she may cushion the shock of diagnosis, return a sense of control, and even provide a sense of valuable space and time to make critical decisions. But second opinions can be a problem if they delay treatment beyond a time that is medically wise or if they lead to "shopping around" for third, fourth, or fifth opinions, deferring the reality of the diagnosis and a reasoned course of treatment.

It is important for individuals and their families to be comfortable with both their physicians and their hospital. This became clear when my father was diagnosed with cancer. While we had great respect for his physician, we were not comfortable with the local general hospital that was handling my father's operation. As a family we decided that it would be best if my father were treated at a major medical center even if such treatment meant switching to another physician. My father's physician was understanding and supportive of my father's and our family's decision. Although we did not wish to hurt the doctor's feelings, my father's health was our first priority. The situation was successfully resolved. My father recovered from the surgery. But even if the ending had not been so happy, insisting that our father be treated in a more sophisticated medical facility was the right thing for us to do. Had he died, at least we would have known that we had done all we could to make sure he had the best possible care.

Deciding on Treatments

After a diagnosis of life-threatening disease, clients will need to make decisions about treatment. Treatment plans differ according to the illness involved. In some cases, treatment plans may be relatively unobtrusive. Some conditions require little more than monitoring. With others, medication or lifestyle modifications may be recommended. When a friend had a heart attack, for example, his doctors prescribed medication, placed him on a diet, and recommended that he review and simplify his lifestyle, eliminating unnecessary stress.

With many conditions, however, other approaches are necessary. In many cases surgery, radiation therapy, or chemotherapy will be required. Whatever therapies are available, individuals should explore their feelings and fears about them. An individual may fear surgery because she fears anesthesia, loss of consciousness, postoperative pain, visible damage (scars and the like), loss of function, aftereffects on employment and finances, or any combination of these things. Radiation may be feared because of the procedure itself (treatment from a machine with no human present), concerns over side effects such as sexual dysfunction and/or sterility, or effects on later health. Chemotherapy can engender similar fears. In all these cases individuals may be afraid that the cure will be worse than the illness.

This is particularly important when diseases have options for treatment. For example, prostate cancer can be treated with several different options, depending on the age of the patient and the stages of the disease, that range from watchful waiting to surgery or radiation. It is critical for counselors to explore with clients treatment options to ascertain that clients are making choices based on evidence rather than emotional reactivity.

It is important that clients discuss and share these fears with physicians. Sometimes these fears may be based upon past experiences that are no longer valid or are perhaps not relevant in this case. Clients might be needlessly troubled or, worse, even refuse lifesaving therapy because of baseless misperceptions.

It is also critical to discuss other options and choices that might be available. Again, second opinions may prove valuable. I also strongly believe that people who are very active participants in health decisions, who maintain a strong sense of control rather than simply passively accepting a physician's advice, who actively research and discuss treatment options are not only likely to cope better, but may, in fact, live longer.

Clients may also need to carefully consider risks and side effects. Physicians are usually very careful about outlining *all* the possible things that could happen as a result of therapy, since physicians are morally and legally required to inform one of risks. Not everyone will experience side effects in the same way. Siegel (1986) emphasizes the importance of positive thinking. He believes that if one focuses on all the bad things that can or might happen, this can be self-fulfilling. Siegel recommends that one develop mental attitudes that stress minimal discomfort. Siegel also teaches positive ways to envision therapies, for example, imagining radiation as a warm, golden beam of healing light.

These treatment decisions can often be confused by the fact that one is getting contrary advice on treatment from physicians and others and even through the Internet. It is important for clients to examine any conflicting advice. Sometimes these conflicts are more apparent than real. Some alternate treatments, such as diet or imaging, may be done along with conventional medical therapies—often allowing clients an active sense of participating in their treatment. In recent years a great deal of attention has been given to holistic and unconventional therapies. My own view is that when these treatments are adjuncts to conventional medical treatment, do not discourage medical treatment, and carry no medical risk, interest and involvement should be encouraged. When my father was ill with cancer, my gift to him was teaching him imaging. Imaging means using a person's imagination in a very active way. Its underlying assumption is that there are strong associations between mental and physical states, and mental attitude may be able to enhance the functioning of the immune system. In my father's case, we developed images that were familiar and comfortable to him. He imagined his immune cells as soldiers seeking out and destroying enemy cancer cells. Each day he set aside time to develop this mental image of a large but successful battle.

At other times, though, there are medical disagreements about what is the best way to proceed. Here counselors can assist clients in finding the information needed to make an intelligent decision. Information from physicians about possible risks and benefits will be essential. Counselors can sometimes suggest options that can be discussed with physicians. For example, perhaps there is time to try less radical approaches, leaving more radical alternatives for later stages of treatment, if needed. It is critical to spend time examining these choices, even given the anxiety often felt in this period and the pressure to make a decision quickly. If a client has fully explored his or her options, the client is less likely to second-guess or regret these decisions later. Counselors should accept the limitations of their own role, however. They are there to assist and facilitate the client's decision, not to offer advice or to impose a decision.

It is also important to know how treatment might affect other aspects of life. Often if potential problems are identified, compromises may be found that might alleviate some concerns. For example, if someone is concerned that therapy might impair work or school, it might be scheduled on a Friday or just before a long holiday weekend so that side effects have subsided by the beginning of the next work or school week.

If a client does make a decision to seek an alternative method of treatment *instead of* a more traditional approach, it is important to understand and evaluate that choice. Sometimes it may result from social pressures such as advice from family or friends. Other times such approaches may result from feelings of helplessness or panic that move a client to seek treatment, however unproven, that seems to offer more than traditional medicine. Sometimes if a client can find a physician who provides emotional support and allows one to clearly review all treatment options, that may mitigate a desire to attempt unconventional approaches.

Other Life Choices

The diagnosis of life-threatening illness may also force the client to review other decisions: "Should I proceed with the wedding?" "Should I pursue this relationship?" "Should I quit school or work?" are examples of the kind of questions clients may need to consider.

There are two contrasting coping tendencies. One is to keep things exactly the same, proceeding with life as if there were no existing crisis. This approach is unlikely to work, because disease already has created or soon will create changes that must be confronted. Pretending that they do not exist impairs the kind of realistic planning that may allow a renewed sense of control. Although one cannot control the fact that a diagnosis has changed one's life, to some extent one can control *the way* it changes life. One client of mine provides a good illustration of this important point. Insisting that his diagnosis changed nothing, he worked as hard or even harder in his small business. But when he was hospitalized as a result of exhaustion, he finally had to admit that his diagnosis had changed his life. Now he was now able to realistically plan his workday. He limited himself to about four hours a day, regulated the tasks he did, and hired additional help. His new plan allowed him to marshal his resources and cope more effectively with his health crisis. When he recognized that he could still make good decisions, even in the middle of a crisis, he regained a sense of his own coping abilities.

Other clients may wish to make definitive decisions regarding all possible contingencies, often ignoring the inherent uncertainty of this phase of their lives. Sometimes it is better to wait, prioritizing issues that need to be settled now and leaving others for a later time. It is important to recognize that similar decisions can have very distinct meanings and implications to different individuals or at different times in the illness. The decision to quit work can represent a premature and unhealthy withdrawal or a life-enhancing decision about priorities. It may profoundly affect financial stability by limiting income, access to health insurance, and the availability of other forms of help. Given the uncertainty of this phase, it is often worthwhile to remember that decisions can be tentative and limited. Instead of asking oneself, "Should I quit work?" one might better focus on more limited possibilities, such as taking a temporary leave of absence, scaling back commitments and work, a shorter day or week, or even working at home. Review and discuss these decisions with all those who may be affected by them.

Finally, clients should consider other contingencies. Clients should review their medical insurance and explore options if they are uninsured or underinsured. This also may be a good time for clients to review or create wills and to consider issues of guardianship, health proxies, power of attorney, advance directives, and the like. It is always worthwhile to periodically review titles, leases, wills, and insurance policies to see whether decisions on property, beneficiaries, guardians, and executors reflect current relationships. An illness is simply one more opportunity to reexamine these earlier decisions. However these options should be addressed with a client, it is critical not to overwhelm a client at the onset of a life-threatening diagnosis.

EXPLORING THE EFFECT OF ILLNESS ON SENSE OF SELF AND RELATIONSHIPS WITH OTHERS

The diagnosis of life-threatening illness changes the client's sense of self in many ways. One may feel betrayed by the frailty of one's physical body. One may feel stigmatized by disease. Critical identities may seem threatened by the illness: a teacher may be anxious that he or she will no longer be able to teach; an avid skier may fear the end of that activity. It is important to discuss these concerns with caregivers, especially physicians and counselors, and to raise them in self-help groups. This may provide opportunities to ventilate these feelings, find reassurance, and sometimes develop new strategies to deal with the problem. One 55 -year-old man facing a colostomy was worried that the operation, if he chose to have it, would effectively end his career. He discussed this concern with his physician, who recommended a support group. In the support group he found reassurance that his fears were both natural but groundless.

A life-threatening illness is likely to change relationships with other people. They may not know how to respond, especially in the early phase of illness, to the newly diagnosed person, perhaps someone who is in the paradoxical position of looking well and yet being seriously ill. Some friends or family may feel awkward and uneasy, anxious about the disease, fearful of how it may change the relationship, unsure of how to act or what to say. Feeling such discomfort, they may very well avoid both the ill individual and even other family members.

If clients are feeling disappointed by the reactions of others, it is usually worthwhile to explore this issue early, because often these things can escalate later on in the illness. That is, later on people may be avoidant in part because they feel guilty about their previous avoidance! Counselors can assist clients to not only ventilate these concerns, but also to develop strategies for dealing with change. Sometimes humor can break the ice. At other times it may be worthwhile to gently confront the issue. One friend diagnosed with leukemia had to confront his fishing buddies. They admitted that they had had extended conversations among themselves as to whether he was well enough to be invited on a trip. He needed to gently remind them that he could make that decision himself, but first they would have to invite him. Life-threatening illness can bring isolation or greater intimacy. What actually happens is the responsibility of everyone: the ill person, family, and friends.

VENTILATING FEELINGS AND FEARS

At any phase of illness clients may experience strong emotional reactions. Individuals and families may have all types of feelings ranging from relief that the uncertainty "is over" to deep depression at the results. Indeed one of the critical roles of the counselor at the time of diagnosis is to provide a safe place for clients to express their shock, disbelief, and denial of the diagnosis.

In fact, almost any emotions may be experienced throughout the course of illness. There is no one set of normal reactions, nor any one sequence of emotional experiences. Each person will respond in his or her own individual ways.

Dealing with emotional reactions can be difficult. Often clients experiencing illness face a double bind. They are filled with feelings, but may find limited opportunities to share them. There can be many reasons for this situation. They may be reluctant to share their feelings and their fears, especially with those whom they most love. Or family and friends may find it difficult to listen. Family and friends may deny the sick individual's negative feelings, telling him or her not to feel angry, guilty, or sad—as if such feelings can be so readily dismissed.

Often self-help groups or counselors can provide the emotional distance and objectivity that people need if they are to ventilate their true feelings. Three things are essential: understanding one's feelings, expressing them, and using them constructively in the course of the illness.

Individuals experiencing life-threatening illness need opportunities to talk over their concerns in a trusting, nonjudgmental atmosphere. Once these feelings are openly expressed, an individual can move on to explore both the sources of these emotions and the ways that this affect will influence treatment.

Counselors should try to assist individuals in using feelings constructively in the subsequent treatment of illness. For example, emotions such as fear and guilt can immobilize or motivate. Anger can isolate one from others, imperiling relationships, or it can be focused against the disease. A case illustrates the ways in which individuals can deal with their feelings and fears. A 30-year-old male was diagnosed with pancreatic cancer. He initially responded with a fear of future pain and suffering, and with guilt that his present pain was punishment for his prior lifestyle—one that included the frequent use of recreational drugs. In counseling he was able both to express these concerns and to explore his fear and guilt. Honest, realistic communication with his physician alleviated his anxiety somewhat.

He recognized the likely course of the disease, but was reassured by his physician that the doctor would do everything possible to minimize pain. Instruction in self-hypnosis and imaging gave him some sense of control over possible future pain.

Counselors should recognize that any and each emotional reaction could have both constructive and destructive manifestations. As an individual client expresses and explores his or her feelings, he or she is able to minimize destructive aspects and facilitate effective responses toward the illness.

INCORPORATING THE PRESENT REALITY OF THE DIAGNOSIS INTO ONE'S SENSE OF PAST AND FUTURE

The diagnosis of illness affects not only the client's present but also the client's past and future. The very nature of dealing with life-threatening issues may compel one to focus on past issues. Previous ways of coping with crisis, expectations of support, and experiences with illness are topics that involve considerable history. They bring clients back to unresolved issues, perhaps dealing with dependency, sexuality, or relationships that are now reactivated by the diagnosis. Clients may wish to discuss these reemerging issues with counselors and therapists, particularly if they seem to be interfering with the way one currently is functioning. For example, Louis, a 25-year-old man, newly diagnosed with muscular dystrophy, found that he needed to work through his fears of abandonment. Louis had been placed in foster care when his mother could not cope with his ill brother. Based on this early experience, Louis feared that his wife would abandon him too. His fears and his constant demands for reassurance actually threatened his marriage. Through therapy, he was able to understand the source of his fears and work on resolving these early issues.

The diagnosis of life-threatening illness also calls the client's future life into question. Not only health, but also all facets of the client's previous lifestyle, such as priorities and relationships, are now opened to review. Some individuals who recover from illness often speak of the diagnosis as a positive and pivotal turning point in their lives. The illness provided an opportunity, however unwelcome and unsought, to review and to change their lives. In one case, a woman who had been a workaholic reprioritized her time so that she could spend more time in leisure activities with her children and her friends.

Even when recovery is not expected, one can decide how one wishes to spend the time that one has left. Clients may decide to reprioritize time and activities, perhaps spending more time with family and friends. Not only does this affirm personal control but it also may alleviate anxiety, bolster social support, and provide useful diversion, making remaining time more enjoyable and meaningful.

The ability to see past the crisis, to seize the opportunity, to make changes, is a critical factor in maintaining a positive attitude. The same human needs that existed prior to the crisis still exist now. Clients may find it helpful to continue to plan for the future, even if decisions are constrained by a more limited time frame. Planning provides a sense of diversion and reinforces hope. For example, one man with cancer researched and planned the cruise he and his wife intended to take when he recovered. He lived to take that cruise. Looking beyond the illness, resetting priorities, and reviewing what the client may want from life, even if it does not enhance survival, can improve the present quality of life.

The crisis of diagnosis is fundamentally a spiritual crisis. Clients may often experience a renewed faith and use spiritual techniques, such as prayer or meditation, in adapting to the diagnosis (Cotton et al., 2006). Spiritual assessment and exploration is critical. Counselors should explore their clients' spiritual history, helping them to identify the ways their spirituality may be complicate adaptation, perhaps by a sense of moral guilt or feelings of spiritual abandonment, as well as ways that spiritual practices, beliefs, and rituals facilitate adaptation to the new reality of illness.

THE END OF THE ACUTE OR DIAGNOSTIC PHASE

The acute phase of life-threatening illness, centering on diagnosis, is by its very nature self-limiting. Although it may take a period of time, perhaps weeks, the uncertainty of the acute phase will be at least partially resolved and individuals and their families will face new realities.

These realities can differ. In rare situations the event precipitating the diagnosis may result in death or a swift decline into the terminal phase of illness. Here loss may be sudden such as with a fatal heart attack or death on the operating table. This leaves survivors to deal with diagnosis and death almost simultaneously. Or the illness may progress so rapidly, or the disability, perhaps from stroke, is so pronounced and irreversible that the individual and family must grieve the extensive losses that have occurred and prepare for the person's likely death.

Then there are situations in which recovery is considered complete. Here the person may have recovered from a heart attack or stroke or have been successfully treated for cancer. In these situations, people may face varied risks of recurrence. However, even with recovery, there still seems to be considerable aftereffects from an encounter with life-threatening illness. Koocher and O'Malley (1981) studied almost 120 survivors of childhood cancer. They found that these people still suffered from various residues of the disease including physical scars, fears of relapse, psychological impairment, and discrimination in employment as well as in obtaining health and life insurance. Even full recovery may leave physical, emotional, psychological, social, and financial scars that may reverberate throughout one's life.

In many cases, though, individuals and their families will have to cope with the ongoing presence of disease, its treatment, and consequent levels of disability. Here the person enters the chronic phase of illness, a phase with its own challenges and tasks.

REFERENCES

Cotton, S., Puchalski, C., Sherman, S., Mrus, J., Peterman, A., Feinberg, J., Pargament, K., Justice, A., Leonard, A., & Tsevat, J. (2006). Spirituality and religion in patients with HIV/AIDS. *JGIM: Journal of General Internal Medicine, 21*(Supplement 5), S5–S13.

Ferrarra, A. (1984). My personal experience with AIDS. *American Psychologist, 39,* 1285–1287.

Koocher, G., & O'Malley, J. (1981). *The Damocles syndrome: Psychological consequences of surviving childhood cancer.* New York: McGraw-Hill.

Pattison, E. M. (1969). Help in the dying process. *Voices, 5,* 6–14.

Siegel, B. (1986). *Love, medicine, and miracles.* New York: Harper and Row.

Weisman, A. (1986). *The coping capacity. On the nature of being mortal.* New York: Human Sciences Press.

Counseling Clients in the Chronic Phase of Illness

THE CHRONIC PHASE: AN OVERVIEW

It is a tedious time of testing and treatment. There are bimonthly chemotherapy sessions, which leave Joan, a 54-year-old cancer patient, sick and exhausted for days. In between those times, Joan cares for her home and maintains her position as an elementary-school guidance counselor. Her latest prognosis is guarded but optimistic. Within six months, the chemotherapy will end. But it will be five years, perhaps longer, before she knows, with only reasonable certainty, whether she will survive this bout with cancer. Meanwhile her days are filled with a low level of continued stress punctuated by occasional waves of anxiety. Her nights are times of fitful sleep and troubled dreams.

Joan's experience is an increasingly common one in life-threatening illness. Most people will neither quickly recover from the disease nor rapidly deteriorate. For most, between the diagnosis and the outcome of the disease there will be a long chronic period during which one struggles with the demands and side effects of treatment, the symptoms of the disease, and the daily business of living. Weisman (1980), in his study of responses to cancer, described the early part of this chronic phase as "accommodation and mitigation." For Weisman, the challenge of this period is to accommodate the illness with previous coping skills and roles. Often by this time, the crisis posed by the diagnosis is mitigated. The ill individual is simply striving now to find ways to live life with the ongoing presence of the disease (Weisman, 1980, p. 87).

Perhaps the most dramatic change in life-threatening illness is the existence and extension of the chronic phase. Not too many years ago the period between diagnosis and death for many illnesses was typically measured in months, and these months were mostly lived within hospital walls. Now that period may be measured in years, allowing hope for a still-undiscovered cure or ongoing remission, and much of it may be lived in the person's own environment, permitting the resumption of work, school, and other roles.

AIDS provides a good illustration of this important point. Persons diagnosed with AIDS may live decades now. Throughout this time, they may harbor hopes, hardly unrealistic, that newly developed treatments will continue to extend life or even cure the disease. They may work or go to school, as well as continue to develop relationships. There may be long periods when symptoms seem under control and health seems good. Although the disease is present and likely to shorten life, the individual continues to live.

This new reality of life-threatening illness has blurred the distinction between chronic and life-threatening illness. The chronic phase of life-threatening illness can be defined as that period between diagnosis and the final outcome. Here the client attempts to cope with the demands of life while simultaneously striving to maintain health and prevent and/or adapt to the deterioration of health caused by the presence of life-threatening disease. The chronic phase involves many of the same issues and struggles common to all chronic illness.

The quality of life in the chronic phase is likely to be deeply affected by the nature and symptoms of the disease. These two factors were explored earlier and deserve mention here again.

The trajectory or pattern that the illness takes often shapes the experience of the chronic phase. In diseases that show a slow but steady or relentless pattern of decline, individuals and their families may have to cope with the psychological distress of constant and continued deterioration. "Every night," one young muscular dystrophy victim told me, "I go to bed knowing I will wake up weaker." In these patterns, there may be a sense of great weariness, of having lived too long. To capture her mood, one client once paraphrased the words of the Native American leader Chief Joseph when he surrendered to U.S. forces: "I have fought too long forever." Not only are these slow periods of decline difficult for ill individuals, they are difficult for their families and others involved with the persons as well.

Other patterns or trajectories may shape this experience in other ways. Patterns marked by relapses and remissions, as well as those of relative stability, are followed by sharp declines, which create their own unique problems for ill individuals and their families. Relapses are times of great anxiety. One woman with MS said, "I never know with each relapse how far I will decline, how disabled I will come, how dependent I will become . . . and I always think 'Will I be able to recover? Will I have to enter the nursing home?'" A man with leukemia, a disease characterized by remission and relapse rather than the declining plateaus of MS, echoed her concern: "Each relapse I say 'How long [to live]' and with each remission I ask the same question." Moreover, both noted the effects of the illness on other aspects of life. A client with AIDS, for example, described how hard it was to plan, to readjust, and even to relate to friends and family. "I have had," he once dramatically announced, "more deathbed scenes than Sarah Bernhardt." In each illness, though, the nature of the trajectory will define the types of difficulties and experiences individuals encounter.

The quality of life in this chronic phase will also be greatly affected and defined by the particular symptoms of the underlying disease. In situations in which one is asymptomatic or experiences minor symptoms and little pain, it may be possible to continue to maintain a good quality of life, one that approaches the standard of life prior to the diagnosis. In other cases, where symptoms are persistent, recurring, and disruptive, and pain is chronic, the quality of life may be disrupted. Regardless of the level of disruption, it is natural that many individuals and their families can be affected by chronic anxiety.

In the early phases of the disease, or in periods of remission, the nature of life may not change dramatically from earlier, preillness times. Often this is very reassuring to individuals and families, a reminder that a good quality of life can be maintained even in the face of life-threatening illness. Hope may reassert itself. Individuals may become busy in treatment and even engage and explore alternate modalities of treatment such as imaging or other attitudinal approaches.

Some individuals may also use this time to plan for the possible events and contingencies likely to occur as the illness progresses. Illness often compels individuals to make financial arrangements and to address other pressing concerns such as child care. People may need to anticipate medical and care needs and allocate and prioritize time. This planning may mitigate some of the loss of control experienced at the time of diagnosis. It is important to remember, though, that some individuals and family members may approach this in a different way, preferring to take each day one at a time.

Life in the chronic phase is often punctuated by varied crisis points. Crisis points can include the complications, deteriorations, and relapses brought on by the illness, as well as the side effects and complications of treatments. Even unrelated and minor illnesses can create crises. For example, the symptoms of a common cold can cause consternation either as a threat to the precarious balance between health and illness or as a harbinger of death, causing anxiety that this simple symptom evidences a final decline.

To others, increasing dependency and perhaps even life events can create psychological distress and crisis. To a young man with muscular dystrophy, the dependency symbolized by a wheelchair can be profoundly distressing. In another case, a man with cancer was devastated when he learned he would be moved from an acute-care institution to a chronic facility instead of going home. This placement reinforced his perception of his deterioration and increased dependency. It reminded him that remissions would no longer be total and that preserving normalcy would be increasingly difficult.

Although the chronic phase can be difficult period, it can also be perceived as a time of opportunities. The chronic phase often provides opportunities to return to work or school. It can be an opportunity to resume or renew relationships. It can even be an opportunity to fulfill a previously unfulfilled dream. Living with disease is always a difficult, unwanted challenge. However, it is a challenge that can be met if one emphasizes that one is living with disease.

The chronic phase can be viewed as a transitional and uncertain phase. Throughout this period, individuals and families experience significant changes and challenges. Individuals must confront a series of tasks that reflect that struggle:

1. managing symptoms and side effects
2. carrying out medical regimens
3. preventing and managing medical crises
4. managing stress and examining coping
5. maximizing social support and minimizing social isolation
6. normalizing life in the face of disease
7. dealing with financial concerns
8. preserving self-concept
9. redefining relationships with others throughout the course of the disease
10. ventilating feelings and fears
11. finding meaning in suffering, chronicity, uncertainty, or decline

MANAGING SYMPTOMS AND SIDE EFFECTS

Throughout the chronic phase, clients must constantly cope with the presence of disruptive symptoms and treatment side effects. Often the most intrusive of these is the presence of pain. In the chronic phase, pain control is particularly critical because it can encourage adherence to a needed regimen that disrupts other roles and it can enhance psychological functioning and morale. But although pain control is critical in the chronic phase, it can often be difficult.

The first step in pain control is always an assessment of both pain and the behavior that results from the pain. Pain is quite complex, more than simply a physical sensation. One must assess the ways in which pain is influenced by psychological states, spiritual concerns, or social factors. For example, pain can be exacerbated by anxiety or depression. Stress can affect the perception of pain. Even social factors can play a role. Some families may act to reinforce either "pain" or "well" behaviors, perhaps by only responding to the individual's complaints. Often, assessing the patterns of pain (for example, when does pain most often occur) can be a good way to determine influenc-ing factors. For example, in one case a client experienced most severe pain on weekends. Two contributing factors emerged upon analysis. First, the pain preceded chemotherapy always scheduled on Monday, suggesting that anxiety over treatment contributed to pain. Second, other family members were available and solicitous on weekends, suggesting that they too often reinforced pain behaviors by their constant inquiries, sympathy, and solicitous attention. In other cases, clients may be reluctant to even share that they are in pain. I have always found the question "Are you comfortable?" to be more open and potentially more revealing than "Are you in pain?"

Once an assessment is made, the counselor can work with fami-lies and others in developing pain-control strategies. In some cases medication will be called for, but medication is likely to be only one strategy in an overall plan of care. Counseling may be a useful strategy as well, allowing one to address underlying psychological, spiritual, or social factors. Both individuals and their families may need to learn principles of positive reinforcement so that well behaviors rather than pain behaviors can be activated and used. Diversion, relaxation tech-niques, and hypnosis are other possible additional strategies. Even exercise may be useful, since it provides diversion, loosens muscle tightness, and reaffirms activity and control.

One very successful strategy that can be used is imagery. Here the client uses his or her own imaginative processes to alleviate pain. Imagery begins similarly to relaxation techniques. One sits quietly in a comfortable position with closed eyes. Slowly and deeply breathing through the nose, one attempts to relax all mus-cles, often starting at the feet and moving to the face. When one is relaxed, one is guided to use imagination. In some cases, the image evoked is a pleasant diversion. For example, a client can select and imagine himself or herself beside a mountain stream or on a Caribbean island. Naturally, such images are drawn from the client's own experiences and fantasies. In other cases, the client may imagine a healing presence that removes the pain, perhaps, for example, a religious figure. Other forms of imaging may involve conceptualizing the pain on a scale, then imagining the scale value declining as the pain moderates.

There are two points that one should remember. First, effective pain control will often involve a series of strategies. Second, these strategies will have to be customized to the individual client. Religious images may be a very useful technique for some, but for others such images would convey little meaning.

Although pain may be a significant factor, it is not the only symptom with which individuals may have to cope. Clients may encounter a series of side effects and symptoms.

If a client is experiencing any symptoms or side effects, it is important for the client to share information about them with his or her physician immediately. Often clients may be reluctant to do this, not wanting to appear to be a complainer or because the client mistakenly assumes that the problem is part of the illness. Counselors should probe here and remind clients that physicians can frequently use this information to better understand the client's condition and to guide treatment. Many times physicians may be able to take steps to alleviate side effects. Many side effects of treatment or symptoms of disease can be mitigated by patients' actions or controlled by medication. It may be important to remind clients that physicians may have to experiment with a number of approaches before they find what works best for them. Clients should also not take any nonprescribed drugs, even over-the-counter drugs, without discussing it with a physician.

When it is not possible to mitigate symptoms, counselors should assist clients in trying to understand the ways in which these symptoms are affecting the client's life. In some cases, symptoms may be minimal and easily hidden, but in other cases they may be very apparent and highly disruptive. Individuals may not only experience the disruptive effects of the symptoms on their other roles, but may also feel a sense of stigma that deeply affects not only their own sense of identity and self-esteem but their interaction with others. To cite an example, I know a young man who was disfigured by facial lesions. He felt so stigmatized by these lesions that he hid himself in this apartment, avoiding the visits and social support of friends and family.

Counselors can assist clients in developing strategies to deal with intrusive symptoms. In some cases, this may involve simple behavioral modifications. Anselm Strauss (1975), for example, in his study of chronic illness, described how an individual experiencing diarrhea had to find stores that permitted easy access to rest rooms. In other cases, lifestyle modifications may be more intensive. One client of mine learned to schedule important meetings prior to lunch because he became tired later in the day. In other cases, environmental modifications may help. One man with limited mobility due to his disease found it necessary to modify his home environment so that he could function on one floor. Sometimes such modifications may involve the cooperation of others. One young boy suffering from leukemia underwent chemotherapy every Friday afternoon. Usually he wasn't functioning well until Tuesday. On Fridays, he was so anxious that he found it hard to concentrate on schoolwork. His teacher was extremely helpful with this problem, because she scheduled significant tests and assignments on Wednesdays and Thursdays. Once symptoms and their consequences are explored, often one can work to control them.

CARRYING OUT HEALTH REGIMENS

One of the most critical tasks in the chronic phase is adhering to a medical regimen because such regimens are a significant factor in whether a cure or a significant prolongation of life can be achieved. Regimens may range from heavy treatment, such as weekly chemotherapy, or massive changes in lifestyle and diet that adversely effect the quality of life, to minor lifestyle changes and simple monitoring. In most cases, individuals must undergo some treatment and adhere to a medical regimen that is itself an intrusion into daily life and a constant reminder of illness. Recently many caregivers have begun to speak of "adherence" or a "therapeutic alliance" to a medical regimen rather than the traditional term "compliance"; adherence or alliance emphasizes the sense of partnership so critical to success, rather than simply following a prescribed set of rules provided by caregivers—it denotes collaboration rather than obedience.

Adherence can be difficult for many people, but certain groups have special problems. Adolescents may find treatment restrictions not only burdensome but a threat to their emerging independence and quest for social acceptance. In addition to these types of psychosocial barriers, there may be situational barriers as well. People experiencing too many crises or operating under severe constraints may find adherence difficult. Persons with limited incomes, for example, may find the costs of special diets prohibitive. Others may find instructions and directions confusing. And those with chaotic lifestyles characterized by constant crises, such as IV drug users, may find compliance virtually impossible. People who are experiencing multiple chronic illnesses may find it difficult to balance the demands of many simultaneous regimens.

Whereas adherence may be more difficult in these situations, studies (Hayes, McDonald, & Garg, 2002) suggest that almost half of all individuals do not fully adhere to the medication treatment regimen, with adherence even lower for behaviorally demanding regimens or lifestyle prescriptions. Individuals, families, physicians, and other caregivers must therefore create a partnership—a therapeutic alliance—to help make adherence work.

This partnership begins when individuals clearly identify and discuss their fears and beliefs about the regimen with their physicians. Often, one significant psychological barrier to adherence is the belief that action will have little effect on the disease. Since this belief will lessen the motivation for adherence, it can become self-fulfilling. A regimen half followed is unlikely to be successful. Physicians can help by being realistic and truthful about goals, side effects, costs, and expectations. If an individual is told the truth, for example, that symptom relief may be partial, that pain will decrease though not disappear, or that the disease will be slowed but not eradicated, he or she will have realistic expectations and therefore be more likely to follow the regimen. When one recognizes the regimen is doing what is expected, one is more likely to continue to adhere to it.

Tailoring regimens also means fitting them as much as possible into an individual's lifestyle. Physicians sometimes make arbitrary decisions on when medication is to be taken without ever discussing how the regimen fits into a person's life. Sometimes issues are minor. One elderly friend had to take medication three times a day. The physician wrote on the prescription "Take at 8 a.m., 4 p.m., 12 a.m." This caused some conflict: my friend was generally asleep by midnight, and at 8 a.m., he was out of his house on a brisk walk. He was reluctant to call his doctor and unsure that he should arbitrarily change the times, but a brief phone call, solved his problem: the doctor altered the times for medication to 7 a.m., 3 p.m., and 11 p.m.

In another situation a client did not take medication because it made her groggy and interfered with her work. When she discussed this problem with her physician, he shifted medication time to the afternoon. My client learned to adjust her work around it. Both cases were readily solved; yet both sets of difficulties, however minor, could have been avoided if physicians and their patients simply talked with one another. Personalizing regimens is usually not difficult, but it does require a level of communication between physicians and their patients that allows for fitting treatment needs to the individual's lifestyle.

The partnership, however, goes beyond an individual and his or her physicians. Sometimes it involves other caregivers such as nurses. They too may need to be involved in training and educating individuals about their regimens. Often individuals will need ongoing support. For example, one visiting nurse was extraordinarily helpful to an older man who was taking triweekly shots of interferon. He was expected to inject himself and this made him very anxious. His nurse was very reassuring, constantly showing him the technique, and promising that she would be there as long as he needed her. Even after he mastered injecting himself, she would call periodically to monitor his success and reassure him. Such continuity, empathy, support, and communication between individuals and their caregivers can facilitate adherence to a regimen.

This therapeutic alliance also may involve family. Sometimes persons within an individual's circle discourage adherence. In one case, for example, whenever Rita was undergoing radiation therapy, an aunt would wonder aloud whether it was worth it. In another case, Tom, a young man undergoing chemotherapy, was often encouraged to drink by a friend, despite that Tom had indicated that drinking interfered with his treatment. In such cases, it is important to identify destructive individuals and develop effective strategies for dealing with them. In the first case, Rita was able to share her feelings with her aunt. In the second, Tom found he could not continue what he realized was a destructive relationship.

In some cases, family members may be expected to participate in the regimen, but they may be untrained, find their role emotionally or physically difficult, or simply have overwhelming demands on time. They too may need training and perhaps counseling support to fulfill new role as caregivers.

A client's level of adherence is unlikely to be stable. It is important to review constantly what factors may be facilitating or limiting adherence. Sometimes it may be medical; for example, individuals can feel very discouraged after a crisis or continued deterioration. Sometimes it is psychological; when people are feeling very bad, or even perhaps very good, they may find it difficult to adhere. Sometimes there are other reasons. Perhaps adherence declines in time of high stress or activity. Changes in the social environment may affect adherence. For example, the death of a spouse may influence the surviving spouse's adherence. In one case, the husband supervised his wife's medication. When he died, her adherence became much less regular.

Again, alliance means that clients should continue to discuss problems as they arise with physicians and caregivers. Identifying barriers to full adherence is often the first step to finding ways to address them. One divorced man struggling with cancer found that his adherence declined when his children visited. He was so involved with them that he often forgot his medication. Once he identified the problem, he and his nurse set up a pill box and a set of alarm clocks.

It is also important for clients not to become discouraged if they find it difficult to adhere to a regimen. One man with emphysema was not supposed to smoke or drink. On vacation with friends, he lapsed and did both. Upon reflection he was discouraged, thinking he could never fully adhere. Yet in discussions with his physician, he was able to identify factors that had led him to abandon his regimen, develop strategies to avoid problems in the future, and return to his regimen. Falling off a regimen, even for an extended period of time does not mean that one cannot return to it.

Alliance also involves respecting individual choices. For example, there may be cases in which individuals wish to attempt alternative, nontraditional therapies such as diets or imagery. When such therapies offer no recognizable harm and they are complementary to rather than competitive with conventional therapies, they should not be discouraged. Participating in such therapies may provide an ill individual with a renewed sense of control and hope. Respecting individuals' choices and seeking to facilitate them, for example, by accommodating diets in hospitalizations, may enhance coping and encourage general adherence with the medical regimen since it reinforces the full partnership in treatment.

There may also be situations in which individuals make a decision not to adhere to treatment or to try a competitive nontraditional therapy. When such cases involve competent adults, counselors can explore with individuals the reasons for and the risks associated with such decisions. In some cases, an individual's reluctance to accept treatment may involve depression, anxieties, or other feelings that can be addressed, or misinformation that can be corrected. Other times, individuals may distrust the medical establishment and feel that it has little to offer; thus, they feel that little will be risked in trying something different. Again it is worthwhile to explore these feelings. In other cases, compromises or simplifications of the regimen may resolve concerns.

There may be situations, though, that are not so readily resolved. Here an individual has made, in his or her terms, a rational decision, perhaps a very different one than a caregiver or a family member might make, not to adhere with a part of the regimen, to end treatment, or to seek unconventional therapy. For example, in one case, a 60-year-old man with leukemia who had already survived two prior (and unrelated to this occurrence) bouts with cancer decided to forgo further chemotherapy for this third encounter with malignancy. He reasoned that the treatment would impair any remaining time he had while promising only limited opportunity for success. Such decisions must be respected. But caregivers and counselors should encourage individuals to explore reasons for the decision, to discuss its effects on family, and to review other possible options for treatment.

Sometimes people decide not to participate in conventional therapies because they believe "nothing can be done." They must be convinced that things *can* be done within the context of conventional medicine—perhaps not to cure, but possibly to extend life, to alleviate symptoms, and/or to control pain. Physicians and other caregivers must encourage openness, because only when the individual expresses his or her true feelings and beliefs can they be addressed.

In summary, adherence should be regarded as a continuum. On one end are those who fully adhere. On the other end are those who do not adhere at all. Most clients will be between these poles, adhering to varying degrees. Understanding where one is in that continuum, what factors influence the degree of compliance, what risks and benefits are associated with the present state of adherence, and what one can do to maintain and/or enhance adherence with caregivers often helps. This ongoing assessment of adherence also provides continued opportunities to receive education and instruction.

Although adhering to a medical regimen is primarily the responsibility of the client and his or her physician or other medical personnel, counselors should acknowledge that they too are part of this therapeutic alliance. When individuals have difficulty with adherence, counselors may wish to explore factors and situations that inhibit adherence. However, counselors should remember certain behaviors such as exhortations, all-or-nothing comments (for example, "Will you follow the diet or not?"), or threatening comments (for example, "If you don't follow this regimen you will surely relapse!") are countertherapeutic and are not likely to be effective in improving adherence. Adherence will be improved in a context that emphasizes full partnership, honesty, good communication, clear empathy, and mutual respect.

PREVENTING AND MANAGING MEDICAL CRISES

The chronic phase is often punctuated by a variety of medical crises. If these crises are poorly managed, they can adversely affect both physical and mental health. Effective prevention and management of medical crises, on the other hand, can often reaffirm a sense of control and raise morale.

Counselors can assist clients in preventing many medical crises through careful education and preparation. Clients should be encouraged to discuss with their physician potential danger signs and symptoms that mandate immediate attention. This can become a useful opportunity to assess symptoms, strategies, and possible difficulties that may arise. By paying prompt attention to potential problems, carefully adhering to treatment regimen, and maintaining an effective lifestyle, an ill individual can prevent many crises.

Not all medical crises can be avoided, however. It often helps to do some contingency planning with caregivers and family that identifies possible sources of informal support and medical assistance. For example, clients and their families may need to know whom to contact if the primary physician is not readily available. If clients are traveling, they need the names of local physicians and medical centers in case emergencies arise. If clients live alone, they may wish to consider having someone offer periodic reassurance calls.

Developing a flow chart can be a very effective technique for both individuals and their families. When I worked with foster parents who were caring for HIV-infected children, this proved a very popular intervention. Here physicians and other caregivers identified possible medical contingencies and difficulties and outlined appropriate responses. In some cases, the action may be as mild as "inform the physician at the next visit"; in other cases the action to be taken may be to seek immediate emergency care. One side benefit of such a flow chart is to reassure the families that not every symptom or event constitutes a major crisis. Families can add their own notes such as who can be contacted, who can provide needed support (for example, transportation, meals, and the like), who should be notified. These charts should be kept in a place familiar and available to other family members. Such a chart can foretell a sense of panic that can immobilize people in a chronic phase and reaffirm a sense of control in a chaotic time. Even the very exercise of creating a chart is an intervention that reasserts the client's control.

It is best to do crisis planning in a noncrisis context, early in the chronic phase. When creating a contingency list, it is important to remind all concerned that these events are contingencies that may possibly occur, not sure predictions. Making the list or flow chart should be an interactive process with families fully participating. Many find this kind of planning hopeful, because it emphasizes all the actions that one can take to prevent and control possible crises. But other clients may feel threatened by addressing future crises. If this process begins to seem too threatening, one can merely list and post medical personnel that should be contacted in case need arises.

In short, although managing medical crises primarily is an issue between clients, their physicians, and medical teams, counselors can play a supportive role. That role includes assessing whether clients are open to this form of contingency planning, assisting clients in finding and organizing information, and in understanding fears, anxieties, and other barriers that may inhibit effective responses to a crisis.

MANAGING STRESS AND EXAMINING COPING

Living with disease is quite stressful because the client is trying to maintain a quality of life with varying degrees of diminished capacity, energy, and resources, as well as pain, psychological distress, and the increased demands of treatment. Often life in the chronic phase is full of small crises, constant problems with which the individual must deal. Managing stress is often a critical problem.

It is helpful to begin to deal with this problem by assessing both the client's current sources and symptoms of stress and the client's styles of coping with stress. Again, clients often find it useful to think about earlier challenges and crises that were resolved successfully. Not only can such a mental review enhance coping by reminding clients of past successful coping skills, it can also reduce anxiety by reminding clients of the times they had surmounted prior problems. Counselors should assist clients in understanding the ways that current lifestyle and current state of disease may inhibit or facilitate effective stress management. Proper diet, activity, exercises, diversion, and even humor may be adaptive mechanisms that can help build stress resistance. Counselors may also be able to teach effective techniques for stress reduction such as biofeedback, relaxation, or medication. In addition, clients should identify and alter or avoid situations that exacerbate stress.

In this period, counselors may have to challenge a client's unrealistic expectations. One cannot do everything that one did prior to the illness. It is important to recognize that energy is going to be expended in fighting the illness even when symptoms are not apparent. If a client is coping with time-consuming treatments, disruptive symptoms, or increased fatigue, maintaining previous activities and involvements is even harder. In these circumstances, surrendering certain activities or delegating responsibilities may help reduce stress. When these measures are only marginally effective and stress levels remain so high that health or sleep is advisedly affected, there may be reason to recommend medication.

However, there are alternatives to medication that clients may wish to try. One woman unable to sleep well since her diagnosis was reluctant to take sleeping pills both because she had younger children (and feared she would not wake up if they needed her) and because she wanted to minimize any drugs she was taking. She found sleep-relaxation tapes a helpful alternative. Since stress levels will fluctuate considerably during the chronic phase, stress should be constantly monitored throughout the illness.

MAXIMIZING SOCIAL SUPPORT AND MINIMIZING SOCIAL ISOLATION

During the chronic phase, clients and their families may experience a deep sense of social isolation. Often individuals and families have the perception that social support is more readily available in times of crisis such as the initial diagnosis.

There are many reasons for this perception. In the context of a clear crisis, need may be more apparent and appropriate ways to respond more clearly defined. If someone is hospitalized, friends have clear norms about what they are expected to do. But when an individual returns home, friends may be unaware of the continued needs of the patient and uncomfortable or unclear about what they should say or do. Other factors too may contribute to a sense of isolation. Separation from work or recreational roles may limit opportunities for interaction. The financial pressures of chronic illness as well as decreased energy levels or other symptoms of disease may also decrease individual and family interactions with others. Fears may further isolate the individual, as friends and family avoid patients and become worried, often needlessly, about possible contagion. The ill client must assess who in the network of family and friends can and does provide support. As mentioned earlier, the client can begin by listing the names of those persons the client counts as part of his or her support system. Often this simple act can give a person a comforting sense of just how extensive the network is. The individual may also wish to explore variables such as geographic distance, other roles, and obligations that might affect the ability of members in the network to provide support. The client may wish to examine the different relationships he or she has with varied members that may affect the level of perceived support and the types of support each person can best offer.

For example, some family members and close friends may have extensive ties, bound by mutual obligations, affections, and past support. With other persons, ties and expectations of support may have to be more limited. Once the network is defined, an individual can assess the ways in which he is using his network. Sometimes the problem is that others may not be able to provide the help needed. They may, however, be more comfortable in assisting in other ways. Again the technique, described in the prior chapter, of noting the types of support (listeners/doers/respite) is useful throughout the illness.

Here we may seek to add one more category—*saboteurs.* Saboteurs refer to friends who are destructive at this point in the illness. Saboteurs, for example, may sabotage adherence to a regimen in direct and indirect ways. Directly they can discourage adherence to a regimen. One adolescent client with juvenile diabetes had friends who would urge him to join their underage drinking, an action that would negatively affect his insulin levels. Other saboteurs operate in an indirect manner, challenging hope that might make clients less likely to adhere. One client, undergoing difficult but ultimately successful treatment for breast cancer found her mother-in-law's frequent comment after every treatment quite discouraging. She would always say, "Don't worry; when the worst happens, your children will be taken care of."

Another way to approach the issue of support is to ask the client about *surprises* in support. I usually begin by asking about negative surprises—the persons that the client thought might be there but are somehow missing. This offers opportunity for the client both to explore any feelings, such as disappointment or abandonment, and to assess factors that might be inhibiting expected support. It is also critical to explore positive surprises—persons who have responded better than could be expected. In one case, for example, a divorced father was pleasantly surprised by the support he received from his teenage son. This support helped validate his role as a noncustodial parent.

Reviewing one's network may also mitigate another potential problem. Some individuals, particularly older persons or individuals with younger families or dependent members, may have serious concerns about how others will survive their death. Reviewing one's network can be a useful way to build reassurance that the needs of others will continue to be met even if one should become seriously incapacitated or die.

It is also important for clients to avoid social isolation as much as possible. One may begin by assisting clients in assessing one's degree of involvement prior to the illness as well as the changes that occurred after diagnosis. This can suggest factors that contribute to isolation. Again, these factors can be varied and can include physical incapacitation, stigma, immobility, shrinking social roles, others' discomfort, fears or anxieties, or other psychological factors that inhibit interaction. Once these factors are identified one can begin to develop strategies to lessen this social isolation and reengage in social life.

Throughout this exploration, one needs to remember that there is an important distinction between isolation, which is an objective state, and loneliness, which is a subjective feeling. Clients can be relatively isolated, having few opportunities for interaction, but not feel lonely; or clients can be isolated and lonely. Others can have considerable interaction with others but still feel a deep sense of loneliness. This last state often reflects situations in which one interacts extensively but still feels that basic needs are unmet. And this, too, reinforces the connection between issues of isolation and support.

Finally, counselors may help clients identify sources of formal support to complement and supplement informal networks. These can include social service agencies, disease-related organizations such as the American Cancer Society, and self-help groups. Self-help groups can be particularly helpful in providing both resources of social support and activities and interactions that ease social isolation.

NORMALIZING LIFE IN THE FACE OF DISEASE

The central difficulty in the chronic phase is living with the disease. As the chronic phase begins, clients must try to accommodate the demands of daily life to the new reality of that disease. This struggle continues throughout the chronic phase, especially if further deterioration raises new complications.

Roles, relationships, and identity are often the major issues in attempting to maintain a normal life. Throughout the chronic phase, the disease can constantly assault a client's sense of self. Symptoms can be so intrusive that they may impair the ways in which the client views and relates to others. The client's sense of sexual identity and sexual relationships may be affected as well. Others can react with embarrassment, awkwardness, or even rejection, not knowing how to relate to the now-ill individual. Important roles may be compromised by the nature of the disease, its symptoms, and its treatment. The ill individual may be unable to function effectively in school, at work, or in other significant roles. Living a life as normally as possible is a key challenge of chronic illness. One of the first things that counselors can do is to fully explore the ways in which the disease has affected the client's life—considering the effects of the disease on the client's sense of self, roles, and relationships.

One of the biggest changes may be in the client's sexual relationships. Health, body image, self-concept, relationships with others, and sexuality are all closely associated. Changes in one area may affect all the others. For example, declines in health or certain forms of treatment may affect sexual desires or performance. Changes in body images such as scarring, particularly when it occurs in parts of the body associated with sexuality, may have similar effects. Even the attitude of one's partner can be affected by the disease. For example, one woman was reluctant to have sexual relations with her husband following his heart attack. She believed that the excitement would endanger his health. Her anxiety affected her sexual desire and ultimately her relationship with her husband.

The key to resolving sexual difficulties lies in honest communication. First, that means establishing honest communication with physicians and other medical caregivers. When I train caregivers, I stress the importance of taking a good sexual history of patients and periodically monitoring the effects of the illness on sexual behaviors and relationships. Patients should be encouraged by the counselor to discuss their sex lives. Often such discussion can clear up any myths or misunderstandings that might be impairing sexual expression. Similarly, self-help groups or counselors can also be helpful in examining the ways in which an illness might influence sexuality.

Of course, honest communication is essential between ill individuals and their partners. Each needs to openly share feelings and experiences about what is comfortable and what causes discomfort. Sometimes patience and compromise are also necessary. One woman, for example, was reluctant to undress in front of her husband following a mastectomy. He constantly reassured her that her operation made no difference to him. He found himself angry and frustrated that she did not accept his assurance, and she felt pressured. In counseling, they were able to reach some compromises. She recognized their needs for intimacy and her husband recognized her need for privacy at this point in her life. She undressed privately and in the dark. Recognizing her needs, he no longer felt that his assurances were ignored.

This case also illustrates two additional points. First, sometimes counseling can be very effective in assisting couples as they examine their sexual relationship during the course of illness. Second, couples can sometimes learn through a counseling process that sexual intimacy is multifaceted and does not always have to be expressed through sexual intercourse. One client shared that one of the most erotic and intimate experiences he ever experienced was his wife's gentle massaging and kissing at a time when he was too frail for other sexual acts.

Other roles and relationships may change as well. In focusing on the ways in which the disease has changed a client's life, one can determine factors that inhibit normalcy and develop creative solutions to difficulties. For example, one man who had returned to work while he was struggling with cancer believed that his supervisors were being overprotective, sheltering him from work challenges that he felt would be a welcome diversion. In counseling, he explored his own reasoning as well as that of his supervisors. He role-played various ways in which he might approach them until he found an approach that he thought would be both personally comfortable and effective. He then was able to resolve his work difficulties. Families and friends may be overprotective, perhaps even overbearing, inhibiting one from reaching one's potential and sometimes even inducing dependency.

In other cases, though, the client may be reluctant to accept the fact that the continued deterioration of health or the demands of treatment may have made the continuance of a previous lifestyle difficult if not impossible. Here the counselor may need to realistically explore what roles can be maintained and what roles will have to be modified or even surrendered. In some cases, one may discover alternate opportunities that allow one to maintain, perhaps in a limited fashion, important roles. In one case, for example, a college professor, already on reduced load, was reluctant to give up his two last classes. His dean, however, was deeply concerned both that he was so debilitated that teaching would be difficult and that he very well might not survive until the end of the semester. As the dean and professor discussed their mutual concerns and needs, they were able to develop an effective solution: both courses would be team taught with an adjunct (or part-time) instructor selected by that professor.

Not every situation can be so easily resolved. Decisions to leave work can be constrained by financial reasons. One young man who had developed a form of muscular dystrophy in his 20s found that the physical demands of his work increased his sense of weakness and fatigue. Although he was in the early stages of the disease, his physician advised him to take a less physical job. However, given his lack of education, only construction work paid a wage that allowed him to maintain his financial independence. Leaving this work provided stark alternatives: he would lose his medical insurance, and he also would have to return to a conflicted home that he had left only two years earlier. Even telling his boss about his condition did not seem viable to him since he doubted whether he would be permitted to keep his job if his condition was known.

Again, self-help groups can be effective resources in assisting one in normalizing life. Support and self-help groups can often provide "tricks of the trade" or strategies that one can use in normalizing life. In addition, they can offer acceptance, moral support, and models of successful adjustment. Often they are reservoirs of creative and effective problem solving. However, everyone must make a decision as to whether such groups are personally helpful. For some, these groups may reinforce an unpleasant sense of being different.

The key to normalizing life in the face of disease lies in negotiating the conflicts between the client's wants, the client's needs, and the client's abilities. Counselors can begin by assisting clients in assessing what they want to do, what they need to do to maintain a quality of life, and what they are able to do at this point in the illness. Once these wants, needs, and abilities have been clarified, counselors can facilitate clients as they find creative solutions that allow living as normally as possible within the constraints posed by the disease and treatment.

DEALING WITH FINANCIAL CONCERNS

The most significant stress within the chronic period is often financial. Life-threatening illness often has adverse financial effects. Medical bills mount at the same time that income is reduced. Incidental expenses are legion, including transportation to and from hospitals, meals eaten out in the course of visits and treatment, special diet supplements, perhaps increased child-care costs, environmental modifications, and even such things as new clothing perhaps necessitated by significant changes in weight or other physical symptoms of the disease.

Four approaches may assist in helping to cope with financial difficulties:

First, it often helps clients just to become aware of the costs of illness. In many cases, clients may be experiencing financial pressure and may not yet have identified the increased demands that cause it. Often just listing the money spent on incidental expenses in a given time period can be a revelation. Once these costs are determined, one can develop a budget. In some cases, this may be the first time that clients have even had a need to budget.

Second, counselors can assist clients in identifying possible resources within their circle of family and friends as well as community resources. Transportation costs might be reduced if one used friends or community resources for rides. The local chapter of the American Cancer Society may, for example, provide transportation at little or no cost. If eating out costs too much, clients can pack a lunch. Understanding what the illness actually costs can help clients plan alternate strategies for reducing cost.

Third, clients may also need to identify and explore their resistance and reluctance to use social services or support. Americans like to think of themselves as self-sustaining and independent. These beliefs may become even stronger during life-threatening illness. With everything else in disarray and while coping with physical dependency, it can be difficult to recognize another form of dependency. Yet it is precisely at this time that clients need help the most. Counselors should help clients to review when independence is functional and when it is not functional. Again, sometimes counselors can help explore this and even serve as advocates in arranging supportive services.

Finally, sometimes the services of financial planners can be helpful in assisting one in making decisions on how and when to tap into financial resources. Sometimes clients may need their help to learn how to set up journals to document medical and related expenses for tax purposes. There may even be financial instruments such as reverse mortgages or viaticals (where an ill person sells his or her life insurance to a broker for a partial settlement) that might alleviate a financial crisis.

Again, these decisions are not purely financial. Selling stocks or annuities may also involve letting go of future dreams. Estate planning can reaffirm one's own mortality and occasionally reopen old issues. One client, for example, was reluctant to sign a will since he had hoped to include a bequest to a sister. But he was unwilling to make such a bequest since they were still not reconciled. Yet not to include her in the will suggested an unwelcome finalization of their present alienation. In summary, financial and estate planning, necessitated by the current illness, can raise psychological and relational issues that one may need to address. Understanding that discomfort, and exploring it with family or counselors, is part of this process.

One of the more difficult financial problems may involve health insurance coverage. Even with insurance, the costs of a major illness can be staggering. Because many insurance companies are trying to control these costs, they may challenge certain costs incurred by individuals. For example, many insurance companies may refuse to pay for treatments they regard as experimental.

Insurance hassles can be highly upsetting. They can become one more stressful thing for an ill client to deal with, generating strong feelings of anxiety, anger, and even betrayal. Counselors obviously cannot solve such issues for clients, but the counselor can assist clients in dealing with the stress that might be generated and help to identify resources such as insurance agents, benefits coordinators, or lawyers to aid clients in finding information and asserting their legal rights.

PRESERVING SELF-CONCEPT

Sometimes in the chronic phase, clients will begin to internalize a self-definition that includes the disease and deterioration experienced. To many people the central aspect of their self-concept is now that they are "a person with a disease," different and stigmatized by that fact. I remember one twelve-year-old boy who had leukemia. At the time he was in remission and as active as any young adolescent. Nothing in his appearance indicated the disease, but its impact was seared into his psyche. He frequently began conversations with the phrase "When I was normal . . ." thereby revealing the degree to which the presence of disease was now a central part of how he viewed himself.

The more clients continue prior activities and relationships, the easier it is to preserve self-concept. Some individuals also find it helpful to use varied techniques to preserve their physical self-concept. For example, if a client loses hair in chemotherapy, wearing a wig may help. Families and caregivers can have a significant role in preserving an individual's sense of self, because the more caregivers and family members treat a person as normal, the easier it is for that person to maintain a sound sense of self. Counselors should periodically question clients about the ways in which the disease has influenced their sense of self—validating feelings when necessary and developing strategies for minimizing effects when appropriate.

REDEFINING RELATIONSHIPS WITH OTHERS THROUGHOUT THE COURSE OF THE DISEASE

During the chronic phase, the effects of the disease may also impinge on the client's interactions with others. Life-threatening illness has the potential to severely affect social relationships. Others who know the diagnosis may have difficulty interacting with someone who is both seriously ill but still appears healthy and vigorous. Preston (1979) discusses what he calls the "Gregor effect." He draws from Kafka's famous story "Metamorphosis," in which the protagonist, Gregor, wakes up one morning to find himself transformed into a giant cockroach. But it is his family's subsequent treatment of him as an insect that really modifies his own self-perception. Their behavior reinforces this new reality. Treated differently he becomes different. The Gregor effect implies that the diagnosis of disease becomes a stigma, a mark that impinges on all other social roles and affects all other relationships and interactions. In her book *The Private Worlds of Dying Children* (1978), Myra Bluebond-Langner notes this change: "Until the diagnosis was made (about the second or third day after admission), the children were, in their own eyes and in the eyes of their parents, not different from other children. . . . Once the diagnosis was made, however, everything changed. People, especially the family, started to treat the children differently, who then noticed the change" (p. 172). In short, the presence of life-threatening illness can change relationships with others. The new status, the illness role produced by the diagnosis, adds uncertainty to every relationship and every other role. These changes can continue throughout the course of the illness.

The key issue for clients is to recognize that every significant change in their life has a ripple effect that influences every other part of life, including every relationship. Life-threatening illness is a significant change, one that generates many ripples.

It is important for clients to understand the ways in which the illness has affected other relationships. Perhaps others are uncomfortable—not knowing what is expected of them or how to act; they may either avoid the client who is now ill or act differently. Here, honest communication can sometimes help. In some cases, changed situations, such as leaving a work role, can change relationships. Without the common bond, the relationship may not generate the interest or time to sustain itself. A philosophical attitude can sometimes help. One client undergoing treatment for cancer expressed it well: "There are," he said, "some friends who are there for me when I'm sick—others who are there for me when I'm better; I've learned to treasure both."

VENTILATING FEELINGS AND FEARS

At every phase of illness, clients have to cope with feelings and fears. These feelings and fears may be quite varied and include many of the responses noted in an earlier chapter. Counselors should be aware that the nature and the intensity of these feelings may vary with the course and trajectory of the illness.

Often these feelings will intensify at crisis points within the illness or in periods characterized by continued deterioration. At such times, fears and feelings associated with disability, dependency, and dying may loom large, perhaps even becoming overwhelming. In such periods all assumptions, rationalizations, and other defenses may be challenged. For example, clients may reassure themselves that if they adhere to the treatment, or continue certain activities such as prayer or meditation or change behaviors, the illness will be arrested. These defenses may allow one to effectively defend against the disease for a while and resume a normal life. But physical deterioration or a medical crisis can overwhelm such a defense, generating strong affect and anxieties.

Different types of treatments can be associated with changes in affect or anxiety. In some cases treatment may ease primary or secondary emotional side effects. For example, depression may be a side effect of some medications, and others can cause fatigue or irritability. Hospitalization, too, even if routine, can reinforce fears of dependency and death. Clients may exhibit a great deal of ambivalence about treatment even when the treatment seems relatively unobtrusive, routine, and successful. They may worry about the psychological and financial costs of the illness to their families.

Even at times in the illness when clients are in remission, they may still experience many emotions and anxieties. Clients may be unrealistically optimistic, anxious, irritable, highly depressed, or have any variety of possible responses. The very fact that things are going well may make some clients anxious—causing them to look for bad news or an expected blow. The point is that counselors should not assume in these relatively tranquil periods that clients will be free of emotional stress. In fact, in seemingly tranquil periods one may have more time to reflect upon feelings and fears. During this time, too, clients may have less emotional support from others, who may be constantly encouraging one not to think negatively, thereby denying one's honest and natural emotional responses.

Since the course of disease is likely to change, clients must adjust to the constant changes posed by the disease. Whenever clients experience these changes, it is important to discuss their feelings and fears, particularly the meanings that they give to such changes. Perhaps the change is viewed as only a temporary setback, or perhaps the change is perceived as an ominous omen, foreshadowing continued decline and eventual death, dashing any hope of recovery or even relative stability. These meanings may not be the same meanings that counselors or medical professionals place upon the change. But, in any case, it may help to review with clients the changes and their meanings, assist clients in assessing the validity of their concerns and fears, consider the effects that these changes will have upon one's life, and determine strategies for dealing with these changes. In addition, with every significant change in illness, one may need to review the viability of any previous decisions, for example, whether or not to work, and to reconsider contingency plans.

Thus, throughout the chronic phase, counselors should allow and encourage their clients to ventilate and explore their emotions in a nonjudgmental and accepting atmosphere. And because feelings and fears may vary considerably, depending on the nature and course of the disease, the counselor should follow the ill individual's lead. It is not unusual that individuals ride an emotional roller coaster, shifting back and forth between times when they feel positive and upbeat, and other times when they feel depressed, angry, or lonely.

In some cases, just ventilating these emotions may allow clients a sense of resolution and comfort. Counselors can also assist clients in identifying confidants with whom they can share their feelings and fears.

In other cases, listening may not be enough. Individuals may need to develop ways to resolve their emotional conflicts or to develop strategies for handling their anxieties and feelings more effectively. In one case, a 30-year-old Hispanic male with testicular cancer was deeply troubled and consumed by guilt, attributing the disease to sexual sins. Encouraged to explore ways of resolving that intense guilt, he reached back to his past religious traditions, engaging in the sacrament of Confession with a sympathetic priest. Following his penance and absolution, he felt emotionally healed. In another case a 50-year-old female who was battling cancer was able to recognize her anger and its effects on her family, and to develop alternative strategies—in her case, pounding on dough—to defuse her feelings.

FINDING MEANING IN SUFFERING, CHRONICITY, UNCERTAINTY, OR DECLINE

With continued chronicity and uncertainty, clients may have to constantly rework issues and tasks raised within the chronic phase. They may need assistance in understanding the peculiar stresses of long-term uncertainty and the implications of that uncertainty for their behaviors and relationships. Such uncertainty may impair any ability to plan. Hypersensitivity and distrust may be generated by long periods of uncertainty. Some clients may believe information is being withheld and scrutinize every remark of both family and caregiving staff searching for clues. They may have a sense that the illness is taking too much time and become angry, depressed, or resigned.

Whatever the experience of illness, the ill person has a need to try to understand and interpret that experience. "Why am I suffering?"

"Why did this happen to me?" "Why did it happen now?" These questions are attempts to struggle with the meaning of the disease—or, even more fundamentally, with issues of purpose and meaning in life or death. Each client will need to struggle with these questions on his or her own, either answering the questions in a way that is personally meaningful or deciding that these questions are ultimately unanswerable. To some clients, illness and the consequent suffering may simply be random acts, whereas to others it can be a punishment, an occasion to learn or grow, an opportunity to connect with the suffering of others and develop empathy, or even part of a large, yet unknown, cosmic plan. It is not the counselor's role to offer an explanation for suffering. Counseling offers opportunities for reflection and insight. Frankl (2004) emphasized that although one may have no choice *about* suffering, one has choices *within* suffering. To Frankl, persons who can find meaning in suffering are best able to cope. Questions such as "What have you learned from this experience?" "How has this experiences changed you?" "How has this experience made you different?" can challenge clients to find meaning and purpose in their illness and, by that, make that suffering a transformative experience.

THE END OF THE CHRONIC PHASE

The chronic phase has several possible resolutions. In some cases treatment, although it may have been long and painful, can produce a total cure. Some ill individuals may experience a partial recovery. In other cases, the condition can stabilize, leading the individual to experience an extended period of chronic illness and ongoing uncertainty. And, finally some will experience continued decline—entering a phase where care becomes solely palliative.

In summary, the chronic phase is a long, uncertain, and difficult period for both individuals and their families. But it is also a time of opportunities—opportunity to fight to regain health, opportunity to make the best of the time that one has, and opportunity to live and experience life in its fullest sense even when fighting disease and possible death.

REFERENCES

Bluebond-Langner, M. (1978). *The private worlds of dying children.* Princeton, NJ: Princeton University Press.

Frankl, V. (2004). *Man's search for meaning* (new ed.). Bel Air,. CA: Rider & Co.

Hayes, R., McDonald, H., & Garg, A. (2002). Helping patients follow prescribed treatment: Clinical applications. *JAMA: Journal of the American Medical Association, 288,* 2880–2883.

Preston, R. (1979). *The dilemmas of care.* New York: Elsevier.

Strauss, A. (1975). *Chronic illness and the quality of life.* St. Louis: Mosby.

Weisman, A. (1980). Thanatology. In O. Kaplan (Ed.), *Comprehensive textbook of psychiatry* (pp. 129–139). Baltimore: Williams & Wilkins.

10 Counseling Clients in Recovery

INTRODUCTION

At any phase in life-threatening illness a partial or full recovery may occur. Perhaps the original diagnosis was wrong or too pessimistic. In other cases initial treatment may be successful in effecting a cure, perhaps immediately following the diagnosis or after a chronic phase. On rare occasions, even in the terminal phase a recovery may be experienced. Recoveries may be partial or complete. In some cases one may retain no apparent ill effects from the disease. In other cases, however, one may experience diminished abilities, carry physical scars, or bear psychological injuries.

Recovery and *cure* are perhaps among the most welcome words in life-threatening illness. I remember the great sense of celebration when we learned my father would fully recover. Happily, these words are used more and more often. However, it is important to recognize that although these words are used more often, recovery does not mean that clients simply return to the life led before. Any encounter with a crisis changes people. Persons are no longer the people they once were. Even a recovery leaves certain issues that must be explored and tasks that must be completed as one attempts to move on with one's life. These tasks include:

1. dealing with the physical, psychological, social, financial, and spiritual residues of illness
2. coping with ongoing fears and anxieties, including fear of recurrence
3. examining life and lifestyle issues and reconstructing one's life
4. redefining relationships with caregivers

DEALING WITH THE PHYSICAL, PSYCHOLOGICAL, SOCIAL, FINANCIAL, AND SPIRITUAL RESIDUES OF ILLNESS

There are often a series of aftereffects to life-threatening illness and treatment. There may be physical scars or permanent disabilities. Clients may need to develop responses to these physical effects. Clients may also have to grieve secondary losses that result from these physical changes. One young woman whose leg was amputated, for example, grieved the loss of her athletic career. This activity had been both an important part of her self-identity and the center of her social life and friendships. Others often invalidated these expressions of grief, reminding her that a leg was a small price to pay for recovery. Although this sentiment may be true, it did not make her loss any less real. Once the crisis of the illness was over, she was left to consider that cost. Only then, once the threat was past, could she realize what she had lost and grieve about the way her life had changed. She recognized that her sense of self-identity was changed by her bout with life-threatening illness.

There may be other emotional and social scars as well. Clients may continue to experience a range of emotional responses, often including anger and guilt. They may be angry that one had suffered, guilty about lifestyle factors that they believed contributed to the illness, even guilty over recovery—especially if peers in treatment died.

There may be social disruptions as well. Clients may feel disappointed by the response of family and friends. In some cases spouses or lovers who were supportive during the crisis may feel free to leave now. Friends too may feel uncomfortable with the recovered person, perhaps even fearing disease. In other cases, recovered individuals may find their friends' concerns trivial or unimportant, affecting mutual support and ultimately the relationship. After a bout with cancer or another life-threatening illness, it can be hard to be sympathetic when friends or families experience seemingly minor problems. One client shared with me her friend's exasperation. She would always try to comfort her friend with the comment, "Well, at least it's not life threatening." After a particularly difficult day, her friend rebuked her, saying, "Do I have to have cancer to get sympathy and support?" The incident reminded my client of both the perspective she had gained from her illness and her need to be aware of others' needs.

Some may find it difficult to establish new intimate relationships, perhaps because they fear the future. Others may be reluctant to become involved with someone they fear may become ill.

Employment and careers can also be changed by the illness. One may have lost or left a job during the illness. Coworkers may be fearful. One may encounter discrimination because of medical history that affects the ability to obtain a position, change jobs, or advance. Some people may experience demotions or dismissals.

There may be financial effects. Obtaining life insurance or medical insurance may be difficult. One may have exhausted savings and piled up considerable debts.

There often are spiritual residues to life-threatening illness. One's sense of security may be threatened. The way one looks at life may change. One's faith and beliefs may be altered. Some may find a deeper sense of spirituality, whereas others find their religious perspectives challenged.

These effects can sometimes be long lasting. A colleague and his wife decided not to have children. He had had extensive chemotherapy and radiation treatments during a struggle with cancer during adolescence, and so he and his wife feared possible birth defects. Although this fear may or may not have been realistic, it does illustrate how one's encounter with life-threatening illness may affect decisions and choices even decades later.

Counseling can be very helpful during the recovery phase, providing an opportunity for individuals to explore these remaining issues. Often it is helpful just to have concerns recognized and validated. Many times, individuals who have recovered from life-threatening illness are made to feel ungrateful if they complain. After all, they are told, they are lucky to be alive. This may be true, and most individuals recognize this truth, but it still does not change the fact that illness and recovery extracted a fearful price. I have found that just asking clients about the effects of an illness—all the effects, physical, psychological, social, spiritual, and financial—reassures them that it is acceptable, even in recovery, to recognize the high and continued cost of illness.

Once these concerns are recognized and explored, counselors can assist clients in developing ways in which to deal with them. Perhaps a client can discuss concerns with family, friends, clergy, or coworkers. In some cases there may be administrative or legal remedies to particular problems such as job or insurance discrimination. It is important that each individual make decisions about the ways to handle these aftereffects of illness that are comfortable for him or her. Not every solution will be the same for everyone. For example, some individuals will find prosthesis or reconstructive surgery important to their sense of normalcy and their own self-image, whereas others may find reconstruction or prosthetic devices unnecessary.

Self-help groups such as Cancervive for persons who have recovered from life-threatening illness can also be helpful. These support groups can help individuals realize that they are not alone in coping with their concerns. The stories and accounts of other members may provide ongoing inspiration as well as successful strategies for dealing with the problems that persist in recovery.

COPING WITH ONGOING FEARS AND ANXIETIES, INCLUDING FEAR OF RECURRENCE

It is very normal and natural following an experience with life-threatening illness for an individual to continue to have a strong sense of anxiety, depression, or other similar reactions. There are several reasons for this. An experience with life-threatening illness reminds one how quickly illness or death can threaten.

Second, the individual may experience continued anxiety about recovery and activity. What can one do? How much should one attempt? What is really pushing the limit? Is this recovery progressing at an expected and/or acceptable pace? These questions can continue for a considerable period of time after a recovery. Sociologist Rodney Coe (1970) once compared recovery to adolescence, describing it as a continuous, often anxiety-ridden, test of reemerging strength against ongoing, increasing life demands.

Finally, there may also be high anxiety about the recurrence of illness. Individuals may be highly sensitive toward symptoms that are associated with the return of illness. For example, a woman who had recovered from cancer particularly feared stomach pains because she believed such pain was a likely sign of metastasis. Many persons who have recovered from life-threatening illness suffer anxiety whenever they have a routine doctor's appointment. One client who had recovered from cancer shared that she had a panic attack every year before her annual checkup with the oncologist. Patients recovered from a heart attack may be very anxious about chest pains, arm pains, fatigue, shortness of breath, or other related symptoms; recovered stroke victims may be highly agitated by symptoms associated with stroke, such as numbness, headaches, or blurred vision.

Clients need not only validation but also strategies to deal with these fears. Counselors can validate the importance to discussing these anxieties with others. Counselors also can challenge gently unrealistic or an even superstitious belief, such as that if a fear is expressed, the feared outcome may occur. In come cases, once clients recognize the source of fear, they can be encouraged to speak with their physician; physicians can frequently provide helpful information about the pace of recovery or the real risks of recurrence. They can also help one to assess changes in lifestyle or preventive health behaviors that might minimize chances of recurrence or new disease. These changes may also give one a renewed sense of control that lessens feelings of vulnerability.

Many individuals may also find imagery and meditation useful. Imaging continued health and recovery, taking time to relax and meditate, pursuing diversion and exercise are all ways to reduce anxiety, manage stress, and reaffirm personal well-being.

Self-help groups may also be valuable. They can allow opportunities to discuss and to explore concerns in a trusting and accepting atmosphere. Again, other survivors can provide reassuring role models.

EXAMINING LIFE AND LIFESTYLE ISSUES AND RECONSTRUCTING ONE'S LIFE

One of the natural desires in recovery is to turn the clock back; to go back to the way things were prior to the illness. Although this is a natural and normal wish, it is unlikely to be achieved. Often too much has occurred during the illness, changing both recovered individuals and their families, to simply resume earlier patterns of life. Clients must recognize that although one cannot go back to the way things were, they can establish a new lifestyle with a different and new sense of normalcy.

The illness may have changed relationships with family or friends. Each person affected by the illness has changed—and perhaps grown as well. For example, children may have learned to be more independent during the course of a mother's or father's illness. Often family roles have also changed. In one case a young wife took on increased responsibilities for the family's business when her husband became ill. Following his recovery, she had no desire to relinquish her interest in that business.

Sometimes a return to the past may not even be desirable. Perhaps poor health or lifestyle practices contributed to the illness. For example, in one case a 41-year-old man had to realize that a return to his previous stress-ridden job and unhealthy lifestyle would likely re-create, in short order, the conditions that led to his heart attack. Like many persons recovering from illness, he needed to identify and change negative health practices.

Finally, illness sometimes changes one's personal priorities. Things that seemed important in the past may no longer seem so essential now. Many times people will grow through the illness, reestablishing personal priorities. For some an encounter with life-threatening illness can be a positive turning point in life. Joe, a middle-aged man who recovered from cancer, now spends considerably more time with his wife and family. The illness experience reminded him just how important family was to him.

In recovery, it is important to reflect upon and review the illness experience. What has the illness taught? How has the experience changed you as a person? How has the illness affected your relationships with others? How has the relationship changed your spiritual beliefs and practices? What insights have been gained? Reflection can often help integrate the client's experience of illness into his or her own sense of personal biography. In my counseling with persons who have recovered, I often use three questions that I have adapted from a very special colleague, Dr. Catherine Sanders, who used them in her grief counseling. The questions that I ask clients to reflect upon are:

What do I need to leave behind as I begin this new phase of life? This question allows one opportunities to consider the negative residuals of the illness experience. Perhaps there is a sense of vulnerability or anger that one recognizes would impair the sense of restoration and complicate recovery.

What do I want to keep from the illness experience? Not all aspects of the illness experience were likely to have been negative. One may have discovered renewed appreciation of life or family or friends. One may have developed new insights about oneself. One may have identified or improved significant strengths. One may have found renewed faith.

What do I want to add? The illness or its aftermath may have identified certain areas that need to be addressed. In some cases these may result from reordered priorities resulting from the experience. In other cases individuals may no longer have the opportunity to resume old roles, perhaps because of continued physical disabilities or other reasons. Individuals then need to address what new skills, values, or attitudes they may need to adapt to this new world.

As counselors review these questions with clients, counselors should caution clients to avoid rash decisions. It is critical to allow time to become aware of the person one has become as a result of the illness and to adjust to the new realities that exist. Clients may regret radical changes that are made in the emotional aftermath of recovery. In one case, a 50-year-old man recovering from cancer wanted to leave his business, return to school, and obtain an education degree. His counselor intervened to help him think more deeply about this change and how it would radically affect his family's financial stability and lifestyle. Together they also reviewed motivations for the career change, found a program in which he could take courses and maintain his job, and thereby plan a much smoother, and almost equally fast, career change.

REDEFINING RELATIONSHIPS WITH CAREGIVERS

Throughout the course of the illness one may have forged very close relationships with caregivers. Once a client recovers, it may be difficult to redefine these relationships or to say goodbye. The client may become anxious and resentful as caregivers' attentions begin to focus elsewhere. The client may feel a sense of abandonment, perhaps exacerbated by the caregivers' delight in the recovery and kidding comments that there is no longer reason to see one another. Maintenance of the relationship can even have a magical quality to some individuals, who believe that it will ward off recurrence.

Families, recovered individuals, and caregivers should avoid abrupt goodbyes. All may need to discuss their feelings about the relationships and ambivalence about termination. Each may wish to validate one another, focusing on what they have learned from the illness struggle. Each may need to redefine the relationship.

Sometimes individuals and families may have a need to acknowledge caregivers by giving appropriate gifts of thanks. This often enables individuals to reciprocate, at least symbolically, the help they have received. Although this is understandable and appropriate, it may make some caregivers uncomfortable. It helps if hospitals, hospices, and nursing homes have explicit policies on gift giving because individuals may be hurt or offended if caregivers refuse inappropriate gifts. Stated policies offer caregivers a clear rationale in accepting or refusing a gift. In some cases, caregivers may even use such policies to appropriately redirect gifts. One recovered furrier, for example, wanted to give a favorite nurse a fur coat. She found the gift excessive and in violation of hospital policy but was able to suggest giving the coat in her honor to a hospital auction.

Not all situations end so graciously, nor are all feelings so positive. In some cases individuals may have unresolved feelings including anger at staff. Here it may be important to take action that brings a sense of satisfaction. Individuals may wish to discuss their concerns with counselors, caregivers, or administrators. In one case a family was very upset at the emergency room of a local hospital, which had misdiagnosed their mother's heart attack. The emergency room had sent her home with a diagnosis of indigestion. Her personal physician insisted, upon hearing the report that same morning, that she be admitted to a larger university hospital. His action probably saved her life. Her family decided to deal with their anger by meeting with the local hospital's administrator. When cases do not involve gross negligence or malpractice, individuals may need to find other ways such as perhaps writing a letter that may never be sent, or adding an entry to a journal about their experiences and feelings.

In summary, recovery raises significant issues for individuals and families. Even in recovery there are tasks that must be worked through so that individuals can recover—not only physically, but psychologically, socially, and spiritually—and go on to resume changed, but hopefully enhanced, lives.

REFERENCE

Coe, R. (1970). *Sociology of medicine.* New York: McGraw-Hill.

11 Counseling Clients in the Terminal Phase

INTRODUCTION

At a conference I once attended as a student, a speaker described the terminal phase as the time when there is "nothing more to do." Even then, I thought that was a very unfortunate way to view the terminal phase of illness. Although there may be little to do to effect a cure or even to prolong life significantly, there is still much that can be done to keep the individual physically comfortable and to provide psychological, social, and spiritual support. Even in this terminal phase, individuals can still live their remaining days with both quality and meaning. For some individuals and their families, the terminal phase can be a significant time, one that allows ill individuals to die with dignity and a sense of completion, one that offers families opportunities to say their goodbyes in ways that will ease their deep sense of loss and grief.

The terminal phase begins when the medical goal changes from curing a person or maintaining that person in remission to providing palliative or comfort-oriented care. Now the chance of recovery or remission is remote. Death is not only possible; it seems predictable, even imminent.

This does not mean that the death is always easily predictable. Many persons, especially older persons, may suffer from multiple chronic conditions such as heart disease, high blood pressure, and diabetes, for example, in addition to perhaps a diagnosis of cancer. Managing multiple diseases is complex and does not always allow a predictable prognosis. Rather than ask for a predictable time frame, it is sometimes helpful to assess whether it would be a surprise if the patient died within the next six months. Such discussions can allow families to consider options such as hospice.

Usually the terminal phase is first recognized and defined by medical staff. Based on the conditions, symptoms, tests, and responses to treatment, physicians modify their definition of patients from "sick" to "dying." This changed prognosis is usually communicated to other medical staff and even to families and patients through direct means such as physician comments and sometimes through indirect means such as changes in treatment, subtle comments, or even evasions. One man, for example, told me that he first recognized his declining state when his physician ceased making his usual optimistic comments.

Often dying persons do not need a physician's confirmation of their state. Aware of the changes they are undergoing, they sense their impending death. Individuals may have a fair degree of medical knowledge and recognize not only internal cues but also external cues about their condition. One client told me that his first inkling of impending death occurred when he commented that next spring he wanted to plant an herb garden. His wife grasped his hand tightly, and with tears glistening in her eyes, she cried out "Of course you will." "She never," he wryly commented, "showed much emotion about my gardening." Moreover, ill individuals may have a high degree of sophistication about illness gleaned from interaction with other patients during the course of the illness, their own reading, the Internet, and TV. They begin to acknowledge the imminence of death even if they vary in their acceptance of that fate (Schroepfer, 2006).

Although individuals, families, and medical staff often share the perception of the transition from ill to dying, this is not always the case. Sometimes the person or the family may be reluctant to admit that the individual is now dying. Other times, individuals or their families may perceive that death is near even when medical staff feel that the patient is not dying or when medical staff recognize their patient is dying but still continue, perhaps inappropriately, to treat the person medically as if a cure or significant remission were expected.

In the beginning of this transition to the terminal phase the physical decline of the person may not be perceptible, or it may be seen as just another stage in a long, continuous decline. The person seems to be slowly fading away. As the physical decline continues, though, it is likely to accelerate and become more noticeable. When family and friends recognize accelerated decline, they focus increased attention on the dying person.

In the final period of the terminal phase, individuals may slip in and out of consciousness. By now staff, the family, and often the individual himself or herself recognize that death is near, that the last weeks and days are at hand. This is the period for leave-takings. Family, friends, and staff share their final farewells with the person, sometimes even when the patient is comatose. In some religious systems there may be a desire for final rituals such as last rites, receiving the Eucharist, or being blessed.

In this terminal phase, the client, even though dying, still retains basic human needs for contact and communication. A colleague, Edie Stark, at a professional conference, conducted one of the most valuable exercises I ever experienced. Edie asked this assembly of death educators and counselors, "What do dying persons need?" Soon the blackboard was filled with responses: "Understanding," "Honesty," "Good Care," "Touch," "Respect," "Listening," "Contact," "Love," "Relief from Pain," "Diversion," "Humor," and a host of other terms were quickly listed. "Now," Edie continued, "What does a living person need?" Edie had made her point: a list addressed to a living person's needs would be the same. Basic human needs do not change simply because the status or definition of a person changes. As long as we live, certain basic human needs remain the same.

Some human needs, though, are sorely challenged in the terminal phase, often by a misguided sense of protectiveness or by family or even medical staff's own needs. One key need that is too often forgotten in this period is the need for open communication.

DISCUSSING DEATH

The question of whether individuals know and recognize their state is now often moot as a result of changes in medical practice. Most of the early research in this area took place at a time when standard practice was to "protect" the person from the information of impending death. Research (Glaser & Strauss, 1965; Sudnow, 1967; Doka, 1982) has indicated the impossibility of this task as well as the negative effects of such policies. Often the practice of protection served to further isolate the dying person. For example, I once studied nurses' interactions with dying people in a hospital that discouraged discussions of death. I found nurses often avoided uncomfortable conversations by avoiding dying persons.

In other cases, inhibitions on discussions of death impaired the person's ability to finish personal business. When my aunt was dying of cancer, she became insistent about seeing me. I was somewhat surprised by the request because our relationship was cordial but not close. When I arrived at the hospital it was clear that my aunt wanted to see me alone. As my uncle left he whispered that my aunt did not know she was dying. As soon as he left she turned to me and said, "You know I'm dying." I took her hand and did not say anything. My silent assent prompted her to make a request. She had become ill right after a move into a new community and she never had the opportunity to formally join a church. She had been active in church all her life and it was important that she die a church member. But whenever she mentioned her desire to her husband, he told her she could join a church once she got well. Her request to see me was a last-ditch effort to break the bonds of pretense.

However, patients should never be forced to face death when they choose not to do so. There are some caregivers, and even family members, who feel that the failure of the patient to openly acknowledge and discuss death is a sign of a denial deemed unhealthy. Nothing can be less true or more destructive. The reality of middle knowledge means that patients, even in the last days of their lives, will move in and out of the awareness of death's imminence—sometimes accepting that truth, other times denying the inevitable prognosis. Open communication focuses on the needs of the patient—that is what the patient wishes to address rather than the desires of formal or family caregivers. The goal of open communication is to keep the dialogue open. A response of "yes" to a patient's query of whether he or she is dying leaves little more to say. Questions that allow the dialogue to continue would be much more in the interest of the patient.

When my father was dying, we (and my father was very much part of the decision) chose hospice care. While the care was excellent, there was one moment I wished would have turned out differently. My father, a highly independent man until his final illness, asked his hospice nurse one day when he would be able to drive. In a way, it was an unusual question. He was now so weakened that he barely left his bed. The nurse, surprised at the query, responded that he would never drive again—he was dying. He became angry. Always a gentle soul, he never complained, but turned his head and never really spoke to her again. It would have been far better to respond in a different way. "You really must miss driving." "It is hard to be so immobile." "Where would you wish to drive?" Any one of those responses would have both been honest and kept the conversation open.

Dying individuals themselves should be allowed to set the tone for conversation. By their own comments, individuals will indicate what they want to talk about and when it is comfortable to do so. My advice to families and caregivers has always been to do a lot of listening. The goal is to allow for open communication.

Open communication means many things. First, it allows "give and take." Two things can inhibit that process. One is when others take a protective attitude, being reluctant to truly communicate, limiting opportunities for interaction, even using evasion and deception. Communication, though, can also be inhibited when others overwhelm the patient, answering questions with so much information, so much *truth* that the patient cannot digest or even hear all that is said.

In communicating with dying persons there are some key guidelines that should be recognized:

■ **Let the Individual Set the Tone.** Often an individual's questions and comments will indicate what he or she wants to discuss. Because of "middle knowledge," it is important to recognize that the needs may change with different visits, and even with different stages in a single conversation. It is not unusual to have a meaningful conversation about an individual's fears and anxieties about dying one day only to return the next day and discuss a cruise a patient wishes to take when recovered.

Some people will choose never to talk about death. One man, recognizing that he had cancer, went over his affairs with his family. But from that initial point he made it clear that he wanted to avoid conversations about death. Such defenses as denial or avoidance have to be respected unless they endanger the person or others.

■ **Listen and Reflect.** A chaplain told me that one of the most significant encounters she ever had had with a dying person was when she simply sat and stroked the dying woman's hand while that woman share her feelings and fears. Many times caregivers may find the simple act of listening difficult. They so want to say something, anything, to contribute to the conversation, break the silence, solve the problem, or bring some comfort. Yet often a receptive silence, perhaps combined with some supportive touch, can be far more effective.

Similarly, when caregivers do respond, it is often helpful to respond in ways that allow the individual to reflect. Responding to a question such as "Am I going to die?" with another question such as "Are you scared?" conveys the message that one is willing to discuss any concerns, while still allowing the individual the freedom to choose what to talk about. Such a response also permits both the dying person and the other person engaged in conversation an opportunity to really understand what is being asked. Sometimes patients do not really want their questions answered.

■ **Remember One's Own Role.** In court cases hearsay and specu-
lation are not allowed. The same should hold true for communication. Questions best answered by physicians should be directed to
them. Encourage direct communication. Sometimes this may mean
being an advocate, informing medical personnel of a patient's needs
or helping individuals find ways to address their concerns.

■ **Communication is Nonverbal and Paraverbal as well as Verbal.**
Counselors can communicate much by paraverbal factors such as
tone, loudness, and cadence as well as nonverbal actions such as
expression and by other nonverbal behavior. Clear discomfort, avoiding patients, limiting opportunities for privacy—all communicate
much louder than words a reluctance to hear someone's concerns.

■ **Always Allow Hope.** In one's responses to dying persons, take
care not to extinguish hope. Nothing you say should extinguish the
hope that someone holds, however unrealistic it may be. One counseling intern felt that she had violated honest communication because
she had responded to a clearly dying person's comment, "I hope I can
recover," with the statement, "I hope so too." She had not failed: she
had allowed the person to set the tone, and she had responded in a
reflective way, with an answer that was sensitive to the patient's own
needs at that moment. Moreover, she was kind. One wise instructor
once told me "hope should not expire before the patient."

DECISIONS IN THE TERMINAL PHASE

When patients move into the terminal phase, they and their families
may have to make several decisions that can affect not only the quality of the patient's remaining life but also the ways in which families
adjust following the death. Often the decisions, such as whether the
patient should enter a hospice program and at what point interventions should be ended, are critical.

Should the Person Enter a Hospice Program?

Whereas other phases of life-threatening illness may be experienced within the home and community, the terminal phase is usually

experienced within institutions. Almost 80% of people die in hospitals or nursing homes. Many observers have noted that hospitals, because they emphasize intervention, aggressive treatment, and cures, are ill suited to care for the dying. In these settings dying persons often receive less attention from staff because staff is discomforted by death. Psychosocial needs of the dying are often ignored. In an atmosphere that emphasizes a medical model with cure or control of disease as desired goals, palliative care, and particularly pain control, are sometimes underemphasized. Patients may be subjected to overzealous maintenance or overly aggressive treatment as medical staff seeks to ward off death.

Obviously, the reality of how dying persons are handled varies among institutions. In any case, numerous variables influence the ways in which institutions both view death and treat their dying clients. Nonetheless, the observed failure of hospitals to adequately handle death led in the early 1970s to the hospice movement. As a social movement hospice care has had phenomenal success in the United States, growing from a single hospice in 1971 to more than 3000.

Hospice in the United States is more of a philosophy than an institution: although hospice care takes place in free-standing hospices and in special hospice units of hospitals and nursing homes, much hospice care is provided at home. Hospice has a philosophy that emphasizes palliative, comfort-oriented care, placing great attention on the management of pain and distress. Hospices have also stressed holistic care that addresses psychological, social, and spiritual needs as well as medical and physical needs. Hospice programs have pioneered a team approach in which physicians, nurses, social workers, counselors, and volunteers join with the dying persons and their families in the determination of care. This is a distinct difference from the physician-centered mode of care generally found in hospitals. Hospices often emphasize maintaining the continuity of the dying person's life by attempting to provide much care at home; institutionalization is generally a last resort. Hospices also recognize a continuing need to provide services, such as bereavement counseling for the family, after the death.

Sometimes people are reluctant to use hospice programs. Many may not have heard of the hospice philosophy or even be aware that hospice programs exist within their community. Sometimes caregivers are reluctant to discuss hospice programs with families since they believe the topic might upset them. Families and dying individuals may believe that entering a hospice program means "giving up." Or they may be troubled by the erroneous belief that once an individual enters a hospice program, he or she will not be able to leave it and will lose eligibility for conventional heath care.

As a result of such misinformation, many people who would benefit from a hospice program fail to enter one, or enroll so late in the illness that hospice really cannot provide them with a full range of services. Enrolling a person in hospice when the individual has only a few days to live and is semicomatose or comatose means that the person cannot draw upon the counseling services and social support that hospice can provide to increase the quality of remaining time.

Hospice programs can be a wonderful resource for a dying person and family. Hospice physicians and nurses often excel at keeping individuals physically comfortable. Counselors, chaplains, and social workers can assist patients and families to meet psychological, spiritual, and social needs. Volunteers can often help with care, providing needed respite for families. Bereavement counseling and support groups can assist families after the death. Many times family members are so impressed with hospice services that some become hospice volunteers themselves.

Physicians, hospitals, and social service agencies can offer referrals to local hospice programs. Many programs are listed in the phone book. Many hospice programs can accept Medicare or other insurance. Information about local hospices can also be obtained through the Hospice Foundation of America or the National Hospice and Palliative Organization.

Although hospices are a welcome option, they may not be appropriate for every person in the terminal phase. Many hospice programs, especially home care, require the participation of a "primary caregiver," such as a spouse, other relative, or friend, who can provide ongoing care. Many individuals, particularly elderly ones, may not have such a person. In some cases hospice care will be inappropriate for medical reasons—perhaps neither the dying individual nor the family are ready to recognize that there is no hope for cure or significant extension of life. Certain conditions have to be met if a person is to die at home. Family members have to be willing to nurse their loved one, have basic training in fundamental nursing skills, and have information about the dying process. Special equipment may be required. And both moral support and flexible, multidisciplinary assistance will be needed.

In recent years, many hospitals have begun palliative care units. These programs seek to apply the principles common to hospice within a hospital setting. They may offer an additional option for care at the end of life.

Ethical Issues at the End of Life

Patients, their surrogates, and families may have to make a series of ethical decisions at the end of life. These ethical decisions may include such as issues as what medical interventions might be implemented, refused, or withdrawn; whether or not artificial hydration and nutrition should be begun or withdrawn; whether to donate bodies, tissues, or organs; whether or not to accept palliative sedation in which the patient is totally sedated to ease intractable pain; and possibly whether the patient might take actions to hasten death such as, where legal, physician-assisted suicide.

It is beyond the scope of this book to fully explore the ethical implications of such decisions (see Doka, Jennings, & Corr, 2005). However, there are some counseling considerations that counselors should consider as they assist clients, surrogates, and family members.

Jennings (2008) argues that current end-of-life ethics are highly individualistic—emphasizing the ultimate autonomy of the patient. Jennings then calls for a more ecological perspective that understands the effect of these ethical decisions on the larger community of family and friends. For example, health surrogates—the person entrusted to make health decisions when the patient lacks the capacity to do so—are expected to follow any advance directives of the patients. In the absence of a clear advance directive, or in seeking to apply the patient-expressed wish to an often more ambiguous medical reality, the surrogate is expected to simply assess what the dying person would choose, or if that is unknown, what a "reasonable person" would wish.

Interestingly, although the surrogate has responsibility for the decision, there is no attention paid to what the surrogate's or the family's values and preferences are. This is a critical point, because the ethical decisions that are made at the end of life may seriously influence the consequent grief of the family (Doka, 2005).

Counselors then support clients in several ways as they struggle with these ethical concerns. First, they can provide information and assist in clarifying options and choices. Second, counselors can encourage a deliberative and inclusive process in which individuals who are dying (when they are able), families, and surrogates consider not only the wishes and values of the dying person but also the implications of these decisions upon the intimate network. Third, counselors can advocate for families. Many times medical staff may wish to quicken this process. Families may need space and time to process these decisions. Finally, even after the death, family members and surrogates may need to review their decisions.

Counselors should also acknowledge the stake that staff members have in these decisions. For counselors who work in health-care facilities, staff may need support so that these decisions do not create a sense of moral distress. In assisting families, particularly in decisions such as hastening death, counselors must be aware of their own values as well as local policies and legal mandates. Recently many professional ethical codes have begun to consider end-of-life ethics. Several of these codes allow counselors to counsel clients considering assisted suicide as long as they do not actually participate in a criminal act. Counselors taking on such a role may wish legal advice before they proceed as to whether even counseling in such situations violates state or local laws or runs afoul of professional licensing entities. Finally, counselors must concede the ways in which this process may be challenging for them as well and exercise good self-care.

TASKS OF THE TERMINAL PHASE

In the terminal phase the medical goal has changed from curing illness or prolonging life to providing comfort. The tasks in this phase reflect that transition. Comfort—physical, psychological, social, and spiritual—is the paramount concern. To achieve that comfort, individuals must face numerous problems that may challenge that goal. Among the tasks of the terminal phase are:

- dealing with symptoms, discomfort, pain, and incapacitation
- managing health procedures and institutional procedures
- managing stress and examining coping
- dealing effectively with caregivers
- preparing for death and saying goodbye
- preserving self-concept
- preserving relationships with family and friends
- ventilating feelings and fears
- finding meaning in life and death
- dealing with symptoms, discomfort, pain, and incapacitation

The terminal phase is generally characterized by constant physical decline. Dying individuals need to cope with the increasing intrusiveness of symptoms. They are likely to become progressively weaker and more fatigued. Physical deterioration may occur as well, affecting both identity and self-esteem. Throughout this period the dying may become increasingly dependent upon others.

Several issues may emerge as caregivers assist their patients in dealing with these issues. First is the issue of pain control. Some degree of pain may be a constant companion throughout the experience of life-threatening illness. Perhaps it was the first symptom that signaled the onset of the illness. Often it is an intermittent or ongoing problem throughout the chronic phase. In the terminal phase, with little activity and diversion, pain can become a pervasive reality.

Pain and suffering are multifaceted realities, experienced on many levels. On a physical level pain may be experienced acutely, in sharp intense periods, and/or chronically. Spiritual pain may result as people struggle with the meaning of life and death. The dying person may suffer the psychological pain of dealing with anxiety and loneliness, and social pain in coping with interpersonal loss. There may be financial pain, as when individuals worry about the financial impact of their illness and death on their families.

Often neglected in the study of pain is what might be called gender pain. This pain is caused when someone is treated not as a person, a man or a woman, but as an object. Any modesty the person may feel is discounted or ignored. One of the best illustrations I know of this occurred on a grand rounds several years ago. A group of doctors, unannounced and unanticipated, surrounded the bed of a seven-year-old leukemia patient. Yanking up the boy's shirt, the head physician stated, "Notice the spleen." After each resident had poked around a bit, they all left. There may be other manifestations as well. People may feel the loss of body image, a loss often exacerbated by the neglect of gender-related rituals such as manicures, hair grooming, or shaves. Individuals may also recognize that their sexual needs are ignored. They are no longer allowed to enjoy lovemaking or even cuddling or other forms of intimacy. This too can add to a person's pain and subsequent withdrawal.

One wise nurse practitioner, Phyllis Taylor (1983), defined the ever-present reality of all these forms of pain as "the most critical problem in the terminal phase." According to Taylor, pain sets up a destructive cycle that saps coping resources. Pain, in all its forms, often results in insomnia since pain is most intensely experienced at night when there is little diversion. This leads to greater irritability, causing family and friends to further isolate the person. This isolation increases the patient's depression, lessens coping abilities, and further exacerbates pain. Pain management, therefore, is the basic precondition to maintaining the quality of life and social relationships.

In the past 20 years, there has been incredible progress in pain management. A range of strategies including pharmaceutical, surgical, radiation therapy, as well as alternative therapies exist to alleviate pain. There is increasing recognition that since suffering is holistic, pain management must be team oriented as well, employing social workers, counselors, and chaplains along with health professionals. Today's medicine often does have the wherewithal to offer all but a small minority of patients both pain control and some degree of mental clarity. In cases where pain is intractable, palliative sedation may be an alternative.

Yet, although there is an ability to manage pain, there is often a significant gap between knowledge and practice (Doka, 2006). Counselors then have a role as advocates. They may need to remind medical staff that, now that the terminal phase has been reached, medical goals have changed from curing illness or prolonging life to palliative goals. Counselors may suggest alternatives, such as hospice care, in which palliative goals are clearly recognized and the dying individual's comfort is the basic priority. Previous medical concerns such as the danger of addiction or the physical risks associated with pain medication, although possibly legitimate during the acute or chronic phases, have less viability in the terminal phase and so may be gently challenged. Research has indicated that contingent strategies, that is, offering the terminally ill medication on request, can reduce anxiety and eliminate the need to display pain as antecedent to medication, thereby actually reducing the amount of medication requested.

Once pain is controlled, individuals can address other issues associated with physical decline. Individuals may need information on the meaning and nature of varied symptoms. Is this symptom or disability permanent or might it possibly subside? Is it to be expected? Can it be treated? What other symptoms might be expected? In addressing these cognitive concerns, caregivers must be sure of the person's real questions. The question "What will occur?" may be a request for information, a cry for reassurance, or a desire to plan. Only when counselors take time to fully understand the context of questions can they provide answers that are both honest and meet an individual's needs. For example, a man suffering from cancer once rather casually asked me if the back pain was normal. In discussing his concerns he revealed that he had deep fears that this pain might mean the cancer had spread to his spinal cord, evoking fearful images of an uncle's death from a different form of cancer, a death that left his uncle incontinent and paralyzed.

Questions about symptoms may reveal underlying feelings too. Individuals may need to discuss what these symptoms and increased dependency mean to them and what they are feeling. There may be behavioral dimensions as well. They may need to develop ways that they can more effectively cope with new and increasing limitations and incapacitation. Even limited intervention can help maintain dignity and reinforce a small sense of control. One man, for example, facing deteriorating bladder control, was able to develop an "emergency" code on his nurses' button that allowed him a "fighting chance" to get to the bathroom in time. And finally, in the face of continued evidence of physical decline, individuals may wish to review treatment decisions and contingencies such as durable power of attorney, living wills, or decisions not to resuscitate.

Managing Health Procedures and Institutional Procedures

Because, in some cases, the terminal phase may be lived within institutions, clients must cope both with the stresses of institutional life and with sometimes painful institutional procedures. Goffman (1961) has described the varied disconcerting aspects of institutional life, such as the facts that treatment is based on organizational rationality rather than individual choice, institutions control very basic behaviors such as eating, and that all 24 hours are spent within a single limited environment. Goffman also notes that these factors can generate a sense of role dispossession and depersonalization. In a hospital, one can be reduced to an object of medical care, losing personhood in the process. One's previous life and position can seem lost. These stresses can be exacerbated in certain units such as intensive care where rules are far more stringent.

The first question individuals and families must consider is whether the institution is an appropriate place. Alternatives to institutionalization in hospital and nursing homes, such as home care or placement in a hospice or palliative care unit, may minimize or eliminate many stressful conditions.

When such options are not available or useful, other strategies may assist in reducing institutional stress. Counselors can assist families and dying individuals in identifying and exploring factors that create stress. Once these issues are identified, one can develop strategies to cope more effectively with them. In some cases, a caregiver can serve as an institutional advocate or assist in empowering ill individuals or their families to create exchanges. For example, one man found his room stressful because it overlooked a busy street. His wife was able to assist in getting the room changed. In other situations no easy solution may be possible and counselors may have to assist individuals in developing more effective ways to adjust to the stress.

Often, issues of depersonalization and powerlessness can underlie a person's concerns. Thus empowering individuals and families to deal with these issues, or serving as an extension of the power of the person, serves a twofold function. Not only does it resolve the immediate problem, it also reaffirms an individual's sense of power and control at a time when he or she may feel such control is missing. The individual's concern with control has other implications. It suggests the importance that even minor factors can have in exacerbating stress. For example, one man was very upset with bureaucratic slowness in replacing his broken TV. Staff could not fully appreciate his concern, since his roommate was graciously sharing his TV. However, for the individual in question, the failure to replace the TV reinforced his own sense of powerlessness and depersonalization, exacerbating his stress. Counselors can help to reinforce a sense of control by providing choices whenever possible. Such choices may include scheduling times for treatment, having a role in selecting staff, and deciding on the presence of others in treatment.

Even knocking on an open door returns power to people. I learned this lesson early. In my clinical training I met a successful businesswoman now dying of cancer. Each morning I knocked on her door and asked whether I could make an appointment to talk. She would open up her appointment calendar, and we would negotiate a time. Personalizing the environment may also mitigate institutional stress. Determining a suitable form of address, allowing personal effects, and allowing modifications of the environment increase comfort and lower the stresses of institutional life.

Managing Stress and Examining Coping

In addition to managing institutional stress, dying individuals must cope with all the stresses to dying. Roberts (1988) has pointed out that dying is an insolvable crisis insofar as nothing the individual can do can change the fact of impending death. To Roberts, the crisis of dying can overwhelm a dying individual's coping mechanisms.

Caregivers, counselors, and family members need to respect and to support each individual's attempt to cope with the crisis of dying. Although individuals' ways of coping may differ, caregivers and families should remember that their major goal in this phase is to maintain comfort.

No individual's methods of coping should be challenged unless they affect the health of others or the dying person's well-being. It is worthwhile for family and caregivers to explore with dying persons ways to reduce any stress they are experiencing. In some cases dying persons may wish to minimize stress by withdrawing from stressful situations. For example, one man dying from cancer decided that he really had to withdraw from his small business. As difficult as it was for him to give up that role, it eliminated a great deal of additional stress. In other situation modifications in the person's environment may eliminate some sources of stress. In one situation the hospital where a young boy was dying from cystic fibrosis relaxed its rules on both the number and the ages of visitors.

In still other situations, providing additional psychological, social, and spiritual support, or strategies such as diversion and imaging, can help the dying person cope with any stress. For example, one dying woman found visits from an unstable sister upsetting. Not wishing to bar her sister's visits totally, she did arrange for other relatives to be present whenever her sister visited.

Although it may be worthwhile for individuals to examine their ways of coping, individuals may not have the energy or time to develop new coping styles. In these cases caregivers should emphasize adapting coping style to the crisis. For example, if someone is responding to a crisis with inappropriate anger, it would make sense to try to direct the response into different channels rather than spending a great deal of time in exploring the roots of that anger. As much as possible, use support and respect current coping strategies.

One particular stress in the terminal phase arises from the sense that time is running out. Caregiver and family sensitivity to that issue can considerably reduce a dying individual's level of stress. I once read a handout at a hospice conference. The handout listed a variety of comments and requests from dying persons. A second column listed typical responses. A third column listed a suggested response. The requests were things like "I would love to smell a rose" or "I'd enjoy a pepperoni pizza." Typical responses were statements such as "Tomorrow I will pick you a rose" or "Thursday the menu includes pizza." The suggested response was always the same: "Do it now!"

Dealing Effectively with Caregivers

Individuals and families have to deal with numerous caregivers. Throughout the terminal phase they may have to cope with physicians, nurses, therapists, technicians, psychologists, social workers, chaplains, volunteers, and more. All these people will have their own personalities and characteristics. And in many cases, patients and families will be forced into interactions in which they have little control, with persons whom, to varying degrees, they may find difficult. Too many, even well-meaning helpers can overwhelm individuals who now have limited resources.

Counselors can assist individuals and families to honestly and openly share and explore their relationships with varied caregivers. This provides opportunities to consider factors that might facilitate or impede relationships with caregivers, to examine any underlying patterns in relationships, and to identify and solve any problems with difficult relationships. Often such examinations may even provide insights into their own relationships with each other and with other informal caregivers among family and friends. It may assist in identifying personal factors and stereotypes that might affect interaction with caregivers. Family members and ill individuals must also recognize and explore the possibility that they may be projecting their own unresolved feelings and conflicts on to staff. For example, as an individual slides into a terminal decline, both the family and the dying person can feel tremendous anger. This hostility can be directed toward caregivers. Sometimes one particular caregiver becomes the focus of this anger. One older woman I counseled was able to recognize that her dislike for one particular nurse was a projection of unresolved feelings toward her sister. In another case an African American man was able to recognize that his negative reaction toward the various nurses and aides was connected to antipathy for West Indians.

In some cases staff may not recognize personal feelings and behaviors that inhibit their reactions to certain individuals. Caregiving staff may need assistance in understanding why others perceive their own interpersonal styles negatively. They may need to identify their own hidden agendas, and reaffirm the fact that individuals have their own ways to face impending death, perhaps including defenses, such as denial, that some caregivers find troubling. Naturally, family must interact carefully and gently so that they do not needlessly complicate their own relationships with these caregivers and exacerbate any existing conflicts between the patient and these caregivers.

There are other things family members can do to build positive relations between the dying individual and staff. It is important to help staff to see the individual as a person rather than simply as a patient. Personal effects of the individual can generate a sense of individuality. One male patient's "grandpa pajamas" were a constant conversation starter with staff. Another simple but effective strategy for families is to fill a small bulletin board with pictures of the individual's family and the individual himself or herself engaging in favored activities. Such simple things can often facilitate interaction and the discovery of common interests shared by the patient and the caregiving staff. Moreover, pictures and the like serve as a constant reminder of the personhood of the patient.

Preparing for Death and Saying Goodbye

There is a process of anticipatory bereavement that complements the process of anticipatory grief. In the latter, individuals mourn a loss that is anticipated. In the former, individuals take objective actions in anticipation of, or in preparation for, that loss.

Some dying person may wish to get his or her affairs in order in preparation for death. "Putting one's affairs in order" can mean different things for different people. It may mean arranging financial affairs: making sure papers are in order, that the family is aware of critical details, that final decisions regarding business are carried out. It may involve actions regarding family relationships: the dying person may seek to reconcile with an estranged relative, receive a visit from a loved one who has moved far away, or say goodbye to every member of the extended family. They may wish to plan their own funerals.

Counselors can have vital functions when dying persons approach this task. In some cases they can assist individuals in their work, perhaps by serving as intermediaries. In other cases they can review with the persons the decisions he or she has reached; in cases where decisions may be hastily made or impaired by physical or mental disabilities resulting from the illness, caregivers can help guide the individual to make better decisions. The decisions individuals make at this point may be of critical importance since they may affect the individual's spiritual need to die appropriately. Counselors can help them to define what is appropriate for them, as well as empower them to control that process as much as possible, and they can interpret their actions and wishes to other family members or staff. For some individuals "dying appropriately" may mean peacefully accepting death. For others it may signify a desperate struggle right up to the very end.

Throughout this period there may be additional moments of crisis and distress, caused perhaps by the knowledge that there is nothing more to do medically, by new disabilities that presage further dependence, by medical crisis, or by final decline. One man, for example, who described himself as resigned to death, found his equilibrium disturbed when further physical deterioration left him incontinent. He openly wept at this new indignity, complaining that he was destined to leave life as he entered, in an infantlike state of dependence.

In the final phases some individuals may find it important to say goodbye. Other individuals may seem to hold on, perhaps waiting for a particular individual to visit or a significant date to arrive. Some may seem to withdraw. Counselors may have a role in helping interpret these and other behaviors to family and friends, as well as providing support, referral, and assistance at the time of the death.

It is important, however, not to force such issues. Some clients will continue to function as if death will never come. Counselors need to understand and respect that strategy as well and perhaps even help families to understand the basic truth that everyone chooses his or her own way to die.

Preserving Self-Concept

In the terminal phase, self-concept is assaulted in many ways. Physical deterioration resulting from the disease can damage self-image and self-esteem. Such deterioration, often joined with decreased energy levels and increased disability, may lead to withdrawal and disengagement from social roles and relationships. The underlying condition or the fact of impending death can create a sense of stigma, of being different, that can inhibit interaction with others. Erving Goffman in his book *Stigma* (1963) describes this reaction as a "flooding" in which the stigma becomes so overwhelming that it impairs the ability to function in other roles. The dying individual is no longer seen as a wife or husband, a mother or father, a sister or brother, a good neighbor, a teacher, or whatever, but only as someone who is dying. People then become awkward or embarrassed in the dying person's presence, and they withdraw from him or her. A destructive cycle is set in motion in which the terminally ill person, treated as less than human, begins to perceive himself or herself in such a way. This may be particularly evident when severe disfigurement accompanies the illness.

The counselors own treatment of the ill individual will be an important factor in his or her ability to preserve a sense of self. Moreover, it models effective interaction for family members and even medical staff. Treating the dying person as normally as possible is essential. The counselor may again need to serve as an advocate for the patient who is dying. Continued emphasis on daily tasks such as grooming and dental care reinforces a sense of personhood. The use and care of articles such as glasses, false teeth, prostheses, or wigs can reinforce aspects of identity. The ill individual still needs to be treated as a man or woman, and his or her privacy and dignity still must be maintained. Touching can be particularly important, because physical contact emphasizes the important reality that illness or nearness to death has not made the person unclean or untouchable. However, ill persons should never be touched or hugged without their permission, for touch may be physically painful, psychologically uncomfortable, or culturally inappropriate. Observing individuals' comfort with touch, or asking them whether they are open to touch, can avoid creating such discomfort. Finally, models of care that allow individuals mutual participation in treatment not only reinforce a sense of self but also reinforce coping and decrease medical resistance.

As in the chronic phase, ill individuals must consider the effects of illness on other roles and relationships. In this ongoing process individuals may need to decide which roles they must let go, which they can maintain, and which can be redefined. And, they can explore the effects of those changes on their own sense of self.

Preserving Relationships with Family and Friends

For the reasons discussed in the previous section, relationships with family and friends often deteriorate in tandem with the physical health of the individual during the terminal phase. Because the person is perceived now as dying, family and friends may withdraw, have problems with knowing how to interact, or become overly protective and paternalistic.

Counselors can do three things to help individuals to preserve their relationships with family and friends. First, the effects of the illness on relationships should be reviewed. For example, if an individual complains of loneliness, one can examine the degree to which he or she is isolated, as well as factors that may be contributing to isolation or to a feeling of loneliness. In some cases the individual may not be isolated at all. For example, a feeling of loneliness may result from a lack of *meaningful* encounters.

In one case a woman dying of cancer wanted to discuss her feelings and her fears for her family after her death. The family had great difficulty with such communication, often trying to deflect such serious thoughts. As a result, she felt increasingly dissatisfied and lonely even though she had a constant stream of visitors.

In other cases loneliness can result from an objective isolation. Causes can vary from the family's disengagement and discomfort to the person's own behaviors, such as intense anger, that may be driving the family away. Once the effects of the illness on relationships are understood, the dying person, the family, and the counselor can develop approaches to mitigate such effects.

Second, it is important to review family interaction for possible negative behaviors. For instance, family behaviors around meals and eating can be very revealing. Families can often become highly agitated when clients cease to eat. Such an act may have multiple meanings to the family—suggesting perhaps that the individual has now given up or that death in imminent and unavoidable. Family members may not always recognize that needs change and appetite may be affected by illness and treatment. I have sometimes seen families treat a 90-year-old man like he was a nine-month-old baby, frantically trying to convince him to eat. Counselors can not only educate families here on the changing physical needs that result as persons approach death but also help teach them other ways they might nourish the client spiritually and emotionally by affirming their love and support and sharing valued reminiscences. In other cases, family members can focus so much on the bright side that the individual's real concerns are ignored. Third, counselors can be helpful in enabling families, friends, and individuals to interact more effectively with one another. Dying persons and their families sometimes need to be told that they are misinterpreting signals. In one case, a middle-aged man dying of cancer complained to me that his wife was withholding information about the school and behavioral problems of their teenaged son. I discovered that she was reluctant to "dump" more problems on her dying husband, particularly because in the recent past he seemed to balk when these topics came up in conversations. With my assistance they were able to understand past communication difficulties. The husband recognized his own ambivalence: On the one hand, he was the boy's father, but on the other hand, there were days when he just could not cope with another problem. Husband and wife were able to develop a code that could communicate their intentions. Every day the husband would ask about their son, Sean. When she had had problems with Sean, the wife would answer, "You know Sean." The husband would follow up on days when he felt able. On other days, he would simply sigh and say, "That Sean." Moreover, both husband and wife were able to identify alternate sources of support to assist the wife and son. In summary, then, counseling can assist families in recognizing that all human needs remain in force until the very end of life.

Counseling may also include advocacy with hospital staff. In some cases, dying persons may need modifications of procedures or space so as to meet these needs and preserve meaningful relationships. One hospital was very sensitive to married couples' needs to preserve sexual intimacy, providing them with the space and privacy they required. However, a counselor did have to advocate for similar private space and time for a gay couple.

Ventilating Feelings and Fears

Although individuals may experience a wide range of emotions in the terminal phase, anxiety, sadness and depression, and guilt are particularly common in the terminal phase. Pattison (1978) notes that dying persons can have numerous anxieties arising from fear of the unknown, loneliness, sorrow, loss of family and friends, loss of control, suffering and pain, regression, and a variety of other sources. Pattison further suggests that anxiety can be alleviated by the caregiver's supportive presence, a willingness to explore fears in an open and honest way, and a readiness to advocate, when suitable, for more effective pain management or more control.

Sadness and depression, too, are common in the terminal phase. Although sadness and depression are both common and understandable, caregivers should not assume that sadness and depression should never be treated. When the quality of an individual's life deteriorates, physicians, family counselors, and other caregivers should consider possible talk therapies and/or pharmaceutical approaches.

Whereas sadness and depression may be expressed verbally, particularly in reactive depression, or through disengagement and disinterest, it may also be expressed by means of suicidal comments. Suicidal comments are common in the terminal phase, and they should be taken seriously. Suicide rates are higher among those with terminal illness, and possibly more accepted by others (see Range & Martin, 1990; Saunders & Valente, 1987).

When individuals express suicidal thoughts, counselors may wish to assess how viable the threat is. Four areas of exploration are often helpful.

1. Imminence. How soon does the individual expect to attempt suicide? Is it a future thought or a present plan?

2. Provocation. What has occurred to make the suicide viable now? Is the individual experiencing a current crisis or new disability?

3. Plan. Does the individual have a plan? How well defined is that plan?

4. Means. Are the means to complete the plan available? Can the individual physically carry it off?

Three interventions may prove useful in inhibiting a suicide:

1. The comment "I don't want to live" frequently means, "I don't want to live *like this*." Often defining and alleviating the "like this" may forestall suicide.

2. Another approach is to delay and contract. Here the counselor seeks to have the individual delay the suicide and may enter into a contract by which the individual promises to contact the counselor or to perform some other specified preventive action prior to any suicidal act.

3. Counselors, caregivers, and families may seek to "suicide-proof" the environment, removing any obvious sharp instruments, limiting the presence of medication, and providing regular observations.

Other feelings, too, may be found in the terminal phase. For example, guilt may be common. The life-review process may make individuals feel guilty about acts they committed or failed to commit in the past. They may feel responsible, morally or medically, for their deteriorating condition or for their failure to respond to treatment. In such cases, caregivers will want to assist individuals in exploring their guilt. Sometimes this exploration will help individuals to develop a sense of resolution. Having explored their guilt, they may now be ready to dismiss it. In other cases different interventions may be necessary. Some people may need to resolve guilt by speaking to an empty chair or by writing a letter. They may need to search their religious traditions to find a sense of forgiveness. They may need to develop and participate in rituals drawn from religious traditions that provide a sense of atonement.

Although anxiety, sadness, depression, and guilt are common responses in the terminal phase, any emotional response can occur. Whatever the response, counselors can assist individuals and families in examining these emotions, seeing the ways that these emotions affect their life and relationships, and—when necessary—developing strategies that will help them to cope with their emotions more effectively.

In assisting ill loved ones in coping with these emotional responses, counselors should remember both the limited time frame and the overall goal of psychological comfort. With death drawing near, there may not be time to fully explore every emotional response. It is unnecessary that the individual effectively resolve all previous conflicts. Rather, the goal should be to facilitate, to the degree possible, emotional balance and comfort.

In the terminal phase, individuals often mourn their own impending deaths. Rando (2000) described a process of anticipatory mourning, noting that persons may mourn losses that are impending as well as those that have already occurred. Dying individuals can anticipate and mourn their own loss. Not only does the dying person have to cope with the loss of self and the threat of nonexistence, he or she must simultaneously deal with the loss of loved ones, because he or she faces in impending death the termination of all relationships. This grief may be expressed as sadness and depression or in other responses typical of grief.

But, despite that this grief is normal and natural, family and friends may discourage its expression. In some cases, family and friends continue to deny the inevitability of death, urging the individual to maintain a positive attitude. In other cases, the dying person may wish to protect the family, assuming a cheerful demeanor. In such cases, counselors have a special role in providing a safe and supportive environment in which clients can express their reactions to loss.

Finding Meaning in Life and Death

Spiritual and existential needs are often accentuated as clients face death. Often the very fact of death focuses one inward, as one engages in a reflective struggle to meet one's own spiritual needs. These may include three issues.

One spiritual need is to die appropriately. This means dying in a way consistent with one's self-identity. There is no one, right way to die. Not everyone has to "accept" death. Some may fight death bitterly to the end. Others may deny, or even ignore, death. Some will want to preserve life until death can be held off no longer, and others will want to die while they still maintain some control over their destiny. In short, each person will define an appropriate death differently.

Dying appropriately also means being able to interpret and understand the experience of death. Understanding the meaning of suffering and death is difficult in a society in which pain seems to have no purpose and meaning. Phillipe Aries (1981) in a historical study of death points out how images of the "good death" have been reversed. In the Middle Ages the most feared death was one that was sudden or one that occurred during sleep, because in these cases the dying person had no time for spiritual preparation. In that period, the pain experienced was believed to help compensate for sin; pain on earth diminished the amount of time a sinner would have to spend in Purgatory after death. Although a lingering death is more common now, there is often no framework in which to interpret or understand suffering. Now many persons seem to ask for a quick death without pain, even if such a death involves lack of consciousness.

Counselors can assist patients and families in assessing what an appropriate death means for them. Counselors can sensitively question clients when clients are able to be so self-reflective. "What constitutes a good death for you?" "Who would you wish to be around you?" "What would you wish to happen?" Such questions can help clarify what an appropriate death means to that client.

A second spiritual need is a transcendental one—to find hope that extends beyond the grave. Changes in the focus of hope are a hallmark of the terminal phase. Earlier in the illness the person may have expectations (perhaps entirely realistic) of cure, arrest, or remission. In the terminal phase these may still be "desired hopes," but they are no longer considered likely. In other words, the person's hope is focused not so much on physical survival but on the ways that his or her life may continue even after physical death. A young client of mine was diagnosed with cancer. Early in the illness he had hopes of a total recovery. In the terminal phase he began to emphasize his beliefs in an afterlife.

Such hope may be rooted in religious or spiritual beliefs of an afterlife. It is interesting to speculate that much of the interest in near-death experiences may represent a recasting of a traditional theological mode of belief in an afterlife into a quasi-scientific framework that is more reassuring in a secular age.

There are other modes of symbolic immortality. The biological mode defines immortality by reference to one's progeny. In the creative mode, continuance is found in one's creations, whether they are the singular accomplishments of the great or the more mundane contributions of the average. The "eternal nature" and "transcendental" modes, like the theological mode, refer to different belief systems. "Eternal nature" would be a belief that one's remains will, in some way, return to the chain of life. Transcendental beliefs would refer to a wide range of beliefs that assert that death moves one toward union with God or the universe. In the communal mode one's life is seen as part of a larger group; as long as the group survives, each person lives within that community's memory. In the medical mode, a sense of immortality finds expression in the hope that one will live on because parts of one's body, such as the eyes, heart, or kidneys, will live on in others (Lifton & Olsen, 1974).

The third spiritual need is to find meaning in life. Developmental psychologists and sociologists assert that the knowledge of impending death creates a crisis in which one reviews life to integrate one's goals, experiences, and values. This need is met when one can affirm the value of one's life. The failure to find such meaning creates a great sense of despair that one has wasted one's life.

Life review and reminiscence therapy can be highly useful tools in assisting clients in creating a sense of meaning. In addition to that great value, life review and reminiscence serve other roles such as reaffirming the continuity of the person's identity. This is particularly important because it can boost the morale of the patient, restoring his or her self-esteem and perhaps, if done with or around medical staff, reasserting the accomplishments and achievements of the patient in a way that creates a sense of parity with staff (Magee, 1988).

Simple acts, such as asking individuals to talk about themselves and their past, may often be enough to generate a flood of memories. Other actions may also prove useful: reviewing photographs, whether personal or related to a given time period; listening to music popular during a person's early life; journal writing are good ways to engender such memories. Constructing family trees and genograms; asking about the individual's life; reviewing family treasures; sharing family stories and humor; constructing life peaks-and-valley lines; even making pilgrimages to special places can also encourage reminiscence that can validate the person's life. Remember that all senses, not just hearing and seeing, can evoke memories. Touching fabrics or other materials, smelling certain scents, even tasting special foods can all be used to unleash memories.

Counselors may also have to help dying persons construct a sense of meaning. Often individuals may need to review the work they have done, the lives they have touched, even the events they have witnessed to gain that sense of significance. For example, one 90-year-old woman who felt she had not accomplished much in her life was able to take great comfort in the fact that she started her life in the horse-and-buggy era and lived to see man walk on the moon. Counselors can also encourage family members to share reminiscences about the part the dying individual had in his or her life, recalling kind acts or the ways in which the dying individual affected them. One client recalled how reminiscing with his dying dad reminded his father of all the good times that they had shared, thereby resolving the father's concern that he had not spent enough time with his son.

Life review therapy also uses many of these techniques. Here, though, reminiscence is combined with careful history taking and astute observations. For example, the counselor may question why the client skipped through a period of life so quickly or seemed reluctant to engage in conversation about a given event. In addition, in life review, the counselor often seeks to have the client attribute meaning to events. "What did you learn from that event?" "How did the experience change you?"

Sometimes the life-review process can uncover regrets or unfinished business. Often this may be subtle. For example, an individual may constantly repeat a certain story. In one case an older man repeatedly talked about his time as a young officer, reviewing a clash of wills with an experienced sergeant. I noted that this man seemed to figure prominently in his account, and I asked him what troubled him about the sergeant and the experience. He then told me a story of how he resented the man's authority and advice. Once, to assert his own control, he ordered his men to attack the enemy in a certain way that ignored the sergeant's suggestions. His men fell into a devastating ambush, and he had carried a heavy load of guilt since that time.

Counselors may have to assist the individual achieve a sense of resolution if that is a need of the individual who is dying. Counselors need not suggest such if it is not a need identified by the person who is dying. There may be several ways that any necessary resolution can happen. In some cases there may still be opportunity for some form of resolving action. For example, there was still time and mutual motivation for a dying man to reconcile with an estranged sister. In other cases, experiences may have to be reframed. One dying teacher, for example, had strong regrets about his own children's modest educational accomplishments. She was able to find success, however, in the impact she had upon her students' lives and the achievements of some of her educational protégés. Finally, in other cases, individuals may need to spiritually reinterpret their lives. Every faith and philosophical tradition has a concept of forgiveness, including self-forgiveness. Once individuals express regrets or guilt, others may encourage them to draw upon their spiritual beliefs to find that sense of forgiveness and resolution.

In deciding whether to embark on a life-review process it is important for counselors to consider two issues. First, the life-review process is a time-consuming, individually directed, interactive process. There may be questions of whether such a directed process can be successfully completed in the time that remains. Second, the goal should be palliative, thus careful of avoiding psychological conflict.

There are other strategies, in addition to reminiscence and life review, that can be useful to clients in reconstructing a sense of personal life meaning. Some individuals may wish to have living eulogies. Here family and friends are invited to come together in a ritual to share their memories and eulogies prior to the death. Dignity therapy trains volunteers and staff to record the life history of dying patients. Within 24 hours, the story is presented as a bound book or some other generativity document and read to the patient and family. The family then retains the document. Research has shown such an approach to be highly beneficial for patients and families (McClement, Chochinov, Hack, Hassard, Kristjanson, & Harlos, 2007).

Ethical wills allow the client to acknowledge and pass on the values that he or she would like to see preserved and honored within his or her family. Even beyond such formal approaches or documents, counselors can assist clients in developing legacies simply by asking questions such as: "How would you wish to be remembered by those around you?" "What stories do you wish that they would tell about you?" "What are the values you wish to pass on to those you love?" "What are the lessons you would wish they would learn from your life?"

This last task reminds counselors to be generally sensitive to the spiritual needs of their clients. Counselors always, as part of their history taking, should assess clients' spirituality. Clients should be encouraged to address such issues as what they believed caused the illness, the role that their faith has played in helping them both understand and cope with the disease, as well as the rituals and practices they find helpful. Effective spiritual care allows individuals to define their own spirituality and describe their own spiritual needs (Pacholski, 2006). This may range from religious observances (such as prayer, rituals, and the like) to secular acts (observing a sunset or reading poems). When individuals do not have theistic beliefs, it is still important to assess what gives them a sense of meaning and purpose and what helps them cope with their illness. Naturally this should be done in a way sensitive both to their stance and to a possible fear of being proselytized.

This spiritual task reminds counselors and clients that every experience, even those that are painful and fearful, provides opportunities for continued personal development and growth. Without roman-ticizing the experience of dying, counselors can also err when one views a dying person's life in terms of the past tense.

THE SPECIAL PROBLEM OF THE COMATOSE PERSON

Even in the period in which the individual is comatose, communication can still continue. It is unclear when people are comatose how recep-tive they are to external stimuli. But there is anecdotal evidence that suggests some people may maintain hearing, at least on some level. Counselors need not neglect comatose persons. They can encourage family members to continue communication. Family can be encour-aged to stroke or hold or touch the individual while gently speaking to him or her. This period can often be an excellent opportunity for fam-ily members to address remaining with the dying person. Two cases illustrate this point. One involved an 18-year-old boy who always had a difficult time communicating his feelings to his father. As his father lay comatose, he was able to finally verbalize his love. In another case a wife was able to finally forgive her dying but comatose spouse for the ways in which his alcoholism had affected their life and family. In both cases this opportunity to communicate facilitated later grief adjustment.

Family members and other caregivers may also use this period for gentle reassurance or continued rituals. One chaplain used to make a point of visiting comatose individuals on his rounds, stopping at the bedside to hold the person's hand and gently recite a favorite and familiar prayer or psalm.

Sometimes in this period, family or caregivers may wish to address the issue of the impending death. If this is their need, counselors can encourage them to do so. Let me offer a dramatic illustration. One older man continued to visit his wife—a woman who had been comatose but seemingly holding on to life for months. The visits were always extraordinary painful for him. His wife continued to thrash in her bed even though the staff assured him she experienced no pain. Acting on his counselor's recommendation, the husband took his wife's hand and recited the Lord's Prayer and the Twenty-Third Psalm, two favorites of hers. She seemed calmed, because the thrashing ceased.

The woman and her husband had both been orphans. In fact they had met in an orphanage. They had had one child who was killed in World War II. One of the woman's concerns had been leaving her husband alone. Remembering this concern, her husband softly told her that it was all right to let go, to die, because their friends would take care of him. She died that night.

AS DEATH APPROACHES

The last moments of the terminal phase have been called the *death-watch*. If staff members suspect death is near, family members are notified so that the person does not die alone. Even here there are interventions that can assist the dying person and the family. Beth Israel Hospital in New York City has begun a Doula program. *Doula* is a Greek word for midwife. At Beth Israel, the doulas are volunteers who serve as "midwives" for the dying, serving as patient advocates and attempting to assist the transition from life to death.

Musical thanatologists are another innovative intervention during this final period. Based on medieval manuscripts, musical thanatologists play harp music during the deathwatch, which is supposed help control respiration and allow the patient to peacefully transition to death. A recent evaluative study found that although these vigils (as they are called) had no discernible effect of respiration, they did lessen wakefulness and decrease agitation (Freeman, Caserta, Lund, Rossa, Dowdy, & Partenheimer, 2006).

Sometimes, though, such predictions are hard to make so that a deathwatch can last much longer than staff anticipated, or the individual may rally and stabilize for a while, leading to a subsequent deathwatch or even a succession of such deathwatches. The terminal phase ends with the pronouncement of death. But this end is simply the beginning of the end of the first phase of the family's grief.

REFERENCES

Aries, P. (1987). *The hour of our death.* New York: Knopf.
Doka, K. J. (1982). The social organization of care in two pediatric hospitals. *Omega: The Journal of Death and Dying, 4,* 345–354.

Doka, K. J. (2005). Ethics, end-of-life decisions, and grief. In K. Doka, B. Jennings, & C. Corr (Eds.), *Ethical dilemmas at the end-of-life* (pp. 285–296). Washington, DC: The Hospice Foundation of America.

Doka, K. J. (Ed.). (2006). *Pain management at the end-of-life: Bridging the gap between knowledge and practice.* Washington, DC: The Hospice Foundation of America.

Doka, K. J., Jennings, B., & Corr, C. (Eds.) (2005). *Ethical dilemmas at the end-of-life.* Washington, DC: The Hospice Foundation of America.

Freeman, L., Caserta, M., Lund, D., Rossa, S., Dowdy, A., & Partenheimer, A. (2006). Music thanatology: Prescriptive harp music as palliative care for the dying patient. *American Journal of Hospice & Palliative Medicine, 23,* 100–104.

Glaser, B., & Strauss, A. (1965). *Awareness of dying.* Chicago: Aldine.

Goffman, E. (1961). *Asylums.* Garden City, NY: Anchor.

Goffman, E. (1963). *Stigma: Notes on the management of spoiled identity.* Englewood Cliffs, NJ: Prentice-Hall.

Jenning, B. (2008). Dying at an early age: Ethical issues in pediatric palliative care. In K. Doka and A. Tucci (Eds.), *Living with grief: Children and adolescents* (pp. 99–120). Washington, DC: The Hospice Foundation of America.

Lifton, R. J., & Olsen, G. (1974). *Living and dying.* New York: Bantam Books.

Magee, J. (1988). *A professional guide to older adults life review: Releasing the peace within.* Lexington, MA: Lexington Books.

McClement, S., Chochinov, H. M., Hack, T., Hassard, T., Kristjanson, L. J., & Harlos, M. (2007). Dignity therapy: Family member perspectives. *Journal of Palliative Medicine, 10,* 1076–1082.

Pacholski, C. M. (2006). Spiritual assessment in clinical practice. *Psychological Annals, 36,* 150–155.

Pattison, E. M. (1978). The living-dying interval. In C. Garfield (Ed.), *Psychological care of the dying patient* (pp. 163–168). New York: McGraw-Hill.

Rando. T. A. (Ed.) (2000). *Clinical dimensions of anticipatory mourning: Theory and practice in working with the dying, their loved ones, and their caregivers.* Champaign, IL: Research Press.

Range, L., & Martin, S. (1990). How knowledge of extenuating circumstances influences community reactions towards suicide victims and their bereaved families. *Omega: The Journal of Death and Dying, 21,* 191–198.

Roberts, M. (1988, April). *Imminent death as crisis.* Paper presented at the annual conference of the Association for Death Education and Counseling, Orlando, Florida.

Saunders, J. M., & Valente, S. M. (1987). Suicide risk among gay men and lesbians: A review. *Death Studies, 11,* 1–23.

Schroepher, T. (2006). Mind frames towards dying and factors motivating their adoption by terminally Ill elders. *Journal of Gerontology Series B: Psychological Sciences & Social Sciences, 61B,* S129–S139.

Sudnow, D. (1967). *Passing on: The social organization of dying.* Englewood Cliff, NJ: Prentice-Hall.

Taylor, P. (1983, January). The patient's pain: Strategies for caregivers. Presentation to Philadelphia Chapter of the Forum for Death Education and Counseling.

12 Counseling Families During a Life-Threatening Illness

INTRODUCTION

Implicit in all the previous chapters is the recognition that any life-threatening illness is always a family disease because family members are intimately involved in every phase of the illness. Not only the ill individual but also all members of the family will have their lives changed in both subtle and significant ways throughout the course of the illness.

It is important to understand the effects of illness upon each family member and the family as a whole. Only then can counselors assist families in understanding the ways in which the experience of a member's illness affects them as well as the ways in which they influence any individual's response to the illness.

Throughout this chapter, I will use the term "family" in the broadest possible context. I define "family" interactively rather than strictly biologically. Family refers to anyone who is part of a close circle with whom the ill person interacts, shares information, and feels bound to by strong personal, reciprocal, and obligatory ties. Some may define this as the individual's "chosen family" or "intimate network." Such a term encompasses not only lovers, but also friends, and perhaps even others such as ex-spouses, all of whom may become participants in the person's struggle with life-threatening illness. In my counseling one of the first tasks is, in fact, to determine who constitutes the person's circle or intimate network or "family."

THE EXPERIENCE OF ILLNESS: A FAMILY PERSPECTIVE

The family involvement with illness often precedes the period of diagnosis. Families may be involved by noticing and assessing symptoms or by suggesting diagnostic tests. They may be consulted as the person begins to decide upon a course of action, choosing, for example, to delay or seek medical help. The ways in which individuals and families interact throughout this prediagnostic phase can be very revealing, because they suggest patterns that persist throughout the illness. In one case a young man concealed his symptoms and doctor's visits from his parents and other family members so as not to worry them needlessly until after he knew what his problem was. This protective pattern continued throughout the illness, inhibiting the ability of others to provide support and causing his family considerable frustration and even resentment.

In the prediagnostic period families may have to cope with considerable anxiety and uncertainty. Their responses may illustrate coping mechanisms that will be used throughout the illness. Some may deny symptoms or the implications of these symptoms, whereas others fear the worst. Family members may experience other emotions as well. Often there may be guilt associated with their fears. It is not unusual for family members to worry about what the illness will mean for the individual and *what it will mean for them.* When family members harbor such thoughts, these beliefs, however normal and natural, may be defined as selfish, becoming a source of guilt or a cause for conflict.

Even at this early prediagnostic phase an element of uncertainty about the future may be introduced. Already there may be subtle alterations in behaviors between individuals and families. Patterns of communication, sexual relationships, and even power may be affected by the threat of illness.

In the diagnostic period families learn what they and the individual struggling with disease must face. This is not to suggest that all uncertainty is now over. Even a diagnosis may still leave considerable uncertainty about treatment, course, and prognosis.

It must also be recognized that ill individuals may make disclosure decisions that inform specific family members in different ways. Some individuals may decide not to divulge full information about the illness to any family members or to tell the whole truth to just a few members of the family, perhaps developing cover stories to present to other members. Often children and adolescents will be given partial or even untrue information. In one case an older man found he had prostate cancer. He shared that information with two of his three adult children, charging them not to tell his wife or other son. He also selected not to share the information with other relatives or friends; to all others, he was undergoing minor surgery for a benign tumor. He reasoned that he did not wish to worry his wife, who had a heart condition, or cause his other son to return home after he had just relocated in a distant state to begin a new job. In another case, a woman who had breast cancer decided with her husband not to tell their 10-year-old son about her true condition. In such cases, even there may be some logic to that initial position; it may later create negative implications for the family. Counselors often need to assist the client to clearly evaluate the implications of disclosure decisions.

During the diagnostic phase, families must face the possible threat of a family member's sustained illness and even death. They must also face the personal consequences of this illness. The onset of illness can affect each individual's life. Each family member's career and life plans may have to be changed or postponed. There may be new and additional responsibilities, demands upon time, and financial effects. Family members, too, may have to make disclosure decisions, choosing whom they will need to tell and where they will seek support. When a mother is seriously ill, she may have fears that her children's development may be disrupted or impeded. With some diseases, such as AIDS, there may be anxiety about the social consequences and stigma that may result. With other diseases, there may be concerns about the effect of the disease upon the health of other family members. Such concern can exist even when a disease is not infectious. Family members may worry that anxiety and added responsibilities may adversely affect their health or the health of others. In short, the diagnostic phase is a crisis characterized by continued uncertainty and anxiety, affecting in individual ways both the patient and each member of the patient's networks.

It is also a time when family members may begin to experience their own grief about the other member's possible death. As discussed in other chapters, researchers have described a process of anticipatory grief or anticipatory mourning, in which family members react to the threatened or impending loss of someone. This grief may be evidenced in a variety of ways: physical, cognitive, affective, behavioral, and even spiritual. Family members may experience such physical effects of grief as aches, pains, or fatigue. They may find it difficult to concentrate or focus, and they may have dreams about the ill member. They may experience a range of emotions including guilt, sadness, depression, or anger. They may be lethargic or overactive, irritable, excitable, or apathetic. They may face a spiritual crisis, searching for some meaning behind the health crisis. They may become disenchanted with religious—or, more likely, embrace their faith more fervently, for personal comfort or as a part of an implicit bargain with God. These reactions will be individual and affected by the responses of the ill person, their own personality and coping style, the level of information they possess, educational levels, and degree of social support.

The effects of the diagnosis affect the family as a whole. The whole family system is altered. Relationships with the ill member, including power and sexual relationships, may change. Members may take on new roles vis-à-vis one another. Some may become caregivers; others may take on advocacy roles. Often some family members, especially parents of ill children, will begin to search systematically for information about the disease and treatment options. Generally the crisis of diagnosis is a time when interaction and communication among family members is high. In many families the crisis is perceived as bringing the family together, and there is a strong sense of family and social support. For example, sometimes different perspectives, perhaps based upon educational, class, or cultural perspectives between family members, may be tolerated or even treasured. In times of family crisis, members may have greater toleration for these differing perspectives. In some families, however, the stress of the crisis may exacerbate tensions, reactivating preexisting conflicts, continuing old conflicts, or creating new ones.

Although the chronic phase lacks the intense crisis atmosphere of the acute or terminal phase, it is often a very difficult period for family members, particularly those living with and caring for the ill individual. Often the support and solidarity experienced in the crisis of diagnosis ebbs somewhat as the threat of immediate death fades and other family and friends adjust to the continued realities of their own life. The immediate family, however, must accommodate new demands, responsibilities, and stresses to their own daily routines. Although they must continue, as may the ill individual, school, or work, they must adjust to the regimen, treatment, and illness as well as modifications in role responsibilities, quality of life, and daily activities and patterns that the illness entails.

A family's financial state is likely to be adversely affected by the primary and secondary costs of illness. Often the demands of the illness as well as any social or financial consequences may curtail social interaction with others. Bluebond-Langner (1987), for example, notes that many siblings of chronically ill children often find their own social lives and friendships adversely affected by their sibling's illness. She describes how siblings live in "houses of chronic sorrow," places uninviting to visit, and how almost all plans become contingent on the health of the ill sibling. Although Bluebond-Langner's research centers specifically on the brothers and sisters of dying children, the implications of her findings are broader, capturing many of the difficulties experienced by all those who share homes with those in the chronic phase.

The chronic phase is often a period of continued stress punctuated by points of crisis. The tension generated by the illness manifests itself throughout the entire family. It may be evident in acute bouts of depression, sleeplessness, irritability, fatigue, helplessness, and isolation. It may take its toll on emotional stability or manifest itself in abuse or neglect. It is not surprising that grief therapists (see Rando, 1983; Sanders, 1983) found evidence suggesting that long periods of chronic illness may create issues that complicate grief even after the person's death.

Beyond the stress, families in the chronic phase are often on an emotional roller coaster, affected by the ill individual's health as well as the reaction and responses of that individual and other family members. Family members may feel anger over the disease and the sick person's demands, over the effects of the disease on their own life and the life of the family, and at the toll the treatment is taking on the individual and the family. They may feel guilty about their feelings of anger as well as their feelings of ambivalence. The sources of this ambivalence may be quite varied. In some cases they may be ambivalent about the individual's continued life under these conditions, both seeking some finality and resolution but fearing death. Even the changes in the ill individual's physical state may cause ambivalence, sometimes by evoking sympathy and repulsion simultaneously. They may be ambivalent about their own caregiver roles. Family members, too, may have great anxiety about the ill member, their own ability to cope, and their own future.

Denial is a common response in the chronic phase, particularly in its early period or at times when the ill member's health seems stable. Indeed, families may exhibit the same range of physical, affective, cognitive, behavioral, and spiritual reactions that an ill individual experiences.

There are often two significant family issues evident in the chronic phase. The first involves the ill member's treatment regimen. Family members may respond in many ways to a regimen, acting as anything from saboteurs to supporters. Some members can become overprotective, seeking perfectionism, or overcontrol, and other family members may exhibit poor and erratic participation in treatment. Family members' responses to the regimen may also vary during the course of the chronic phase. In the early chronic phase when the individual seems to be doing reasonably well, family responses may range from feelings that the treatment is unnecessary and a burden to an almost magical insistence upon adherence, hoping that such adherence will stave off disease. In the later part of this phase, characterized by decline, family responses may again range from hopelessness ("Why bother?") to unrealistic expectations. Caregivers and counselors will need to be sensitive to the ways that family reactions and behaviors facilitate or complicate the ill member's own response to treatment.

As the individual's health deteriorates and the family member moves into the terminal phase, family members begin to cope emotionally and in other ways with the now-expected death and the ever-growing burdens of care. Although some family members may continue to deny death even in the phase of physical deterioration, most family members will recognize the possibility, if not the probability, of death. They may begin to plan both for the individual's death and for their own life after the loss.

In the terminal phase members of the extended family and the dying individual's network will rally around the dying member and the immediate family. Sometimes this can raise issues and cause resentment between family members. In some cases family members may resent what they view as intrusions. The return of family members who have moved away or who have been alienated can reactivate old or continuing conflicts as well as create new ones. In one case a dying woman made a great fuss over the fact that her son, who lived two hundred miles away, visited the hospital almost every weekend. This caused her daughter, who had been her mother's primary caregiver throughout the chronic period, to feel hurt and resentful, renewing long-held feelings about her mother's preference for her brother.

Throughout the terminal phase family members will cope with a variety of reactions and feelings. There may be a sense of ambivalence and relief that the individual's struggle, and their own, is nearing an end. Guilt, anger, sadness, and depression are common. They may feel awkward in communicating and interacting with the person, unsure of how to behave and react. They may feel drained by increasing responsibilities for the emotional and physical care of the dying person. As the individual deteriorates and begins to disengage and withdraw, family members may feel confused, hurt, and rejected. And, family members may feel exhausted by the illness.

Family members may also be conflicted about behavior should the individual become comatose. If the person is hospitalized, family members may feel the continued responsibility to visit, while at the same time feeling useless and awkward. Counselors and caregivers can often be especially helpful at this time in reassuring family that they will be kept informed and in assisting them in making decisions about time and priorities. Counselors may also wish to assist family members in interacting with comatose persons. Often simple acts such as stroking the comatose person or taking part in routine physical care can assuage feelings of uselessness. And this period can be a meaningful opportunity for family members to take leaves and finish any remaining business.

In the closing period of life, family may have to make or review a variety of decisions, such as continuing treatment, approving autopsies, or allowing donations of body parts. They may have to begin to consider actions that need be taken after the death, such as funeral arrangements and disposition of property. These discussions, too, can sometimes create individual stress and tension as well as conflicts between family members.

As the individual moves toward death, families may have a need to be present, participating in a deathwatch. At such points there may be an intense concern for privacy, such that even routine medical monitoring may cause resentment and anger. Families may wish to participate in varied rituals such as Anointing of the Sick. Other families may not desire such rituals. When a priest unilaterally began to administer last rites, one mother of a dying child was highly disturbed both because she was unwilling to recognize the fact of impending death and because she wanted her local priest, rather than the unknown chaplain, to have that role. At the moment of death, families may want uninterrupted privacy. They may appreciate time alone to say goodbye and complete any private ritual of leave-taking. Although the client's struggle ends with death, family must still cope with their own ongoing grief.

Throughout the entire course of life-threatening illness one needs to be sensitive to the effects of the illness upon the whole family. Families are always trying to maintain a dynamic balance, constantly adjusting to the continued changes brought about both by internal changes such as the growth and development of family members and by external, societal pressures. Life-threatening illness, with all the extensive financial, interpersonal, social, psychological, and spiritual changes that it brings about, can seriously threaten that required balance. This is evident in all phases of the illness, but especially at crisis points such as the diagnosis, the terminal period, and times of pronounced deterioration in health.

It may be evident, too, in times of recovery. Here the recovery of the person, with consequent resumption and reordering of family roles and expectations, may threaten any tenuous balance that had been achieved. It is not unusual that families may experience tension and ambivalence even in recovery.

Family members may share anxiety about recurrences, fearing another family trial. They may be reluctant to share or to give up roles that they had assumed during the illness. Each change throughout an individual's illness produces both individual and interpersonal effects. Family members may grieve the losses that these latter changes entail, for they mean the death of the family system as it once was. One mother dying of cancer recognized her own ambivalence when her teenage daughter began to take up the chore of chauffeuring the younger children. She deeply appreciated her daughter's newfound responsibility but also mourned her own loss of mobility and function, and even resented the shared confidences, experiences, and closeness that were developing between her daughter and the two younger siblings.

One must be particularly sensitive to the effects of an individual's life-threatening illness on children in the home. As I noted earlier, Bluebond-Langner (1978) indicated that siblings of dying children often live in homes of "chronic sorrow" in which parents are constantly depressed about their ill child. Life often revolves around the disease, with plans constantly changing contingent upon the illness. Well children often feel isolated and anxious as a result of the illness, distressed by the treatment, and even guilty about their own good health. Their emotional, social, and developmental needs are often subordinated to those of the ill child. In some cases, well children even feel that they are the targets of their ill sibling's anger. These findings probably have application more broadly to any case in which children are members of families providing care than to those with life-threatening illness.

Professional caregivers can assist families by helping to empower more open and effective parent-child communication, aiding and advocating recognition of the child's needs, and helping families to identify additional or alternate sources of support for children. In some cases this may be other family or friends. Often there may be family members or friends who wish to provide help but are uncomfortable or threatened by interaction with the ill member. They may, however, welcome the opportunity to show support by providing help with children. In addition, many agencies provide programs such as camps, support groups, counseling, and recreational and respite services to such children.

ASSESSING FACTORS THAT AFFECT FAMILY REACTIONS

The previous section outlined some of the ways in which family members may be affected by and respond to a member's illness, but family members' reactions are highly individual, influenced by a wide variety of factors. Rando (1984) reminds us that we need to view the family from two perspectives. First, each family is a collection of individuals. Reaction to another member's illness will be affected by a range of individual variables such as personality, coping abilities, age and maturity, gender, relationship with the deceased, intelligence, education, mental and physical health, religion and philosophy of life, fears, knowledge of and experiences with illness and death, and formal and informal supports. Second, the family as a whole has its own unique structure and characteristics. These latter include such factors as the number and personalities of the members of the family; their developmental states; the family's position in the family life cycle; interactional patterns; values, norms, expectations, and beliefs; equality of relationship, flexibility, and communication; patterns of dependence and independence; coping styles and problem-solving abilities; and resources and strengths. The illness will also affect the family's responses in such areas as the meaning the illness has for the family as a whole; the symptoms and manifestations of the illness; the stigma associated with the illness; the stress and strains of the illness and treatment regimen; the timeliness and course of the illness.

Rando (1984) suggests that several factors seem to facilitate a family system's ability to cope more effectively with life-threatening illness. These include

- knowledge of the symptoms and probable cycle of the illness, and training as to how to provide effective care throughout all phases of illness
- the ability to participate in the care of the ill individual, particularly in the terminal phase, since participation allows a sense of control
- open and honest communication, including the openness to discuss feelings within the family and with the ill family member
- flexible families structures that allow members to readjust roles throughout the course of the illness
- positive relationships between family members and effective and compatible patterns of problem solving and coping
- availability of effective informal and formal support systems
- social and economic resources and the absence of other crises and family problems, all of which combine to maximize effective coping
- quality medical care and good relationships and communication between family and medical systems
- a philosophical or religious belief system that allows a continued sense of hope and provides an interpretive framework for illness and death

This list suggests other factors that might complicate a family's adjustment to life-threatening illness. These factors include

- dysfunctional patterns of family relationships, interaction, communication, and problem solving
- unavailability or ineffectiveness of informal and formal support systems
- stigmatizing diseases that inhibit the family from requesting or receiving assistance

- other familial or individual crises concurrent with the illness
- lack of social or economic resources
- poor-quality medical care and poor communication and interaction with medical caregivers

These factors indicate family groups that may be at particular risk. Families that include members suffering from feared diseases such as AIDS may have to face stigma that will inhibit support throughout the illness and even after death and that even strain relationships with some members of the caregiving community. Family units that have experienced the fragmentation caused by separation or divorce may also experience special difficulties. For example, a single parent coping with a child with life-threatening disease might well face a lack of financial, social, psychological, emotional, and spiritual support. Similarly, ex-spouses and separated couples may face special problems when one person becomes terminally ill. Here expectations and norms about appropriate behavior, responsibilities, and even feelings are unclear. Prior conflicts may strain relationships with other family members. Similarly, cohabiting unmarried heterosexual couples or homosexual lovers may face similar difficulties because members of the biological family may not sanction these relationships. The lack of a legally recognized tie may create other problems as well, arising from the role of the partner in treatment decisions, insurance questions, and reaching out for support from informal and formal sources. Families with distinctly different cultural or economic backgrounds may have serious problems interacting with and communicating with medical staff. Certainly, families experiencing social and economic deprivation or those with histories characterized by conflict will have special problems in coping with life-threatening illness.

Families are all unique, each with its own "personality." Just as no two individuals will respond in exactly the same ways to a succession of stressors and crises, no two families will deal with the ongoing problems associated with life-threatening illness in the same ways. Counselors must try to discover whatever strengths a family has and help the family to best use these strengths. Counselors should simultaneously try to understand, correct, and otherwise compensate for any weaknesses that may inhibit the family's response to that illness.

ASSESSING CAREGIVING

Counselors must take particular care in assessing the functioning, and even health changes, that may result when families are extensively involved in caregiving. Family caregivers may face high levels of stress that can adversely affect their jobs and careers, interactions within the family, and their social outlets—potentially lessening support. In addition, caregiving may have deleterious effects upon the caregiver's physical and mental health (Doka & Davidson, 2001; Levine, 2003–2004). Hence it is critical to assess any health changes not only in clients but also caregivers.

Naturally the experience will have different meaning for each caregiver. For some caregivers, caregiving is a burden—doing odious tasks for someone who wishes that he or she were not so dependent. Others may acknowledge, even in the burdens of caregiving, gifts such as the opportunity to transcend one's own needs, an appreciation of newfound strengths, or the pride in keeping promises and difficult commitments. Counselors should be careful to assess what the caregiving experience means for the individual caregiver.

The meaning of that experience may be dependent on several factors. These naturally include the objective aspects of the caregiving experiences. For example, the sense of burden is likely to be higher when the caregiver's sleep is constantly disrupted or the patient is incontinent, immobile, or demented. There may be other objective factors as well. Culture, for example, defines differently the mutual obligations that family members owe one another as well as the cultural norms that frame the caregiving experience. Individuals from cultures that emphasize high levels of filial piety may be reluctant even to accept professional help or respite.

This assessment should also consider subjective factors. Caregiving will always be interpreted through the prism of past experience and history. It is easier to provide caregiving when prior relationships have been positive. It is much more difficult to be a caregiver to someone when there is a history of conflicted or ambivalent relationships and a perception that the person now needing care was never forthcoming with support in the caregiver's past.

In short, counselors should carefully assess the caregiving experience and the meaning that the experience has for the caregiver. Only then will the counselor be able to suggest appropriate interventions and resources.

FAMILY TASKS THROUGHOUT THE ILLNESS

Families, just like individuals, will have to integrate the experience of a family member's illness into their ongoing life, because throughout the time of the illness the family will continue to function and develop, to cope with all the continuing tasks of life, and to interact with all the issues and needs that existed prior to the diagnose. Families, just like individuals, will have to cope with a series of tasks throughout all phases of life-threatening illness. And families, again like individuals, will have varying degrees of success coping with the variety of problems they face.

The Prediagnostic Phase

Just as ill individuals find it valuable to understand their experiences during the prediagnostic period, families learn by examining the whole family's role in this prediagnostic period. In some cases families may have had a limited or even no role. They may have known little or nothing about the symptoms. If an individual has kept his or her family in the dark, this action could have positive results if it leads the family to reexamine its patterns of communication, so that individuals do not continue to show patterns of poor communication—perhaps from a desire to protect—that limit their ability to reach out for or to accept family support. Discussing factors that influenced someone to withhold information about illness may help the whole family learn to cope more effectively in future crises.

In other cases family members may have been aware of symptoms but minimized or dismissed their significance. Sometimes this occurs because family members wanted to reassure the ill member and themselves that nothing was wrong. Again, discussions can help families identify patterns of behavior and help them to understand the ways in which these patterns can either hinder or facilitate the ongoing response to serious illness.

Similarly, family members may wish to examine ways in which they interacted and ether supported or impeded the ill member during the health-seeking phase. Could they share concerns and reach decisions effectively? Did prior conflicts interfere with decision-making processes? Could they provide emotional, social, and other needed forms of support for the ill member and for each other?

The point of such examination is not to renew conflicts but to understand the ways in which the family functioned. Understand that a family can build on its strengths and compensate for weaknesses, as it engages in a family struggle with life-threatening illness.

The Diagnostic Phase

Understanding the Disease and Treatment

Within a family system there may be considerable differences in the ways that family members understand the illness and treatment. These differences can result from a variety of factors: cognitive, educational, developmental, and generational differences between members; access to different information; emotional and cognitive reactions such as denial that may block understanding; and so on. Assuming that the ill individual is willing to disclose information about the illness throughout the family, family members may need assistance to develop a realistic understanding of the disease. Some family members may have very pessimistic views as a result of misinformation or prior experiences and, therefore, will need some positive reinforcement. Others may be overly optimistic. At this phase of the illness, optimistic responses should be challenged only if they seriously impair family functioning, treatment, or the health of others. In one such case, a woman whose son was HIV positive denied that her son was ill since he was asymptomatic. She also badgered her daughter-in-law because she refused to continue having sex with her son. Her conduct caused division in the family and impaired her son's participation in treatment. Here was someone whose false optimism required correction so that she could understand the risks of her son's condition.

Realistically Considering the Family's Abilities to Provide Support and Identifying Additional Resources

The time of diagnosis is an appropriate time for the family to begin to develop realistic care plans. Diagnosis usually includes an indication of immediate treatment and caregiving needs. Families that are able to effectively plan and meet these immediate needs will have less anxiety about the future and may well develop effective coping strategies that can be applied to subsequent experiences. Families may need to be made aware of various sources of assistance such as social services, specialized services (for example, for children or for the elderly), community services, and illness-related services. Family members should be encouraged to show such information, because individuals will often identify needs based on their knowledge of available services. Counselors can assist families in identifying needs and evaluating care strategies. If necessary, they should assist families in examining any sources of resistance to using identified help within or outside of the family system. Strategies that distribute tasks throughout a family and use outside resources are likely to be more effective both in the immediate crisis and in the long run.

Developing Strategies to Deal with Issues Created by the Illness

The following are some immediate problems that life-threatening illness creates for the family:

Disclosure. Once individuals share information about the symptoms and diagnosis, family members must be concerned about when, what, and how they talk about the disease within and outside the immediate family. Should they tell parents, in-laws, children, or friends? Other family members and the ill member may differ in the degree of secrecy or openness they desire. Counselors can assist by exploring how these decisions will affect each individual. As I stated earlier, sometimes it is best to adopt a policy of limited disclosure: "What information do I need to share with whom, at what point?" Family members need to be advised that information can often spread geometrically. One client's teenaged daughter decided to confide her older brother's HIV diagnosis to her boyfriend. Within a short time news of her brother's condition had spread throughout the community, placing further strain upon the family. The point counselors should emphasize is that disclosure decisions can have numerous implications and effects, and thus merit careful consideration.

An issue that often arises within family systems concerns disclosing information to children. Adult members frequently wish to protect a child from troubling information and perhaps protect themselves from the child's questioning. Such strategies are often ineffective because children can sense the anxiety and tension around them. It is often more productive to inform children about what is happening but to present such information in ways consistent with their own experience and developmental level. Again, limited disclosure is often the best policy. Certainly, children should be fully prepared for what they will experience. Adults should describe the sights, sounds, and smells that children may observe. Whether children visit or not, they should be given other opportunities to show support, perhaps, for example, by sending pictures, making tape recordings, or phoning. Children should also be supported during the visit. After the visit, children need the opportunity to discuss their feelings and observations.

Coping with Professionals and Treatment Decisions. Although these tasks are really the responsibility of the ill member, family members may still have strong feelings about them. Caregivers may assist families in identifying and exploring their concerns and assessing how these concerns are complicating or facilitating the ill member's reaction to illness. It is critical that family members are comfortable about treatment decisions made at all phases of the illness. Should the ill person die, the grief of family members will be easier if they are not haunted by questions about whether alternate treatment decisions, including choices of hospitals or doctors, should have been made.

Life Contingencies. The diagnosis of life-threatening illness affects all areas of the ill individual's life and of the lives of other members of the family, such as a family member's decision to quit a job. Counselors can help families to identify their options and review the implications of various decisions. Family members may also need help coping with the uncertainty often evident in the acute period. Often emphasizing that any decision made can be tentative reinforces and facilitates that understanding. But families may need to recognize their own ambivalence and anxiety about uncertainty.

Assisting Families in Examining their Own Coping Styles

Both individual family members and the family as a whole may exhibit coping styles and strategies that are functional or dysfunctional. Nathan (1990) identifies four strategies often found in the early phases of the illness:

1. The *direct/action-oriented* approach is a problem-solving mode in which family members make realistic efforts to deal with the disease.
2. The *conscious/normalcy* mode recognizes the reality of the situation but emphasizes continuing to live life as normally as possible.
3. A third pattern is called *denial/suppression*. Here members deny the disease.
4. Finally, an *escapist* strategy seeks to distance one from the illness by escape mechanisms such as substance abuse.

Nathan notes the last strategy is often the least productive adaptation. Families need to examine the ways that they are responding as individuals and as a family, identifying where and when their strategies are effective, evaluating the ways in which their coping strategies interact, and considering, when necessary, alternate strategies. Counselors can help by reinforcing, when evident, effective patterns of coping. It is also important in the early phase, to emphasize that coping strategies must be continually reevaluated as the circumstances and family needs change.

Facilitating Communication within Families and Between Families and Ill Individuals

The last two tasks have explicitly addressed the issue of communication. Throughout the diagnostic period, family members may have needs to discuss feelings and fears as well as issues created by the illness. Counselors can assist the family by assessing barriers to effective communication and developing strategies to improve family communication. A variety of interventions may be used to improve communication. In some cases it is useful to ask members to write down their feelings or to develop structured "sharing sessions." Any such intervention should be suggested only after barriers have been identified within the family.

Ventilating Feelings and Fears

Families, too, may need to express their feelings and fears. They may need to explore their ability to discuss their concerns with one another. They need to consider how their reactions facilitate or impair family interactions as well as the response of the ill member. Caregivers may wish to check "feeling rules" or family norms that govern the expression of feelings. Sometimes families can repress such feelings. Counselors can be very useful here, because they have the opportunity to observe and explore any nonverbal behaviors that may be exchanged when feelings are discussed. Counselors can also lead discussions on how family members respond when feelings are displayed.

Exploring the Ways in which the Diagnosis Affects the Ill Person, Relationships with That Person, and Family Life

The diagnosis of life-threatening illness is often a turning point for ill individuals and their families. Life for everyone will now never be the same. Family members need to reflect upon the ways that the diagnosis has affected both the ill member and others within the family system. Some members may not recognize that the person's perspectives and reality have been unalterably changed. And they may be confused or resentful about changes in family life created by the onset of disease.

They also may need to examine their own relationship with the ill individual. Both their perception of the ill person and their behavior toward that person may change as a result of the diagnosis. Parents of dying children, for example, sometimes speak of "diminished expectations." When a child is born, parental expectations may be limitless. Beginning with the diagnosis, though, and continuing throughout the illness, expectations can continually change. By the time of the terminal phase, parents may have considerable fears about their child's future. These diminished expectations can exist in any relationship. These changes in perception can also lead to changes in behavior toward the ill member. One woman, for example, was deeply dismayed when her brother was diagnosed with cancer. She perceived the diagnosis as a death sentence and began to withdraw from him. In other cases, fear, anxiety, and misinformation may affect relationships with the ill member. In some cases, the diagnosis can become the "master status" or the overarching attribute and identity that define the individual. The person becomes not the parent or the sibling or the spouse, but the "disease victim." This label itself can reinforce that role by removing other significant roles from that person.

The Chronic Phase

Assisting in Managing Symptoms and Dealing with Changes in the Course of the Illness

Family members may need assistance in assessing the effects of the individual's symptom upon themselves and the family. Goffman, in his book *Stigma* (1963), describes "the wise," that is, a group of sympathetic others who understand the stigma created by serious illness and can provide empathy and support. In the chronic phase, family members may be called upon to assume such roles. Often they can help the ill member by minimizing possibilities for public awareness of symptoms of the disease. For example, the adult children of a woman with heart disease helped their mother to plan walking routes to church and other events that would minimize physical stress. Family members, too, may help in reevaluating their roles as conditions change throughout the illness.

Assisting the Individual in Adhering with the Treatment Regimen

One of the ill person's basic tasks in the chronic phase involves adhering to the treatment regimen, but this is not solely a task for the ill individual. By necessity, family members usually become involved in the treatment. In some situations, such as those involving a young child or a frail or disoriented adult, family members may have primary responsibility for the treatment regimen. In most treatment regimens family members will have important roles in encouraging or discouraging adherence.

In designing treatment regimens, especially those that mandate family involvement, counselors will do well to bring the whole family into the process. Often family members can provide valuable insight on issues that might influence adherence. For example, in one case a son questioned the timing of medication on weekends when family schedules were different and activities were likely to interfere with adherence.

Counselors must also be careful about assuming that the family member will participate in the regimen. Family members may feel inadequate to the task of acting as "policemen." They may also be very uncomfortable with other possible regimen-related rules. One woman and her adult son were discomforted by the request that he assist his mother in handling her colostomy bags because it violated family norms of modesty. In other situations family members can be overwhelmed by competing demands on their time. Counselors can assist families by carefully assessing physical and psychological comfort levels in assigning tasks, providing adequate training, and assisting members in developing additional support, both for backup and for respite.

Counselors might also want to monitor the ways in which family members and the person undergoing treatment perceive that the family is facilitating or complicating adherence. And they should also be sensitive to the ways in which the regimen is affecting relationships within the family.

Preventing and Managing Health Crises

Throughout the chronic phase, ill individuals may experience medical crises. Families, as well as the ill member, should be informed about ways to avoid crises and how to manage them when they do occur. Often rehearsing strategies for handling medical crises can alleviate anxiety and enhance coping. Once a crisis is resolved, families may need an opportunity to review and reflect upon their ways of handling that crisis. Counselors may need to intervene to assist families with reviewing in a positive manner, so that strategies of scapegoating are avoided, impediments to effective responses are discussed, and alternate approaches developed. Family members may also need to ventilate feelings and fear arising from the crisis.

Reducing Stress and Examining Coping Strategies

Because chronic illness is extraordinarily stressful for all the members of the family system, some or all members of the family system may need stress management. Families should identify sources of stress and ways that stress is manifested, and they should examine their own strategies of coping with stress.

Being a family caregiver is extremely stressful. Not only is the person dealing with constant demands to provide care for the person who is ill, but he or she must simultaneously cope with his or her own sense of loss. Family caregivers may experience an intense range of emotions. They may feel anger and resentment at the person who is ill or at other members of the family system whom they perceive as being unsupportive or unappreciative. They may feel guilt about their own inability to be "perfect" all the time for the ill individual. They may find it difficult to cope with the demands of providing the full range of physical, emotional, social, and spiritual support the ill individual seems to require.

These family caregivers may find counseling and self-help groups useful. They may need to learn how to communicate their own needs to other family members.

Family caregivers and other family members may also find it valuable to learn effective stress-reduction strategies. These can include such things as improving problem solving; increasing planning and communication; withdrawing from stressful situations or delegating; examining and modifying unrealistic expectations of self; and employing effective lifestyle management such as good diet, regular exercise, social support, diversion, relaxation, and meditation.

Primary caretakers, especially, must find ways to allow themselves respite. For example, one retired daughter who lived near her father became his primary caregiver during his illness. She came near to burning out, but through counseling finally did learn to effectively involve her brothers, both of whom worked and lived some distance away. One was able to come on weekends to care for his father, thereby allowing her and her husband a chance to get away to their vacation home. The other brother assumed responsibility for negotiating with hospitals and physicians. By communicating her needs and recognizing the importance of respite, she was able to minimize stress.

In examining the ways families cope; it is important to remember that each family has its own characteristic ways of coping. Recognizing what these characteristic ways are can be the first step toward discovering strengths to build on and weaknesses to be corrected.

Marshaling outside Support and Resources

Throughout the chronic phase families will need to effectively use informal and formal support systems and cope with medical personnel. Effective use of such support can enhance adaptation, reduce stress, and minimize a sense of isolation. This support not only provides needed help and respite, it also has a ritual aspect, affirming that all caregivers are part of a larger group, reinforcing the security of the group in a chaotic time. It is not surprising that family caregivers find that the degree of support a family has prior to the death is an important factor in its adjustment to bereavement after the death. Families need to examine their informal support system, assessing how relationships with friends and families have changed throughout the illness, identifying needs and support available from their informal support network, recognizing barriers to the effective use of such support, and developing strategies to usze such support more effectively. One key issue a family needs to consider is what persons are best suited for which tasks. Not every member has the same level of empathy, patience, commitment, skill, time, and so forth. Some may be good persons to help with shopping or with childcare. Others may help negotiate with medical staff. Still others may be good caregivers or listeners.

A similar assessment should be applied to formal support systems. Counselors can assist families to explore any resistance toward using such services. Family members, for example, may consider themselves best attuned to care for the patient, distrustful of others. They may have to be gently coaxed into respite—first taking a small shopping trip prior to taking a movie or a weekend respite.

This exploration of reluctance to entrust care to others may be a particularly helpful strategy if the level of patient deterioration becomes so pronounced that placement in a chronic care facility is necessary. In such cases counselors may need to review with families their own attempts to care for the person, identifying in nonjudgmental ways limits to the capacity to maintain care in the force of the patient's escalating needs. They may find it important to explore alternatives to institutionalization. If the counselor foresees institutionalization, it may be helpful to have families begin to consider what circumstances and events may necessitate it. Often when families begin extensive caregiving, I ask what factors would make it impossible to continue to care for the person at home. This allows the family opportunity to consider the possibility and to minimize aversive reactions when possibility becomes actuality. In many cases, family members will even feel proud that they actually went far beyond what they once considered impossible. If the patient is institutionalized, it may be helpful for counselors to help family members redefine their roles as caregivers. They have not stopped being caregivers (and by implication—caring); their role has changed now to other caregiving responsibilities such as advocacy. Nonetheless, should permanent institutionalization become necessary, caregivers may have to assist families in addressing new emotional or interactional issues that may arise.

Normalizing Life in the Face of Disease

The simple phrase "normalizing life" conveys one of the more difficult and complex tasks in the chronic phase. It is one that really entails many distinct issues. The first issue is attempting, as much as possible, to normalize the ill member's life. For that member to preserve self-concept, he or she will need to be treated by significant others as "normal." Families need to review the ways that the illness is affecting their perception of and interactions with the ill person. The goal for families is to prevent the illness from dominating their relationship with the ill member so that it becomes his or her primary identity or "master status."

It is also critical to recognize that such treatment can impair an individual's adaptation to illness by damaging self-esteem and coping capacity, and by inducing unnecessary dependence. It is important to continually assess the ways in which the illness itself is affecting interaction with the ill member, the ill member's response to illness, and the general quality of family life. "What changes have occurred in your family since the last visit?" Addressing this question can facilitate an ongoing assessment and attune family sensitivities to the continued changes wrought by the illness. Such a review should also include an assessment of the ways that sexual relationships may have changed between the ill member and his or her partner. And it should also consider financial changes and stresses experienced by the family.

The key to this task lies in normalizing family life *as far as possible.* In some cases, families will place such a great effort on maintaining the "usual" life of the family that such effort actually undermines family life and hinders the ill member's adaptation to the illness. For example, one family I worked with attempted to maintain their previous activities and made no allowance for their father's illness. This lessened the social support available to the father and created additional stress and strain for him. Families should inventory aspects of family life, determine which parts of that life are significant enough to be maintained and which parts must be modified or given up because of the illness, and then allow family members to verbalize their own sense of loss over these changes. This last step is particularly important, since it is an unfair burden not to allow family members to recognize that the loss of previous activities is a source of concern. It is not selfish for family members to miss the quality of life and personal freedom that existed prior to the illness.

Ventilating Feelings and Fear

In any phase of illness, ill individuals and families will need to deal with feelings and fears. Counseling can provide a trusting atmosphere in which these feelings and fears can be discussed and explored safely. Counselors can assist family members in developing effective ways to handle such emotions. Throughout this phase family members may need to examine the many losses that they and their family have experienced throughout the course of the illness. These can include loss of activities, losses of health, and losses of family life and lifestyle. And they may have to grieve about losses that they anticipate, including the death of the ill member. It is not unusual that feelings and fears may change considerably throughout the course of this phase, swinging from optimism to pessimism, depending on the ill member's current condition.

Finding Meaning in Suffering, Chronicity, Uncertainty, and Decline

Just as ill individuals have to cope with finding meaning in sickness and suffering, so, too, do other family members. Each family member may be in a different place in the spiritual and philosophical journeys. Family members need to respect these differences.

Families and Recovery

Families, too, may have ongoing needs even in recovery. The family may have changed significantly throughout the course of the illness. It may be difficult to readjust to the recovered member when he or she attempts to assume old roles and relationships. Patterns of independence or dependence formed in the illness may be difficult to change. Family members may experience a variety of emotions at recovery. They may feel anxious about recurrence or feel very vulnerable and fragile. They may feel angry as a result of unresolved conflicts arising from the behaviors of other members during the course of the crisis. They may be impatient with the recovering member, perhaps feeling that person's recovery is being paced too slowly or too quickly.

In any case, families should periodically discuss how the family is faring throughout the period of recovery. They may need to validate feelings, noting that this phase in the illness process can be a difficult adjustment.

The Terminal Phase

Understanding the Process of Dying

When an individual reaches the terminal stage, family members may need to be informed about the dying process particular to that disease. What can they expect, in trajectory, symptoms, incapacitation, and pain? They may need training as to the ways they can respond to any medical conditions or crises they may encounter. They may need assistance in understanding and exploring their own feelings now that the goal has changed to palliative care. They may need to be able to interpret varied signs concerning the proximity and actuality of death. In some cultures, persons may report omens or premonitions of impending death. In other cases, the dying person may communicate obliquely a sense that death is near. For example, Callanan and Kelley (1992) described *nearing death awareness.* Here the dying person may symbolically communicate his or her awareness of impending death by speaking metaphorically of travel or traveling; reporting visitations or conversation with now deceased family members; or having a sense of impending death. In my father's case, on the last day of his life he began to ask whether he was dying. The question did not seem to be "Do I have a terminal prognosis?" but rather to have much more imminence. When I questioned my father, he simply stated that he felt different. I asked him if there was anything we could do. He asked that the family stay around. We kept him company throughout the day. Later, in the evening, he said he felt better and suggested we all retire to our own rooms. He died that night. Callanan and Kelley (1992) suggest such a dialogue. Naturally the kind of deathbed phenomenon is likely to be more extensive than the archetypical images suggested by Callanan and Kelley. Nonetheless, counselors can have a role in helping families understand and interpret such signs and respond to these communications.

If the family is planning to keep the patient at home, they may find it useful to talk with medical staff about what they can expect in this final period. But the information a family needs at this stage is not solely medical. Family members may need assistance in interpreting the dying person's social and psychological reactions. They may need help in understanding that reactions such as withdrawal, anger, grief, and sadness are natural responses to the dying process (Hebert, Schulz, Copeland, & Arnold, 2008). And family members may need to explore and to discuss with one another their own responses to such behaviors.

Coping with Caregivers and Institutions

The terminal phase often means that family members will again have to deal with a new group of caregivers—those who are actively involved in the care of the dying person. In this phase the dying person may very well be institutionalized in a nursing home, hospital, or hospice. This, too, can create stress for families. As families explore any difficulty or stresses associated with caregivers and institutions, they can develop effective strategies to alleviate problems and stress.

Counselors also should assess the effectiveness of pain management with family members. There are three major reasons for this. First, family members are most aware of the patient and may be able to interpret signs of distress even in patients who are comatose or experiencing dementia. Second, family members themselves may constitute a barrier to effective management of pain. They may have unrealistic fears about the effects of various analgesics. This can be especially important if they are the ones in a home hospice situation who are administering medication. Finally, perceptions that the patient died in suffering or pain are likely to complicate the family's grief (Doka, 2006).

Emotionally Restructuring Relationships with the Dying Person

Emotionally relationships with the patient may be highly complicated in the terminal phase. Family members may be experiencing countervailing reactions. They may wish to stay with the person in the moment, making the best of remaining time while simultaneously wishing to relate to the person as he or she was and trying to now plan for a life without that person. Counselors can assist this process by exploring with family members their own needs and reactions. When necessary, they can gently test the family members' sense of reality. And, when appropriate, they can encourage family members to meet their own and each other's needs. In one case, for example, a hospice nurse was able to explore with the wife of a dying man her own needs to be involved in the ongoing life activities of her teenaged children. She was able to assist the woman in arranging for alternate care, freeing her to meet those needs.

Effectively Using Resources

At any point in the illness it is important for family members to consider their effectiveness in using resources such as other family members, friends, and formal services (self-help groups, counselors, and other services). Whenever conditions change, it is critical for family members to reassess their needs and to reconsider their use of available resources. Again, families may need to be informed about different types of services that may be able to provide assistance. And again, they may need to explore with a counselor any resistance or barriers toward using such assistance. Often in the crisis of the terminal phase, their informal support systems will rally around. This may provide additional aid and support. But family members may also recognize a sense of resentment for a perceived lack of support during earlier phases of the illness.

Dealing with One's Own Emotions and Grief

In the terminal phase, as in any phase of illness, family members may experience a range of emotional responses. As family members face the imminent loss of the dying member, they need to inventory the many losses they have already experienced as well as the losses they anticipate. It is also important, especially after a long illness, for family members to understand that their own reactions to the death may be very ambivalent. They should be reassured that wanting the patient's and their own struggle to end while simultaneously wishing the patient could continue to live in a perfectly normal reaction.

Understanding the Human Needs of the Dying Person

Even though an individual is dying, he or she maintains the same human needs that have persisted throughout life. Humor, love, touch, communication, and care are just a sample of these ongoing needs. Often, though, because families facing the terminal phase are so concerned about the issue of death, they can neglect the individual's other needs. Sometimes formal caregivers can be helpful in assisting families to understand their perception of the dying person and to encourage responses that are cognizant of the dying individual's continuing human needs.

Maintaining Relationships with the Dying Member and Continuing to Incorporate the Dying Person Within the Family System

In many ways this is an extension of the earlier task. Not only do families need to be cognizant of ongoing human needs, they need to continue to maintain relationships and continue to incorporate the dying person within the family. In the terminal phase the dying person may have limited energy and be bedridden. Often dying individuals are physically removed from the flow of family life, either because they are confined to a sickroom at home or removed to an institution. Moreover, family members may seek to protect the dying person from additional troubles or difficulties, thus withholding information and removing the person from family decisions. Communication, too, can become increasingly awkward. Family members may be unclear as to what to say.

It is important for families to openly discuss their relationships with the dying member. To the degree that family members are comfortable participating in activities such as the care of the dying person, or reminiscing, they may provide meaningful interaction for the present, and they may also mitigate subsequent grief. For example, when one family was encouraged to share the ways that their father had influenced their lives with him, they found these special times both enjoyable while he lived out his last days and helpful when they later mourned his loss. This activity seemed not only to ease their communication, but also to be significant for their father and facilitate their later grief. Family members can also participate in other ways that are comfortable for them. Some may choose to be involved in personal care, monitoring medication, providing massages, or helping with grooming. Others may be comfortable in social conversation, or reading to a family member, or even watching television together. That, too, may provide diversion and social support. Still others may find it helpful to pray with the ill person or participate in other religious rituals. Families should also recognize the need to allow the dying individual the freedom to decide whether or not he or she wishes to pursue these activities.

Realistically Planning for the Dying and Death of the Person

In the terminal phase family members may be faced with a series of difficult decisions. Some may involve actions to be taken during this terminal phase, for example, decisions to seek hospice care, or to sign "Do Not Resuscitate" orders, or to terminate treatment. It is critical for counselors to review these ethical decisions as they complicate subsequent grief (Doka, 2005). Families may also need to decide about autopsies or tissue donations. Families may need help in interpreting signs of impending death and in understanding procedures that may take place around the death. This information is critical in any context, but is essential if the individual is at home during his or her final days. Families will need to know whom to call and when. Other decisions may involve issues related to the time of death, for example, funeral plans. Still others may involve decisions about the postdeath period such as decisions about work or selling the home.

The very discussion of these topics can support family members' desire and need to pan. Family members can review the effectiveness of their own problem-solving processes. One man, for example, while facing the death of his wife, became aware that his penchant for unilateral decisions complicated relationships with other members of his family. He was able then to incorporate his children in the decision-making process.

Planning for the Continuation of Family Life Throughout the Terminal Phase and after the Death

Throughout the terminal phase and even after the death the family continues. But that family will be affected by the dying process and changed after the death. It is important for families to explore the ways in which the illness and death affect the family's communication, interaction, and structure. Families will need to consider how these events have influenced the family's goals and plans. And they may need to consider ways in which they will adjust and prevent fragmentation following the death.

Finding Meaning in Life and Death

Family members as well as the dying individual need to make sense out of the dying person's life and death. Coming to terms with the ways in which a person has influenced one's own life, both for good and for bad, is a critical part of grieving and ongoing personal development. When it is possible, that is, when the reflections are positive, sharing such reflections with the person who is ill and with other family members can help each person's search for meaning. When my father had reached a critical point in his own struggle with cancer, our family shared a meal together. We spoke of all the good times we had had, all the gifts he had given us. I do not think that any of us realized all the different facts of his fathering until that moment. Each of us, including my father, developed a better measure of the man. Approaches such as dignity therapy in which the dying individual's story is shared with the family are especially useful since they benefit both dying persons and their families (McClement, Chochinov, Hack, Hassard, Kristjanson, & Harlos, 2007).

Negative feelings, although shielded from the dying individual, should not be bottled inside. They should be shared, but probably with a counselor or a confidant. At this point, it is unfair to complicate other family members' struggles with meaning by adding to their burdens.

Families do not have to face the crisis of illness alone. Counselors can assist families in identifying resources that can support families and ill individuals in their struggle.

In summary, families face considerable challenges when one member is ill. They can face these challenges better if they confront them as a family. Standing together as a family means that each family member feels the freedom to discuss concerns openly and to share in solving problems throughout the course of the illness. This open sharing does not mean that every problem can be resolved to everyone's satisfaction. It does mean, however, that if families set up a process in which each member's concerns are aired and considered, in which family and individual needs are viewed and balanced, and in which appropriate compromises are made, families will find that they are better able to withstand the stresses of life-threatening illness and be more effective in supporting each other throughout this stressful time. There is a myth that illness always brings families together. Sometimes it does, but other times the illness experience can hopelessly fragment a family. It is not the crisis, but the way a family faces that crisis, that knits a family together.

SUPPORTING FAMILIES AT THE TIME OF DEATH

Counselors, when possible, can help families prepare for the actual moment of death. Some, perhaps hospice or hospital chaplains or social workers, may actually be present with families at the moment death occurs. The passing from life to death, whatever one's spirituality, is a sacred moment. Families should be offered the opportunity of creating a ritual to mark that moment. Lighting a candle, saying a prayer, touching the person one last time, or joining hands in a moment of silence are examples of ways that families may choose to mark that moment. Families might be invited to construct their own unique ritual. "Is there anything you would like to do to mark this moment?" In my teaching, I often suggest that counselors follow a "rule of three"—that is offering, if asked, at least three varied suggestions. I have found that such a process seems to empower families to create their own ritual. A statement offering one option (or even two) may be perceived as coercive by the family. Later, family members may need to review any decisions that they made within the course of the illness.

Regardless of expectation, the moment of death is often a confused time when family members cope with shock and disbelief. Counselors can often assist by helping that family in reviewing and assisting them with final details such as death certificates or funeral or alternate arrangements. Most importantly, at the moment of death, counselors can allow the patients the opportunity to grieve. One very special colleague and a pioneer in the field, Patricia Murphy, often shares that in her hospital, in the middle of downtown Newark, it was not unusual for clients to wail at the moment of death. Her young physicians would often be discomforted by such strong emotional displays and suggest a Valium. "By all means," Pat would tell them, "take one—just leave the family alone."

CONCLUSION

This chapter began by reminding readers that life-threatening illness is a family illness, affecting all the members of a family in varied ways at all phases of the illness. The family also has needs, reactions, and tasks that are similar to those of its ill member. Families that recognize their reactions and needs and use their own unique strengths and resources to more effectively cope with the tasks created by the crisis of life-threatening illness may more effectively adjust to the illness and threat of death. And families may find that their own adjustment to any subsequent loss and grief is eased.

REFERENCES

Bluebond-Langner, M. (1978). *The private worlds of dying children.* Princeton, NJ: Princeton University Press.

Bluebond-Langner, M. (1987). Worlds of dying children and their well siblings. *Death Studies, 11,* 279–295.

Callanan, M., & Kelley, P. (1992) *Final gifts: Understanding the special awareness, needs, and communications of the dying.* New York: Bantam Books.

Doka, K. J. (2005). Ethics, end-of-life decisions, and grief. In K. Doka, B. Jennings, & C. Corr (Eds.), *Ethical dilemmas at the end-of-life* (pp. 285–296). Washington, DC: The Hospice Foundation of America.

Doka, K. J. (Ed.). (2006). *Pain management at the end-of-life: Bridging the gap between knowledge and practice.* Washington, DC: The Hospice Foundation of America.

Doka, K. J., & Davidson, J. (Eds.) (2001). *Caregivers and loss: Family needs and professional responses.* Washington, DC: The Hospice Foundation of America.

Goffman, E. (1963). *Stigma: Notes on the management of spoiled identity.* Englewood Cliffs, NJ: Prentice-Hall.

Hebert, R. S., Schulz, R., Copeland, V., & Arnold, R. M. (2008). What questions do family caregivers want to discuss with health care providers in order to prepare for the death of a loved one? An ethnographic study of caregivers of patients at the end of life. *Journal of Palliative Medicine, 11,* 476–483.

Levine, C. (2003–2004, Winter). Family caregiving: Current challenges for a time-honored practice. *Generations: Journal of the American Society on Aging, 27*(4).

McClement, S., Chochinov, H. M., Hack, T., Hassard, T., Kristjanson, L. J., & Harlos, M. (2007). Dignity therapy: Family members perspectives. *Journal of Palliative Medicine, 10,* 1076–1082.

Nathan, L. (1990). Coping with uncertainty: Family member's adaptations during Cancer remission. In E. Clark, J. Fritz, & P. Reacker (Eds.), *Clinical perspectives on illness and loss: The linkage of theory and practice* (pp. 219–233). New York: Charles Press.

Rando, T. A. (1983). An investigation of grief and adaptation in parents whose children have died from cancer. *Journal of Pediatric Psychology, 8,* 3–20.

Rando, T. A. (1984). *Grief, dying, and death: Clinical interventions for caregivers.* Champaign, IL: Research Press.

Sanders, C. (1983). Effects of sudden vs. chronic illness death on bereavement outcome. *Omega: The Journal of Death and Dying, 13,* 227–241.

Appendix

These exercises, consisting of discussion questions, role-plays, and case studies are designed to illustrate some of the concepts developed within the book. They may be useful for workshops, trainings, or class activities.

PREDIAGNOSTIC PHASE

1. Imagine that a test was developed that could identify a genetic marker for Alzheimer's disease. This test, taken any time within the life cycle, would indicate that at some indeterminate point in the future a person who tests positive would likely develop dementia. Naturally, since the test does not indicate age of onset, there is no way to ascertain whether these symptoms might appear at 60 or 90 years of age. Obviously, there is always the possibility that the person may die of another factor before any symptoms of dementia emerge. What would the advantages and disadvantages be of such a test? How would you counsel a client who wished to explore the possibility of the test? Would you take the test?

Assuming you are 40 years old and the test result is positive, meaning you have a high likelihood of one day developing Alzheimer's, how would that influence life decisions now? Suppose you are dating a prospective partner who indicated testing positive. How would that affect the relationship?

2. In the following cases, what issues might be worth exploring based upon the description of prediagnostic behaviors (these may be role-played)?

    a. For the past six months, Matt, a 13-year-old boy, has complained to his mother about an occasional throbbing pain in his left leg. His mother has dismissed it as "growing pains" and wondered whether the pain related to a move to a new school. At his annual physical, Matt noted it to the doctor, who recommended further testing. Subsequent x-rays and tests found that Matt has osteogenic sarcoma (bone cancer) in his leg. Because the disease is advanced, Matt's leg will need to be amputated. Chemotherapy will follow, and the prognosis is guarded.

    b. May is an older woman caring for her grandchildren while her children work. She is also active in the church choir and the mission society of her local church. She has diabetes and high blood pressure. She claims life can be so busy that it is hard to adhere to her regimen. She recently had a small stroke. While recovering, she constantly worries about how the grandkids are faring.

DIAGNOSTIC PHASE

3. In each of these cases, analyze the cultural factors that you think might assist in interpreting the situation. How would you proceed? When there is a need for intervention, discuss interventive techniques.

    a. Julio is a 60-year-old Hispanic man diagnosed with amyotrophic lateral sclerosis (ALS). His family does not want him to know. They insist he be told he has a "nerve disease." What should you do?

    b. Jane Rainbow is a Native American woman who is entering the hospital for minor surgery. She stops her physician as he begins to explain the risks, saying she does not wish to know. How should the doctor proceed? Would you answer differently if the risks were greater?

4. Role-play. Robert is a 23-year-old active church member, but already in his life, he has achieved much. He has been an honor student, Eagle Scout, the recipient of many athletic trophies and scholastic awards. He has just become engaged and holds a new, exciting job. Learning he has leukemia, he keeps asking, "why me?"

CHRONIC PHASE

5. Role-play

    a. *Wife:* As part of your health regimen, you must adhere to a very strict diet. This is essential to control your diabetes as you undergo treatment for cancer. Your husband is always taking you out to dinner, urging on wine, rich foods, and desserts that are not part of your regimen. This has caused some conflict, and you seek counseling so that your husband may recognize the problem and be more supportive.

    b. *Husband:* Your wife of 35 years is now undergoing treatment for cancer. You are pessimistic that she will survive since she has multiple health problems, including diabetes and high blood pressure. As for many married couples, it has not always been easy for the two of you. Twice in the marriage you even separated for short periods. You just want your wife to enjoy the time she has left.

    c. *Counselor:* A couple has come to you recommended by a physician who feels that the marital discord may be adding stress to his patients and complicating her treatment.

6. Case Discussion. Marcie is a 79-year-old woman struggling with cancer. She is facing tremendous pain and discomfort from chemotherapy. Although the prognosis seems promising, she wonders if it is worth all the suffering. Her only surviving son has urged her to seek counseling. Accompanying her, he worries that his mother will decide to forgo treatment—something the mother is considering. What issues, as a counselor, would you wish to explore?

7. John is an active, bright-to-average sixth grader who has recently been readmitted to the school after hospitalization for cancer. The surgery has left a large incision on his chest. John is presently undergoing chemotherapy. His performance in school has always been variable, especially since he entered intermediate school, and he has had a reputation as being manipulative. Since his return, he has been complaining of tiredness, especially in the afternoons and on Fridays, following Thursday chemotherapy, and often forgets or claims he can't do homework. He also demands to be excused from swimming, a class he had always hated. List key issues that you perceive in this case. Is there any information you would wish to have? Outline some possible strategies to more effectively deal with this.

TERMINAL PHASE

8. Stella is 57 years old and has been a housewife for much of her life. As she is now dying of ALS, she deeply regrets that she did not do more with her life. She has come to you as a counselor. What interventional strategies would you use? (Also may be done as a role-play.)

9. A patient no longer has the capacity to participate in discussions about care. Her oldest daughter holds the health proxy but does not agree with her mother's earlier expressed wish to withdraw artificial hydration and nutrition. How would you advise the daughter to proceed? Is a surrogate decision maker bound to these earlier expressed wishes, or is it ethical for her to use her own judgment? She has just come from her home in Florida—about 1,000 miles away. Her younger sister has been a major caregiver for her mother since she resides

in the same city. She believes her mother's long expressed wishes should be followed, but she is reluctant to confront her sister, whom she always found stubborn and somewhat intimidating. What might be some underlying dynamics? If the family came to you, how might you proceed?

10. Thomas is a 60-year-old man dying of cancer. The pain is intense. He has openly spoken of hastening his death. The physician fears that Thomas may be storing pain medications in order to overdose—a strategy that Thomas found on the Internet. What is the ethical course for the physician?

RECOVERY PHASE

11. Jon has recovered from a serious illness. In the middle of treatment, he has promised to join "Prince of Peace Volunteers," a denominational volunteer group, if he recovers. He really does not wish to uproot his life, but fears God will allow the illness to recur if he does not fulfill his vow. He has come to you to sort out his feelings. How might you help him?

12. **Role-play or Case Discussion.** Rita is a 46-year-old survivor of cancer. She has had a successful career in advertising, but since her operation she has not received a promotion she thought she deserved. In addition, although she still retains all her accounts, she is noticing that senior management seems to be shifting new accounts to other executives. She has thought of relocating but wonders about the effects of a job change on her heath insurance coverage. She has been divorced and would like to develop a new relationship with a man, but she is also embarrassed by the small scars that resulted from her cancer surgery.

FAMILY ISSUES

13. **Role-play**
     a. *Bobby:* You are a 16-year-old boy whose father is suffering from multiple sclerosis. Since your father has been disabled

from the disease, your mother is on your back a great deal—asking you to pick up your little brother, take him to practice, or shop. You resent the extra responsibilities and are frightened about the family should your dad continue to deteriorate. Your only relaxation is hanging out with your friends.

b. *Mother:* Your husband has deteriorated rapidly since his diagnosis with MS. You try to keep stress away from him since you feel it exacerbates his condition. You are trying to hold your family together, but it is difficult. You are especially concerned that your 16-year-old son is not acting responsibly. Instead of helping, he is hanging out with a bad crowd. His grades are declining, he is breaking curfew, and even worse, you suspect he is using marijuana and alcohol. You are deeply worried but have kept your concerns, as much as you can, from your husband.

c. *Jeremy:* You are an 11-year-old boy. Ever since your dad became ill, you have been worried about your family. You try to help, but everyone says you are too young. You used to be closer to your older brother, but now he seems moody. You are fearful that your dad will die, but whenever you mention these fears your brother gets angry or your mother cries. You love baseball but are thinking of quitting since picking you up from practice has become a bone of contention between your mother and brother.

d. *Counselor:* A mother has called to see whether you can help in "getting her son in line." She noted the father is ill and confined to a wheelchair. She has agreed to family counseling but indicated it would be too tough for her husband to attend and that he does not need the additional stress.

14. Mildred has been caring for her 82-year-old mother for some time. The mother has Alzheimer's disease. After her mother was found wandering, Mildred has decided to place her in a nursing home. Her younger brother Gary flew in, convinced that this was a bad idea. He has spoken to a case manager and he is convinced that with a little help Mom can remain in Mildred's home "with less stress" than before. This conflict has caused them to see you, a counselor with the local office on aging.

Index